Brazil Under the Workers' Party

Continuity and Change from Lula to Dilma

Edited by

Fábio de Castro
Lecturer, Centre for Latin American Research and Documentation,
University of Amsterdam, The Netherlands

Kees Koonings
Professor, Centre for Latin American Research and Documentation,
University of Amsterdam, The Netherlands

and

Marianne Wiesebron
Senior Lecturer, Department of Latin American Studies, Leiden University,
The Netherlands

First published 2014 by
PALGRAVE MACMILLAN

Palgrave Macmillan in the UK is an imprint of Macmillan Publishers Limited, registered in England, company number 785998, of Houndmills, Basingstoke, Hampshire RG21 6XS.

Palgrave Macmillan in the US is a division of St Martin's Press LLC, 175 Fifth Avenue, New York, NY 10010.

Palgrave Macmillan is the global academic imprint of the above companies and has companies and representatives throughout the world.

Palgrave® and Macmillan® are registered trademarks in the United States, the United Kingdom, Europe and other countries.

ISBN 978–1–137–27380–2

This book is printed on paper suitable for recycling and made from fully managed and sustained forest sources. Logging, pulping and manufacturing processes are expected to conform to the environmental regulations of the country of origin.

A catalogue record for this book is available from the British Library.

Library of Congress Cataloging-in-Publication Data
Brazil under the workers' party : continuity and change from Lula to Dilma / edited by Fabio De Castro, Kees Koonings, Marianne Wiesebron.
pages cm
Summary: "This edited collection interprets and assesses the transformation of Brazil under the Workers' Party. It addresses the extent of the changes the Workers' Party has brought about and examines how successful these have been, as well as how continuity and social change in Brazil have affected key domains of economy, society, and politics. Looking at the factors which drive transformation in a dynamic Brazilian society, this study offers a valuable insight into the paradoxes and debates which emerge when looking at Brazil as a changing country during the past twenty years"—Provided by publisher.
ISBN 978–1–137–27380–2 (hardback)
1. Partido dos Trabalhadores (Brazil)—History.   2. Brazil—Politics and government.   3. Brazil—Social policy.   4. Brazil—Social conditions.
5. Brazil—Economic conditions   I. De Castro, Fabio, 1967–
II. Koonings, Kees.   III. Wiesebron, Marianne.
JL2498.T7.B73 2014
320.60981—dc23   2014025120

Typeset by MPS Limited, Chennai, India.

Contents

List of Figures and Tables

Figures

Tables

Acknowledgments

The first steps on the long road toward publication were taken during a one-day conference that we organized in Amsterdam on 11 November 2010. Most of the authors presented first drafts of their chapters and engaged in lively debate among themselves and the audience.

We are grateful to the Chair of Brazilian Studies Rui Barbosa and its sponsors: the Brazilian Ministry of Foreign Affairs, Continental Juice B. V., Seara Meats B. V., TAM Airlines, and TAP Portugal. Our special thanks go to the then Ambassador of Brazil in the Netherlands, H. E. José Artur Denot Medeiros, for opening the conference.

All texts were revised and updated. We invited a number of authors, not present at the conference, to analyze additional subjects that, in our view, were also of key importance for the purpose of the project.

The book would not have been possible without the financial and logistical support of the Centre for Latin American Research and Documentation (CEDLA), Leiden University, and Utrecht University. The financial support of CEDLA was essential for the technical and language editing, a crucial and demanding task. We thank Sara Koenders and Jennie Levitt for their rapid and skillful editorial support.

Notes on the Contributors

Rebecca Abers is Professor of Political Science at the University of Brasília, Brazil. Her research is focused on social movements, participation, and institutional change in environmental and urban policies. Publications include *Inventing Local Democracy, Grassroots Politics in Brazil* (2000) and *Practical Authority: Agency and Institutional Change in Brazilian Water Politics* (2013) (with Margaret Keck).

Nabil Bonduki is Head Professor of Urban Planning at the Faculty of Architecture and Urbanism at the University of São Paulo, Brazil. He has served in municipal and state political positions as City Counselor and Superintendent for Social Housing, and consultant for housing planning in several committees in Brazil and Africa. He is the author of several articles and books about housing, including the award-winning *Origens da Habitação Social no Brasil* (1998).

Antônio Marcio Buainain is Professor of Economics at the University of Campinas and Senior Researcher at the National Institute of Science and Technology on Public Policies, Strategy and Development. His researches focus on rural development, agricultural policies, family farming, and innovation in agriculture. He has published numerous books and articles in academic journals such as the *Journal of Peasant Studies*.

Fábio de Castro is Assistant Professor of Brazilian Studies and Political Ecology at the Centre for Latin American Research and Documentation, University of Amsterdam. His research focuses on protected areas, local management systems, and biofuel. He has published several book chapters and articles in journals such as *Human Ecology, Human Organization*, and *Society and Natural Resource*.

Junior Ruiz Garcia is Lecturer in Economics at the Federal University of Paraná, Brazil. He studies public policies with special focus on development issues, in particular regional development, rural poverty, and agrarian transition. His recent publications include *Desenvolvimento Rural do Semiárido Brasileiro: Transformações Recentes, Desafios e Perspectivas in Confins* (2013).

Hélio Henkin is Professor of Economics and Director of the Faculty of Economic Sciences at the Federal University of Rio Grande do Sul,

Brazil. His research focuses on industrial development and export promotion policies. He has been the director of the Small Business Services and a member of the Export Council of the Federation of Industries of Rio Grande do Sul. He has published book chapters and papers on industrial and export performance.

Kees Koonings is Professor of Brazilian Studies at CEDLA/University of Amsterdam and Associate Professor of Anthropology and Latin American Studies at Utrecht University. His research interests include violence and insecurity, in particular in Brazil and Colombia, urban governance and participatory democracy, political militarism, and the history and sociology of regional industrial development.

Henrique Dantas Neder is Professor at the Federal University of Uberlandia, Brazil. He is an economist and his research interests lie in social and economic inequality, rural and urban poverty, rural labor market, and impacts of social policies on poverty. His recent publications include *A Nova Cara da Pobreza Rural: Desenvolvimento e a Questão Regional* (2013).

Marcelo Cortes Neri is Professor of Economics at EPGE/FGV, Brazil, where he founded the Center for Social Policies. He is currently President of the Institute for Applied Economic Research (IPEA), and Brazilian Minister of Strategic Affairs (SAE). He has published several books on microcredit, social security, Bolsa Família, rural poverty, inflation and consumption, and the new middle class.

Timothy J. Power is University Lecturer in Brazilian Studies and a fellow of St Antony's College at the University of Oxford, UK. A former president of the Brazilian Studies Association (BRASA), he has published articles on Brazilian democracy in the *Journal of Politics*, *Legislative Studies Quarterly*, and *Political Research Quarterly*, among other outlets.

Lizandra Serafim is Professor of Public Policy at the Public Management Program of the Federal University of Paraíba (UFPB), Brazil. She studies state-society relations, participatory institutions, democracy, and public policies with special interest in urban and health sectors. Publications include *Citizen Participation in Challenging Contexts: Logolink 10 Years, 10 Countries, 10 Organizations* (2012) and *Sociedad Civil y Nuevas Institucionalidades Democráticas en América Latina: Dilemas y Perspectivas* (2009).

Luciana Tatagiba is Professor of Political Science at the University of Campinas, Brazil. Her most recent researches focus on social movements and relationships with the state around housing issues. Publications include *Mouvements Sociaux et Participation Institutionnelle: Répertoires D'action Collective et Dynamiques Culturelles dans la Difficile Construction de la Démocratie Brésilienne* (2010) (with Evelina Dagnino).

Paulo Fagundes Visentini is Professor of International Relations at Federal University of Rio Grande do Sul (UFRGS), Brazil and editor of *AUSTRAL: Brazilian Journal of Strategy and International Relations*. His research focuses on Brazil's South-South cooperation, especially on Africa and has published *A Política Externa do Regime Militar Brasileiro* (2004), *FTAA: The Push for Américas Integration* (editor) (2004), *A Projeção Internacional do Brasil (1930–2012)* (2013), and *A África e as Potências Emergentes: Brasil, China e Índia* (2013).

Marianne Wiesebron is Associate Professor in the Department of Latin American Studies, Leiden University. She carries out research on processes of regional integration and Brazilian foreign policy. She has published several books and journal articles such as the recent article 'Blue Amazon: Thinking the Defense of Brazilian Maritime Territory' in *Austral: Revista Brasileira de Estratégia e Relações Internacionais* (2013).

Introduction: Brazil under the Workers' Party

Kees Koonings, Fábio de Castro, and Marianne Wiesebron

From euphoria to upheaval

At 6 p.m. on 25 March 2013, protestors, mostly youngsters, blocked two major avenues in Porto Alegre, the capital of Brazil's southernmost state of Rio Grande do Sul: the Ipiranga Avenue, close to the campus of the private Catholic University of Rio Grande do Sul (PUC/RS), and the Bento Gonçalves Avenue in the suburb of Agronomia neighborhood, close to the campus of the public Federal University of Rio Grande do Sul (UFRGS). The protestors rejected the annual rise in urban transport fares that had been announced shortly before by the municipal authorities. Bus tariffs would increase from BRL 2.85 to 3.05. The demonstration caused huge traffic jams during the city's already congested evening rush hour. Two days later, a small crowd gathered in front of the *prefeitura* (City Hall) in the city center, where the protestors were confronted by repressive crowd control operations of the *Brigada Militar* (as Rio Grande do Sul's military police is called) upon trying to break into the building. During this opening act of what would soon become a massive wave of protests across Brazil, at least one person was severely injured, material damage was done, and paint was thrown at the municipal secretary of transport who had come out to speak to the protesters. In May and June 2013, the protests spread to São Paulo and Rio de Janeiro, Brazil's two largest cities. In São Paulo, a bus tariff rise of 20 cents (from BRL 3.00 to 3.20) had been proposed to the municipal council on 22 May 2013. On 6 June, between 2,000 and 4,000 protesters took to the streets in downtown São Paulo, mobilized by the local group *Movimento Passe Livre SP* (Free Fare Movement São Paulo), demanding the reversion of the proposed tariff increase.[1]

1

From that moment onward, the protests proliferated across the country and started to attract worldwide attention, especially when the protesters began to use matches of the football Confederations Cup as focal points for their activities. On June 15, in the federal capital Brasília, military police arrested 24 demonstrators in front of the recently finished national football stadium Mané Garrincha during the opening match of the tournament. Since then, the cycle of protests and flareups has been daily fare for Brazil watchers. In particular, Independence Day on 7 September 2013 brought a new spike of nationwide protest activities as did another announcement of bus fare hikes in February 2014. It became clear that 2014 would be a crucial, even historical, year. With the FIFA World Cup coming up, the imminent prospect of economic slowdown after almost a decade of solid growth, and an important electoral season primed to ignite as soon as the final whistle had been blown in the World Cup final at Rio's Maracanã stadium on 13 July 2014, the transport protests became part of a broader mood of introspection. The protests of 2013/14 shone light on a country that had been undergoing two decades of important transformations.

Not only is the cycle of protests interesting in itself but it also helps to reframe a number of key issues that concern contemporary Brazil. It soon became evident that the issue of bus fare hikes was merely a trigger that unleashed a much broader agenda of contest and conflict. As the numbers of participants grew, the range of issues targeted by the protesters also expanded to include other domains of faulty public services: education, health care, security (i.e., public security and law enforcement), and so on. Quickly, a connection was made between these deficiencies and the large amounts of money spent on venues, infrastructure and urban reform directly related to planned sporting mega-events such as the football world cup and the 2016 Olympics (not to mention the perks and prerogatives the public assumed would accrue to FIFA and IOC dignitaries, politicians, and the stakeholders of economic gain and corruption).

When the initial police response turned out to be quite violent, popular indignation focused on the state's lack of concern for basic civil rights and dignity. This issue became hotly debated when more radical elements, calling themselves the Black Block (dressed in black, faces hidden), used the protests to unleash more destructive forms of violence. This generated outrage among those who thought that the protests were the work of disloyal elements ('vandals') to start with. In turn, many protesters made efforts to show their patriotism, for instance by waving national flags in the streets. Another notable feature was the rejection of partisan symbols during the protests; the crowds did not tolerate banners, shirts, flyers, or other any forms of propaganda by political parties.

So far no systematic analysis of the social background and dynamics of the wave of protests has appeared in scholarly publications. Analysts stress the unpredictability of the movement, its rapid spread through the use of social media, and a comprehensive suite of demands centered on comprehensive citizenship through the recovery of the public domain, state intervention, and participatory politics.[2] Apparently, the movement was dominated by young people, very likely students, with largely (lower) middle-class backgrounds. The protests voiced a widely shared concern that the external image of Brazil as a success story of economic growth, reduction of poverty and inequality, and democratic stability, did not match domestic realities. The sporting mega-events, expected to consecrate Brazil's newfound status, had now turned into symbols of waste, corruption, and exclusion, in short, flawed governance.

The Workers' Party and the transformation of Brazil

The events of 2013/14 produced a peculiar paradox for the political party that had been leading the federal governmental coalition since 2003: the *Partido dos Trabalhadores* (Workers' Party, or PT). In 2002, Luiz Inácio Lula da Silva, the iconic co-founder and undisputed leader of the PT (Bourne, 2009), won the presidential election after having lost the previous three; in 1989 against the young conservative populist Fernando Collor de Mello, and in 1994 and 1998 against the prestigious sociologist, ex-senator, ex-finance minister, and leader of the social-liberal PSDB *Partido da Social Democracia Brasileira* (PSDB) Fernando Henrique Cardoso (FHC). FHC had won the presidency in 1994 riding a wave of success from the program of monetary stabilization and reform that he, as minister of finance in the government of Itamar Franco (1992–94), had introduced in June of that year. But since 2003, Brazil has been governed (at the federal level) by the Workers' Party. Lula's inauguration in January 2003 also brought huge crowds to the streets, especially in the federal capital Brasília. These supportive and festive crowds represented the expectation that the Workers' Party would lead Brazil, in the new millennium, in a direction of sustainable economic growth, social justice, and inclusive democracy.

With varying degrees of success, the PT had been pushing such an agenda when in office at the municipal and state levels since the mid-1980s. Founded in 1979 and legalized in 1981, during the closing years of the military regime (1964–85), the party represented a new direction in the politics of the Brazilian (and Latin American) Left (Castañeda, 1993). The PT aimed at social transformation to achieve, initially, a socialist society, and, eventually, a socially just democracy, by working within the boundaries of an electoral democracy (Keck, 1992; Nylen, 2000). Evolving, in general terms, from a social movement-as-political party, through being an opposition party, to becoming a party in office (first at subnational level, then, from 2003 onward, at the federal level), the PT tried to put its key political slogans about the *modo PT de governar* – the PT way of governing – (namely, 'reversal of priorities' and 'popular participation') into practice.

In other words, the main platform of the Workers' Party had been citizenship. In this respect, it had a natural affinity with a host of social movements that proliferated in Brazil during and after the democratic transition of the 1980s. In office at the subnational level, the PT's principal strategies were the provision of public goods and services to the underprivileged sectors of Brazilian society, transparency in office and practices of good governance, and innovative experiments with direct and participatory forms of democracy, such as the participatory budgeting systems in Porto Alegre and many other municipalities (Wampler, 2007). In the process of becoming a party in office, the PT shed most of its initial radicalism; the party's bid for the presidency in the 2002 electoral season was based on a notable turn towards a more mainstream approach of economic policy and global insertion, defended by Lula in his famous *Carta ao Povo Brasileiro* (Letter to the Brazilian People, June 2002).

Despite this concession to neoliberalism – which implied continuity with the economic model of his predecessor FHC (see Amaral, Kingstone and Krieckhaus, 2008) – the PT governments of Lula (2003–06; 2007–10) and Lula's successor Dilma Rousseff (since 2011) sought to address a wide variety of issues in the original spirit of the Workers' Party while at the same time facing certain obstinate realities. These realities include globalized capitalism, sustainability, domestic coalitional politics at the federal level, the complex and often volatile political landscape at all levels of the polity, high expectations, especially within civil society, and a quickly changing global environment in which Brazil actively sought to redefine its position (and increase its leverage) as one of the BRICs countries [Brazil, Russia, India, China] (Armijo and Burges, 2010).

For many, Brazil under the Workers' Party has been a success. Between 2003 and 2010, economic growth was steady, contributing towards Brazil becoming the sixth largest economy in the world in 2011 and transforming the country from being a perennial debtor into a healthy creditor. In social terms, for the first time in national history, Brazil showed a steady decline in poverty and indeed in income inequality.

After 2003, a new middle class arose (Power, 2010) and the millions of beneficiaries of the famous *Bolsa Família* conditional cash transfer program contributed to the re-election of Lula in 2006 (Hunter and Power, 2007). Internationally, Brazil emerged as a proactive power player, no longer automatically aligned to the traditional allies of the north (the US and Europe) but seeking to establish new alliances along a multiplicity of south-south vectors and groupings.

Now, more than ten years into the process, a new generation mobilized to claim exactly the issues the Workers' Party had been advocating throughout its notable march through the Brazilian political landscape during the previous 30 years. President Dilma Rousseff responded to the protests by announcing, on 24 June 2013, an ambitious package of reforms, framed in five so-called 'pacts' (commitments vis-à-vis the nation): (1) fiscal responsibility, (2) political reform, (3) health care, (4) public transport, and (5) education. The political reforms should broaden participation and strengthen citizenship, ban corruption, and increase transparency, all this to be decided through constitutional reform approved by popular plebiscite.[3] This package, therefore, was an effort to align the Workers' Party's mode of governing to the protest agenda. If successful, or at least credible, the reforms should back up the Workers' Party in the crucial October 2014 elections (for president, federal chamber of deputies, federal senate, state governors, and state legislatures), ensuring Dilma's re-election.

The book

This, then, is the background to this book's effort to interpret and assess the transformation of Brazil under the Workers' Party. What has been the extent of the changes the PT tried to bring about? How successful has this been? How, above all, has continuity and change in Brazil affected key domains of economy, society, and politics? The chapters brought together in this volume seek to answer these and many other questions that emerge when looking at Brazil as a changing country during the past ten to twenty years.

The first two chapters examine Brazilian politics and society to take stock of the impact of the rule of the Workers' Party on the stability and quality of democracy and on the interaction between the state and civil society. In Chapter 1, Timothy Power reviews the early presidential years of Dilma Rousseff in light of the legacy bequeathed by her predecessor,

Luiz Inácio Lula da Silva. Dilma is a product of the Lula years but is also heiress to a longer phase of political and economic stability that began in Brazil in the mid-1990s. After reviewing Dilma's successful campaign in 2010, the chapter examines several lessons that Dilma could draw from the Lula years, and concludes by assessing the ways in which she defined herself politically in her first two years as president of Brazil. In Chapter 2, Rebecca Abers, Lizandra Serafim and Luciana Tatagiba, explore the changing relationships between the state and social movements under Lula's presidency. Going beyond the focus on participatory institutions, it is argued that under the PT, state-society interactions took on a variety of forms, namely new forms of protest, personalized negotiations, occupation of government jobs by activists, and formalized participation. The chapter adapts Tilly's notion of repertoires of contention to understand these activities as a repertoire of state-society interaction. The chapter compares these changing repertoires in three policy areas: urban policy, agrarian development and public security, arguing that varying practices of state-society interaction are rooted in the historical traditions of each policy area and subject to creative innovation, especially where social movement activists played a direct role in the governing process.

In Chapter 3 Brazilian politics is moved to the global stage. Paulo Fagundes Visentini offers an analysis of Brazilian foreign policy in the first decade of the twenty-first century. The chapter focuses on international relations priorities and principles between 2003 and 2010, and the possible rupture or continuity of this agenda during Dilma Rousseff's presidency since 2011 to date. The chapter addresses Brazil's actions related to South American integration in the world, examining multilateral alliances such as the IBSA countries (India, Brazil and South Africa) and the commercial and financial G20, and explores Lula's African policy and the BRICS dynamics. It is argued that Brazil evolved from a sleeping giant to an emerging power. However, to consolidate this status, Brazil has yet to face several challenges in its foreign policy and domestic society that may influence its emergent international role.

The next four chapters delve into economic and social development, to examine the alleged synergy between economic growth and equity that was an important cornerstone of the Workers' Party's policies. In Chapter 4, Hélio Henkin discusses the trajectory of Brazilian economic policies throughout the two terms under Lula, in the context of a broader shift that had brought political and economic stability. The chapter analyzes the performance of the Brazilian economy in terms of income distribution and other goals, and looks at the tradeoffs and the choices faced by those creating Brazil's economic policies. In Chapter 5, Marcelo Neri reviews the social performance of Brazil during Lula's two presidential terms. The chapter measures the evolution of income-based social indicators such as poverty and inequality. The main determinants of this evolution and some of the consequences are discussed: the role played by the macroeconomic environment and by different social policies such as education, minimum wage and official income transfers, including *Bolsa Familia*. The chapter notes a movement towards a more prosperous, equitable and predictable society in which people report increasing levels of life satisfaction. In Chapter 6, Marianne Wiesebron addresses several social policies set up during the Lula administration or improved from previous administrations. The conditional cash transfer program *Bolsa Família* is of particular relevance. In ten years, this program reached nearly 14 million families, leading, among other outcomes, to empowerment of women as the program beneficiaries, and better health and education indicators. More recently, under the Dilma administration, more attention has been given to the economically extremely poor. Although more investment is needed to eradicate poverty, and to improve education and health in Brazil, the *Bolsa Familia* has had a remarkably positive social impact for millions of Brazilians. Despite the success of poverty alleviation, one particular domain of society and social policy has proved resistant to positive transformation. In Chapter 7, Kees Koonings looks at the ways violence, crime and insecurity cast shadows over the acclaimed success of Brazil as a consolidated democracy. These challenges reflect the deep-rooted structures of inequality and exclusion. These complex issues are discussed by combining a national-level perspective of patterns of violence and insecurity with a local-level, urban perspective through the case of Rio de Janeiro, including the recent strategy of 'favela pacification'. In addition, the Workers' Party federal program PRONASCI (Programa Nacional de Segurança Pública com Cidadania), aimed at public security within a citizenship framework, is reviewed. The chapter argues that the failure and suspension of this program shows that the reign of the Workers' Party has not provided the silver key to unlock the conundrum of violence, insecurity and fear in Brazil.

The final three chapters of the book analyze key domains of social change in which public policies engage with complex challenges generated by exclusion and contradictions: urban and housing, rural social conditions, and resource use and the environment. In Chapter 8, Nabil Bonduki provides a detailed examination of recent urban and housing policy in Brazil, with emphasis on the national housing policies reformulated during the Lula administration. The chapter explains how this public policy has been shaped since the 1990s, under strong popular participation and high demands for housing, culminating in the creation of the City Ministry, the Council of Cities and the National Housing Fund. The analysis points at constraints and challenges in the implementation of these policies, including the economic crisis of 2008 and strong intervention of the private sector. This trend, which neglects the urban question and exacerbates the dramatic reality of Brazilian cities, became the major challenge faced by the Dilma administration in the housing sector. Moving from cities to the countryside, in Chapter 9 Antônio Marcio Buainain, Henrique Dantas Neder and Junior Ruiz Garcia address recent rural policies in Brazil; rural Brazil is marked by strong income concentration and social inequalities. Notwithstanding the validity of such picture, the examination of a set of databases of social and economic indicators in Brazil reveals the progress registered during Lula's two successive presidential terms. An overall assessment of social and rural development policies under Lula is discussed from a dual perspective. First, by tracing the roots of these policies since re-democratization in the 80s. Second, by analyzing the innovations introduced during Lula's administration and following the implementation of key rural policies during his mandate. Finally, in Chapter10, Fabio de Castro analyzes recent environmental policies in Brazil. In the last decade, the 'environment' has become a core element of national politics in Brazil as it is linked to local demands of traditional communities for social justice, to national demands for expansion of commodity production, and to global demands for mitigation of carbon emission. Three main domains of environmental governance are discussed – protected areas, renewable energy, and climate governance. Lula's terms have been marked by important accomplishments but also by major challenging contradictions as these environmental issues clash with other policies. Since Dilma, contradictions have increased with reduced commitment to social justice towards traditional communities and to conservation measures for mitigation of carbon emission, while rural elite groups have gradually dominated the decision-making process.

Notes

1   Details were taken from (all sites consulted in February 2014): Terra.com (http://noticias.terra.com.br/infograficos/protesto-tarifa/). We used a number of internet sources for this brief review of the 2013 protests. Terra.com provides a detailed map and timeline of events, backed up with news reports, for

the March–June 2013 period. The weekly *Carta Capital* offers an interesting analytical documentary, *Zerovinte*, that seeks to explain and contextualize the protests (http://www.cartacapital.com.br/politica/cartacapital-lanca-documentario-sobre-os-protestos-de-2013-6118.html). Other useful sources of information and documentation are websites of newspapers such as *Folha de São Paulo* (http://www1.folha.uol.com.br/especial/2013/paisemprotesto/), Brasilescola.com (http://www.brasilescola.com/historiab/protestos-contra-aumento-das-tarifas-uma-nova-acao-politica.htm), noticias.uol.com, and the international service of the BBC (http://www.bbc.co.uk/portuguese/noticias/2013/09/130907_sete_setembro_mm.shtml) (all consulted on February 2014).

2   See comments by Renato Janine (philosopher), Vladimir Safatle (philosopher), Sérgio Amadeu (political scientist), and Luiz Gonzaga Belluzo (economist) in the documentary *Zerovinte*, produced by *Carta Capital* (see URLs in note 1).

3   See http://noticias.terra.com.br/brasil/politica/dilma-anuncia-5-pactos-e-propoe-plebiscito-da-reforma-politica,c3576d53bbb6f310VgnCLD2000000 dc6eb0aRCRD.html for Dilma's televised speech on 24 July 2013, during which she announced the reforms.

References

Amaral, A.D., Kingstone, P.R. and Krieckhaus, J. (2008) 'The Limits of Economic Reform in Brazil' in P.R. Kingstone and T.J. Power (eds), *Democratic Brazil Revisited* (Pittsburgh: University of Pittsburgh Press).

Armijo, L.E. and Burges, S.W. (2010) 'Brazil, the Entrepreneurial and Democratic BRIC', *Polity* 42(1):14–37.

Bourne, R. (2009) *Lula of Brazil: The Story So Far* (Berkeley: University of California Press).

Castañeda, J.G. (1993) *Utopia Unarmed: The Latin American Left After the Cold War* (New York: Vintage Books).

Hunter, W. and Power, T.J. (2007) 'Rewarding Lula: Executive Power, Social Policy, and the Brazilian Elections of 2006', *Latin American Politics and Society* 49(10): 1–30.

Keck, M.E. (1992) *The Workers' Party and Democratization in Brazil* (New Haven: Yale University Press).

Nylen, W.R. (2000) 'The Making of a Loyal Opposition: The Workers' Party (PT) and the Consolidation of Democracy in Brazil' in P.R. Kingstone and T.J. Power (eds), *Democratic Brazil: Actors, Institutions, and Processes* (Pittsburgh: University of Pittsburgh Press).

Power, T.J. (2010) 'Brazilian Democracy as a Late Bloomer: Reevaluating the Regime in the Cardoso-Lula Era', *Latin American Research Review*, 45 (special issue): 218–37.

Wampler, B. (2007) *Participatory Budgeting in Brazil: Contestation, Cooperation, and Accountability* (University Park: Pennsylvania State University Press).

1
Continuity in a Changing Brazil: The Transition from Lula to Dilma

Timothy J. Power

Just before 4:00 p.m. on 1 January 2011, Luiz Inácio Lula da Silva removed the presidential sash that had been bestowed upon him by Fernando Henrique Cardoso (FHC) exactly eight years earlier. As Lula draped the sash over the shoulders of his successor, Dilma Rousseff, the symbolism of constancy could hardly be more evident. This was only the second time in Brazilian history that a democratically elected president had transferred the office to another democratically elected president from the same party (the previous occasion had been 60 years earlier, when Lula was five years old and Dilma was three).[1] But Dilma was much more than an ordinary co-partisan from the Workers' Party (PT): she had been Lula's chief of staff for the past five years, and the leading architect of his second term in office. Dilma had been Lula's personal choice to succeed him in the presidency, and in 2010 Lula became the first Brazilian president to serve two consecutive terms in office and then 'elect his successor' – a goal that had eluded his predecessor Cardoso in 2002. The transition from Lula to Dilma thus occurred in a context of unprecedented continuity. Thus, fairly or unfairly, virtually all of the outcomes of the Dilma government – achievements as well as failures – are likely to be judged against the benchmark of the Lula years (2003–10).

This chapter explores the significance of this transition by examining the circumstances under which Dilma came to inherit the presidency from her mentor. The chapter proceeds in five main sections. In the first section, I examine the macropolitical context of the 2010 general election. I argue that the election of Dilma must be understood not only in the context of an intra-PT succession, but rather in the context of 16 years of an emerging social democratic consensus in Brazil that began with the Plano Real[2] in 1994. I explore several points of this consensus that was engineered jointly (though not always smoothly) by the Cardoso and Lula administrations. The next section of the text looks at how Brazilian political elites view this consensus, and illustrates some potential fault lines within the very broad, heterogeneous Lula–Dilma coalition. In the third section, I revisit the course of the electoral process in 2010 and the principal results. In a fourth section of the chapter, I discuss several 'lessons of the Lula years' that are likely to imprint upon Dilma and her coalition government from 2011 onward. These lessons point to new lines of cleavage in Brazilian politics, some of which apparently favor the PT and its allies in the medium run. Finally, I review the first two years of the Dilma government against the backdrop of the unifying theme of this volume: the legacy of Lula.

From crisis to consensus? The reshaping of Brazilian democracy

After 21 years of military dictatorship, Brazil became a political democracy in 1985. As the country now approaches three decades of uninterrupted democratic experience, evaluations of the regime have become noticeably more laudatory. In the late 1980s or early 1990s, Brazil was often described as a precarious democracy, with dysfunctional institutions, poor leadership, and an aversion to necessary reforms (for example, Hagopian and Mainwaring, 1987; Power, 1991; Lamounier, 1996). But from the perspective of 2013, these alarmist descriptions seem dated. After the Plano Real in 1994 ended hyperinflation and ushered in a new era of stability, Brazilian democracy made significant advances in macroeconomic performance, social welfare, executive-legislative relations, and global activism. Moreover, with the passage of time Brazilian democracy has come to be seen relatively favorably in regional perspective, having managed to avoid some of the more spectacular ills that have afflicted several neighboring countries, for example, financial default, party system collapse, populism, secessionism, curtailment of liberal freedoms, and replacement of presidents by dubious constitutional means. Today, Brazil is more likely to be cited with respect to significant economic growth, improving social indicators, stable presidential leadership, and a healthy accrual of 'soft power' on the international stage. It was in this newly optimistic context that the elections of 2010 took place.

The eventual victor in 2010, Dilma Rousseff, was and is the beneficiary of these positive trends. Dilma owes much to her two predecessors in the *Palácio do Planalto*, Fernando Henrique Cardoso (Partido da

Social Democracia Brasileira, PSDB, 1995–2002) and Luiz Inácio Lula da Silva (PT, 2003–10). After the protracted hyperinflationary crisis of 1987–93, a period in which many of the pessimistic views of Brazil understandably gained traction, the Plano Real and the election of Cardoso 'rebooted' Brazilian democracy in the mid-1990s. This led to a new phase in which major reforms were first instituted by the PSDB and allies and later expanded and consolidated by the PT and allies. In the wake of these important policy convergences, it became possible to identify an implicit cross-party consensus that emerged around several key issues of democratic governance in the Cardoso–Lula era. Here I stress the word 'implicit', because the consensus that has emerged is far from being a formal political pact, but is rather a shared understanding about the basic objectives of policy and best practices for implementation. Furthermore, the use of the term 'consensus' should not be taken to imply that the Cardoso and Lula governments were identical in their policy outputs. They were not. The differing emphases and styles of these two administrations show the emerging consensus to be some-what elastic, preserving some space for innovation, experimentation, and credit-claiming within a broadly defined social democratic policy space. The five central points of consensus in the Cardoso–Lula period revolved around macroeconomic policy, social policy, a new federal equilibrium, coalitional governance, and renewed activism on the global stage.[3]

The fundamentals of macroeconomic policy date from Cardoso's experience as finance minister in 1993–94 under Itamar Franco, yet they were not endorsed by the PT until almost a decade later. Cardoso's initial objectives were a fiscal adjustment combined with the introduction of a new currency, the real (BRL). The real was to be aggressively defended by a Central Bank that was granted de facto (though not de jure) independence. In Cardoso's first term as president, the reform program was accelerated by conventional initiatives of privatization, state reform, and market liberalization, most of which required constitutional amendments. In this period, Lula's PT led the minority left bloc in Congress that energetically opposed all of the major Cardoso reforms. However, during his fourth run for the presidency, in 2002, Lula released the *Carta ao Povo Brasileiro* that soberly laid out a rationale for leaving most reforms intact and maintaining the basic lines of macroeconomic policy (Spanakos and Rennó, 2006). Recognizing that Brazil's hands were tied by the 'turbulence of financial markets', Lula agreed to continue inflation targeting and to maintain a healthy primary surplus equivalent to 4.25 percent of GDP. By the end of

Lula's first year in office, financial markets, domestic capitalists, and Wall Street seemed largely convinced of the new PT-led government's commitment to responsible economic policies. The honeymoon was protracted: from 2004 to 2008, Brazilian GDP growth averaged nearly 5 percent annually, and the real appreciated more than 50 percent against the dollar. In this period, an interparty consensus formed around the ideas of continued inflation targeting, fiscal responsibility with a primary surplus, monetary policy in defense of the real, an improved tax take, and no reversals of the 1990s privatizations. Lula decisively followed the Cardoso-era model of keeping the 'economic team' almost completely insulated from day-to-day politics – a practice personally overseen by Dilma in her gatekeeping role as Lula's presidential chief of staff.

Social policy is another area benefiting from broad cross-party consensus. As Marcus Melo (2008) has argued, progress in social assistance derives from a genuinely interactive process in which both the PSDB and PT have innovated, emulated, and expanded signature programs over the past 15 years. The result has been improving quality of policy, especially in conditional cash transfer programs. In the mid-1990s, PSDB and PT governments in Campinas and Brasília, respectively, innovated basic income programs as well as conditional cash transfer schemes (CCTs) that required regular school attendance (*Bolsa Escola*). After *Bolsa Escola* showed promise, Cardoso implemented a federalized version. In return, when in 2003 the Lula government merged *Bolsa Escola* with several smaller CCTs to create the renowned *Bolsa Família* program (Hall, 2006; see Wiesebron this volume), the political opposition was reciprocally supportive. The result is a social safety net that now provides a guaranteed income to over 12 million families covering nearly a quarter of the national population. The two substantive points here are basic incomes for the poor and aggressive investment in the educational system to improve human capital. Combined with the equally consensual policy of providing annual minimum wage increases above the rate of inflation, these policies reduced poverty and inequality in the Cardoso–Lula era, with the indicators improving most rapidly during Lula's second term in office (Neri, 2012; this volume).

Post-1995 Brazil also saw important changes in the prospects for governability, both subnationally and nationally. Samuels and Abrucio (2000) observe that the bottom-up sequencing of the Brazilian transition to democracy empowered pro-decentralization governors and *municipalista* mayors during the constitutional assembly of 1987–88. Rapid fiscal decentralization in this period led to perverse outcomes, creating revenue shortfalls for the central government while encouraging subnational executives to embark on a long spending spree in the late 1980s and early 1990s (Rodden, 2003). To consolidate the fiscal adjustment required by the Plano Real in 1994, the federal government began an aggressive recentralization program that continued throughout the Cardoso years. In 2000, the landmark *Lei de Responsabilidade Fiscal* (LRF) locked in limitations on subnational public employment while simultaneously imposing hard budget constraints on the states. The reconstructed federal pact thus curtailed the blackmail potential of subnational governments, increasing the breathing room for the president during the Lula years. In effect, Cardoso spared Lula the federal headaches that he himself had endured in the 1990s.

Meanwhile, in Brasília, Cardoso improved coordination in executive-legislative relations by adopting explicit power-sharing arrangements with allied parties via a system that has come to be known as *presidencialismo de coalizão* (coalitional presidentialism).[4] In transferring ministerial portfolios and generous allocations of public spending to his coalition partners, Cardoso wrote a sort of 'user's manual' for power-sharing, and Lula read it carefully. One of Cardoso's more controversial initiatives was to establish heterogeneous alliances with no requirement of ideological consistency. This pragmatic tactic was initially ridiculed by the PT: prior to 2002, Lula had never advocated a coalition that reached outside the 'family' of traditionally left-wing parties. Yet in breaking with this tradition in 2002, and in accepting a vice-presidential candidate from the conservative and clientelistic Partido Liberal (PL), the PT won the presidency for the first time. In power, the PT's coalitional strategy was strikingly similar to that of the PSDB in the 1990s. Both parties successfully created interparty support coalitions ranging from 65 to 70 percent of the seats in Congress, allowing both Cardoso and Lula to dominate marginalized oppositions. Dilma has preserved the basic model of oversized, ideologically diverse coalitions.

Finally, the Cardoso–Lula era was marked by a renewal of Brazil's international projection (see Visentini, this volume). This trend was visible not only in key global forums (the UN, the WTO) and in regional integration schemes (Mercosul, Unasul, and CELAC (Community of Latin American and Caribbean States)), but also in areas far removed from Brazil's traditional domains of policy (for example, the commercial outreach to China, or the joint mediation with Turkey of Iran's nuclear ambitions). The new activism was also combined with a dramatic upgrade in the personal engagement of chief executives in the foreign policy-making process ('presidential diplomacy'). In describing this activism as a point of consensus, I am referring not to the *content* of specific foreign policies (which, as I show below, differed substantially from the PSDB years to the PT years) but rather to a widely shared principle that Brazil should be visible and dynamic in global affairs. Cardoso, for example, gave more attention to developed countries, especially the United States and Europe, where he was already well known as an intellectual. Lula, on the other hand, emphasized South-South relations and used presidential diplomacy to reach out to engage with new partners in Asia, Africa, and the Middle East. Lula became the public face of Brazil in the past decade: he was the only chief of state invited to address both the World Economic Forum in Davos and the World Social Forum in Porto Alegre (Scolese and Nossa, 2006, pp. 74–7), and played a key role in winning the 2016 Olympic Games for Rio de Janeiro. From 2011, Dilma faced the difficult prospect of living up to the international reputation of two well-travelled predecessors who in many ways had served as their own foreign ministers.

What does all of this convergence portend for the presidency of Dilma Rousseff? Macroeconomic policy, social policy, a revised federal pact, coalitional presidentialism, and renewed international projection are elements of a broad political consensus in Brazil and have become familiar emblems of the post-real regime. Thus, while it is correct to say that Dilma emerges from the popular Lula administration and from the plebiscitary election of 2010, that is only part of a larger story. Dilma is also a product of a revamped Brazilian democracy, one that is characterized by a bi-coalitional architecture and several important points of policy consensus.

Elite views of post-1995 Brazil

Since 1994, the bi-coalitional logic has dominated Brazilian *presidential* politics, with only the PT and the PSDB producing nationally viable candidates (although results for congressional and gubernatorial posts remain highly fragmented). In each of the past five presidential elections, the share of the first-round vote won jointly by the PSDB and PT has ranged anywhere from 70 to 90 percent.[5] Given this established pattern and given 16 years of Cardoso and Lula, it was natural that the presidential election of 2010 – fought essentially between their respective political heirs, José Serra (PSDB) and Dilma Rousseff (PT) – would be characterized by frequent comparisons of the policy legacies of the two main parties. One year earlier, I participated in an elite survey that anticipated this debate and asked a representative sample of

139 federal legislators to rate the degree of continuity or change between the administrations of FHC and Lula.[6] In Figure 1.1, the response items are ordered from top to bottom according to the degree of continuity attributed by legislators, and the overall congressional mean is indicated by the solid grey circle. On average, political elites see

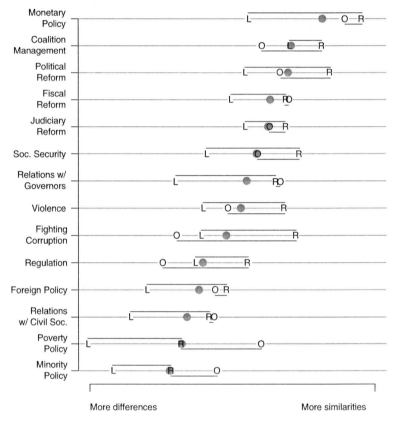

Figure 1.1   Perceived contrasts between the FHC and Lula Governments as of 2009

Notes: The grey circle indicates the average opinion of all legislators in Congress. L is the mean response of left parties, all of which were in the pro-Lula bloc (PT, PC do B, PSB, PDT, and PV); R is the mean opinion of pro-Lula parties of the center-right (PMDB, PP, PTB, and PR), and O is the mean opinion of the opposition bloc (PSDB, DEM, and PPS). The horizontal lines above each set of dots represent the spatial distance between the two pro-government factions, L and R. The horizontal lines below each set of dots represent the distance between the two center-right factions R and O.

Source: Brazilian Legislative Survey (2009), Wave 6.

the degree of continuity from FHC to Lula as being highest in the areas of monetary policy and coalitional presidentialism – two of the main points of implicit consensus discussed above. Looking back on the Lula years, it is interesting to note that these two items correspond directly to the main substantive policy output (the maintenance of orthodox macroeconomic policy) as well as to the main aspect of political process (the management of a heterogeneous support coalition in Congress) of this period. Legislators find the FHC and Lula governments to be most different on foreign policy, relations with civil society, policies toward minority groups, and anti-poverty initiatives.

Figure 1.1 also reports the mean responses for three mutually exclusive categories of legislators, separating the respondents along two important dimensions. I distinguish here among members of pro-government parties of the left (L), members of pro-government parties from the centre and right (R), and members of opposition parties (O). Note that political parties in categories R and O are located in a similar ideological space, within the centre-right of the political spectrum; however, what links together the parties in L and R is their common support for the Lula government in 2009.[7] All of these parties, without exception, have continued their coalitional support of Dilma Rousseff as well. Contrasting the relative positions of these groups allows us to determine whether the reported *perceptions* of legislators are linked more to ideology (left versus right) or to situational politics (that is, the government versus opposition cleavage). To this end, and to represent visually the ideological coherence of the large pro-government bloc supporting Lula, Figure 1.1 highlights the distance between the mean responses of the two different pro-Lula factions. This is represented in the graph by the length of the solid lines drawn from L (pro-government left) to R (pro-government centre-right). Substantively, the length of these lines represents perceptual heterogeneity within the governing coalition led by the PT – the longer the line, the more dissensus within the pro-Lula camp.

Although on some of the survey items we see agreement among the groups in their comparisons of the FHC and Lula governments, there are also some fascinating differences of opinion. For example, there are a number of survey items on which the pro-Lula centre-right clearly distances itself from the pro-government left. The relevant themes here include relations with civil society, tax reform, and the conduct of foreign policy. On these issues, the core Brazilian left sees large differences between Lula and FHC, whereas the remainder of the political class does not. These are policy domains in which ideology – and *not* a simple government-versus-opposition logic – influences how legislators see the recent past. From the perspective of the anti-Lula opposition, these themes could be used to sow dissent within the governing bloc.

Yet Figure 1.1 also shows that there is a cluster of policy issues – including regulatory activity, corruption control, public security, and political reform – in which the perceptions of the pro-government left, surprisingly enough, are closer to those of the *opposition* than to those of the pro-Lula centre-right. In these cases, the spatial ordering of the groups most likely derives from positional assessments of the FHC and Lula governments. The opposition (in 2009) may prefer the policies of Cardoso, and perceives unwanted departure from those policies under Lula. The pro-government left prefers the policies of Lula, and aims to highlight sharp differences between Lula and his predecessor. But the *governistas* of the centre-right – the vast majority of whom supported *both* the Cardoso and Lula governments – allege that there are few differences between the two presidents. This may be nothing more than an attempt to justify the bandwagoning behavior of these opportunistic centre-right parties, many of which supported first Cardoso, then Lula, and now Dilma. For these parties, which join legislative cartels mainly to extract clientelistic benefits from chief executives, it is difficult to find a president whom they will *not* support.

Tensions within the Lula–Dilma bloc are also evident with regard to foreign policy. Our survey item in 2009 was: 'The current orientation of Brazilian foreign policy gives priority to relationships with the countries of South America. I would like to know if you agree or disagree with the following statements related to this topic.' The statements were as follows:

- Regional integration is an efficient way to stimulate the economic development of the country.
- Leadership of the process of regional integration will project Brazil on the global stage.
- Many of the current South American governments are allies in the struggle against neoliberalism, and should be supported.
- The association with some South American countries damages the image of Brazil due to the authoritarian inclinations of their governments.
- It would be more advantageous to deepen relations with OECD countries than with neighboring countries.

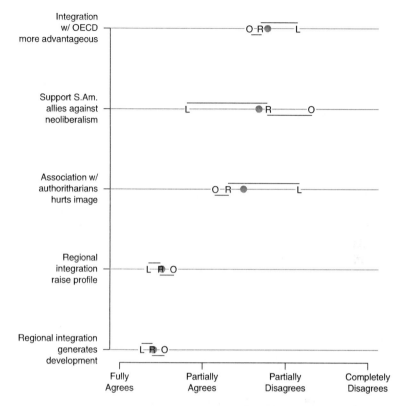

Figure 1.2   Elite opinions regarding Lula-era foreign policy, 2009
Notes: See text for survey statements as well as explanatory notes to Figure 1.1.

One can readily observe in Figure 1.2 that the first two statements are noncontroversial within the Brazilian political class. As mentioned earlier, consensus in foreign policy pertains to the abstract idea of high Brazilian visibility rather than to the content of specific initiatives, which clearly differed from FHC to Lula. All factions agree that South America should continue regional integration efforts and that Brazil should strive to lead the process. However, the remaining three statements, which focus on South-South relations and the recent 'left turn' in South America, reveal a dissensus among political elites with regard to Brazil's international profile in the Lula era. In each case, the centre-right parties backing Lula hold views that are closer to the opposition outlook than they are to the position of the governing PT. These are fault lines or 'wedge issues': they illustrate latent tensions within the heterogeneous pro-Lula alliance.

Therefore, Dilma inherits a Brazil that was reshaped by Cardoso and Lula, but she also inherits a particular political coalition that formed around the successes of the Lula government. This is a coalition that retains centrist and conservative parties (most notably the Partido do Movimento Democrático do Brasil – PMDB) that supported Cardoso's reforms in the 1990s, but that then gravitated rather quickly into the orbit of the PT when this party won the presidency in 2002. On a number of issues, these support parties appear to be in a state of ideological discomfort. This suggests that their ongoing support of Dilma may well be contingent on conjunctural factors, such as continued policy successes and presidential popularity.

The election of 2010: a battle of legatees

Lula came to the presidency as an agent of Brazil's best-organized political party, the PT. Few now remember that Lula even had to face a closed primary election to secure the nomination in 2002 (he fended off a symbolic challenge from Senator Eduardo Suplicy of São Paulo, who won 16 percent of the vote). But over the course of his eight years in office, Lula began to transcend the PT and enjoy unprecedented autonomy from the party. This transcendence occurred not only for the obvious reason – Lula's immense and enduring personal popularity with ordinary Brazilians – but also because sequential corruption scandals in 2005–06 tarnished the PT brand name and marginalized some of the key figures in the party, including several potential successors to Lula (Pereira, Power and Raile, 2011). The *mensalão* scandal of 2005, which brought down the de facto leader of the party, José Dirceu, was the direct reason why Dilma was promoted to presidential chief of staff. Dilma's steady hand during the crisis, which righted the ship and set Lula on course for an easy re-election in 2006, cemented her role as the new heiress apparent. Yet Dilma had joined the PT only in 2000 and had never before held elective office. When viewed against the methodical party-building of the first two decades of the PT – a party of discipline and hierarchy, and one with deep reserves of political talent – it is striking that Lula was able to personally name a successor with weak roots in the party and to do so with no visible resistance. Lula personally negotiated the agreement with Brazil's largest party, the PMDB, to emplace party boss Michel Temer (a former president of the Chamber of Deputies) as Dilma's running mate in 2010.

In 2002, Lula had defeated José Serra of the PSDB, who by then had already served as deputy and senator for São Paulo and had also held two ministerial portfolios under Cardoso. The setback for Serra was only temporary: he was promptly elected mayor of São Paulo in 2004 and then governor in 2006, putting him in a strong position to seek the presidency once again. His intra-party rival Aécio Neves, the popular governor of Minas Gerais and grandson of Tancredo Neves, briefly flirted with the PSDB nomination as well. However, the dominance of the *paulista* faction of the PSDB was impossible to overcome: in all six presidential elections since the transition to democracy, the PSDB has nominated senators or governors from São Paulo. The resources available to a sitting governor of São Paulo are unrivalled in Brazil, so unsurprisingly Serra was victorious in the intraparty struggle. Having run for president before, not to mention governing 22 percent of the Brazilian electorate himself, Serra enjoyed nearly universal name recognition at the beginning of 2010. Dilma, by contrast, was still largely unfamiliar to the general public.

Despite a respectable showing by Green Party (PV) candidate Marina Silva, who campaigned explicitly against the consolidation of a PT-PSDB duopoly, the 2010 presidential campaign was always a two-person race. From the party convention season in May–June until roughly the end of July, Serra and Dilma were in a statistical dead heat, with each having approximately 35 percent of the voting intentions. However, Dilma's name recognition began to rise significantly after the PT convention, and when the free television campaign began in August she began to pull ahead of Serra. This was due largely to Lula's direct media engagement in the final two months, when he appeared regularly on Dilma's TV spots to reinforce his sponsorship of her candidacy and to hammer home a message of continuity. In the televised phase, Serra's rather underwhelming campaign slogan was '*O Brasil pode mais*', or 'Brazil can do better', a tacit admission that Brazil was already achieving something under Lula. Yet Dilma's slogan was the ingenious '*Para o Brasil seguir mudando*', or 'For Brazil to continue changing'. The verb *mudar* (to change) highlighted the declining inequality and rising social mobility of the Lula years, while the verb *seguir* (to follow, continue) suggested direct continuity with her mentor. Lula's efforts to frame the presidential election as a plebiscite on his eight years of rule were clearly successful, and Dilma made little effort to distinguish herself from her predecessor or to suggest new courses of action. On 3 October 2010 Dilma received 47 percent of the valid vote to Serra's 33 percent, while Marina Silva took an additional 19 percent (the best showing of any third-placed presidential candidate since the transition to democracy). Like Lula in 2006, Dilma fell just short of outright victory and was forced into a runoff election on 31 October.

In the short runoff campaign, both Dilma and Serra sought to win Marina's supporters, who were largely urban and middle-class. Although Serra inherited more of Marina's support than did Dilma, this was not enough to overcome the PT's large advantage in the first round. Polls consistently projected a Dilma victory, which she eventually achieved with 56 percent of the valid vote – less than Lula's 61 percent in 2002 and 2006, but still decisive. The 2010 runoff results confirmed some of the new electoral geography that had already become apparent with Lula's re-election in 2006. Dilma won overwhelmingly among poorer and less educated Brazilians; she defeated Serra by 33 percentage points in the Northeast but lost by 8 points in the South. The voter preference data in Table 1.1 suggest that the 2010 election result is strongly explained by income and education, which are reliable and negative predictors of the Dilma vote. Age and urbanization have little impact, while religious affiliation seems to have had a moderate effect (Dilma performed less well among Pentecostals, who were targeted in the final weeks by a negative campaign insinuating that Dilma might support abortion rights). Interestingly, gender does have some explanatory power, but not in the direction expected by simplistic journalistic accounts. Dilma defeated Serra by 16 percentage points among male voters, but by only four points among women. This is very likely a partisan effect rather than a candidate effect: the gender profile is very similar to what Lula achieved in his five bids for the presidency, and the PT has suffered a similar gender gap throughout its history (Braga and Pimentel, 2011).

But the data in Table 1.1 are univariate and descriptive, and multivariate analysis can take us further. In their comprehensive study of the election using the sophisticated *Estudo Eleitoral Brasileiro*, Peixoto and Rennó (2011) argue that the 2010 presidential vote is explained not by 'class voting' but rather by popular perceptions of social mobility. They find that the most consistent individual-level predictors of a Dilma vote in the runoff were, unsurprisingly, PT partisan identification and approval of the Lula government. But when the authors control for subjective perceptions of upward mobility, they find that income is no longer a statistically significant factor, contrary to what is implied by

Table 1.1   Voting intentions on eve of 2010 presidential runoff election

	Dilma Rousseff (PT)	José Serra (PSDB)	Blank/ null/ none	Don't know
Gender				
Male	55	39	4	2
Female	47	43	4	5
Age				
16–24	48	43	6	3
25–34	51	41	4	4
35–44	53	39	4	4
45–59	53	40	3	4
60 and over	49	45	2	4
Education				
Elementary	57	36	2	4
Secondary	48	43	6	3
College	40	51	6	3
Region				
North/Center West	50	42	3	5
Northeast	63	30	3	4
Southeast	48	44	5	3
South	42	50	3	5
County Type				
Capitals/Metro Areas	52	39	5	3
Interior	50	43	3	4
Household Income (in multiples of minimum wage)				
Up to 2	56	36	3	5
2–5	49	43	5	3
5–10	45	48	5	2
More than 10	39	54	6	1
Religion				
Catholic	53	40	3	4
Pentecostal Protestant	47	44	5	4
Mainline Protestant	45	45	4	6
No religion	53	37	8	3
ALL VOTERS	**51**	**41**	**4**	**4**

Source: Data Folha voting intentions poll, 29–30 October 2010 (last 48 hours prior to election), with 6,554 voting-age adults in 257 municipalities (study no. PO3548). Margin of error of 2 percent at 95 percent confidence level; poll correctly predicted final Serra and Dilma shares of the valid vote to within one-half of a percentage point for each candidate. (datafolha.folha.uol.com.br.)

the descriptive statistics presented in Table 1.1. Perceptions of change are more important than material conditions: in other words, electoral preferences in 2010 were largely shaped by the emergence of the 'new middle-class' in the Lula years. Remarkably, this statistical finding had already been anticipated by Dilma's campaign slogan, *'para o Brasil seguir mudando'*, which was clearly intended to invoke ongoing processes of social mobility. If the perception of *mudança* was key to her victory, then her legitimacy naturally depends on *seguimento* of the social changes effected in the Lula years.

In light of these election results and of the rise of the 'new middle class' in Brazil, scholars have begun to advance new interpretations of Brazilian macropolitics. In a recent book, André Singer (2012) interprets the last three presidential elections in Brazil as an electoral 'realignment' that is instituting a sort of a Rooseveltian New Deal in Brazil – a progressive multiclass political coalition captained by the PT, intent on pro-poor policies and growth, and with a renewed role for the state. Paraphrasing Singer, Perry Anderson (2011, p. 7) has recently written that 'Lula's victories in 2002 and 2006 can be mapped with uncanny closeness onto Roosevelt's of 1932 and 1936'. If, following the New Deal parallel, the PT's victory in 2002 was a 'breakthrough' election and the victory in 2006 was a 'realigning' election, then Dilma becomes the custodian of what Singer terms *lulismo* – a social contract built on upward mobility for the poor.

Lessons of the Lula years for Dilma

As Dilma succeeded Lula in the Brazilian presidency in 2011, she enjoyed one great advantage over Lula in 2003: she had been able to observe eight years of a PT-led government in power. Prior to Lula, the only left-leaning coalition government in modern Brazilian history had been the PTB-led administration of João Goulart in 1961–64, which ended tragically in a military coup. After 21 years of military rule followed by another 17 years of centre-right governments under democracy, the possibility of a Lula victory in 2002 had led to alarmism in the international media and instability in financial markets (Martínez and Santiso, 2003; Spanakos and Rennó, 2006). Lula's ability to win the election, to allay domestic and international fears about his policy intentions, and to secure deep mass support and broad interparty coalitions were all novelties in Brazilian politics – they changed the way the left was viewed and understood. Yet Lula had no domestic leftist predecessor to emulate, whereas Dilma does. An attentive Dilma could observe several emergent legacies or 'lessons' from the Lula years. In this section, I review four of these lessons (although I note that this list is by no means exhaustive) before turning to some of the salient issues and cleavages that have emerged as a result of the Lula experience.

A first lesson of the Lula era might be that *the left cannot govern alone.* In purely politico-strategic terms, this may well be Lula's most important legacy to the Brazilian left.[8] Prior to 2002, the PT was 'purist' in all of its presidential bids. In 1989, 1994, and 1998 the party declined to form interparty alliances with any parties outside of the traditional 'family' of the left, and lost all three elections. In 2002, 2006, and 2010, the PT formed broad alliances with parties of the centre and right (notably the PMDB in the latter two contests), and won all three elections. The overall tally was three losses by a relatively sectarian Lula, followed by two victories by a pragmatic 'Lula light', followed by another successful campaign by an ecumenical Dilma in 2010. The 'big tent' strategy practised by the PT since 2002 has been controversial within the party, with many rank-and-file militants continuing to prefer 'historic' alliance partners from the left (Amaral, 2010), yet Lula's immense personal prestige was able to overcome any internal resistance. An objective evaluation would have to conclude that the Lula–Dilma alliance strategy has brought some significant payoffs to the party. Although there has never been, strictly speaking, a 'PT government' in Brazil – only a series of coalition governments in which the PT reserved the presidency and several key ministries – the party has nonetheless been able to win power and reward its supporters consistently over the past decade (Singer, 2012).

Nonetheless, a second lesson of the Lula years might focus on the dark side of interparty cooperation: *politics as usual has a price.* Coalitions that are oversized and 'disconnected' – meaning that the constituent parties of an alliance are not ideologically adjacent to one another – can be unwieldy and politically expensive for the president to maintain. An example may be found in the Lula government's most significant crisis, the *mensalão* ('big monthly payments') corruption scandal of 2005, in which high-ranking political operatives of the PT made illegal side payments to purchase support from patronage-hungry parties in Congress. Of the 18 deputies accused of receiving the *mensalão*, the majority were drawn from three small and traditionally clientelistic parties of the centre-right, the PTB, PL, and PP. One interpretation of the *mensalão* scandal (Pereira, Power and Raile, 2011) is that side payments were used to overcome the ideological distance between these parties and the PT, as well as to soften the impact of the PT's overrepresentation in the

Lula cabinet (the party held 60 percent of ministerial portfolios despite contributing only 29 percent of the Congressional seats held by the pro-government alliance). The cost of entering alliances with the centre-right is the perpetuation of a style of politics based on the exchange of favors, something that the PT had historically rejected prior to 2003. So the second lesson of the Lula years is simply the flip side of the first: while broad alliances win elections and pass legislation, they also imply significant transfers of resources that can skirt the limits of legality. In case anyone had missed this point, the lesson was driven home by no less of an authority than the Brazilian Supreme Court. In late 2012, the court conducted a groundbreaking judgment of the *mensalão* accusations in which several PT luminaries were belatedly convicted of corruption and racketeering during Lula's first term. These names included José Dirceu (Lula's presidential chief of staff and the architect of the modern PT), José Genoíno (former PT president), and Delubio Soares (former party treasurer), all of whom had advocated heterodox alliances with the centre-right. The challenge for Dilma is to maintain the operational benefits of broad interparty fronts while limiting their potential for blowback.

A third lesson of the Lula years derives from the *visible tensions between the PT and its historic base* among progressive civil society organizations. In the 1980s and 1990s the PT served as a sort of clearinghouse or 'umbrella party' for a large number of left-leaning civil society organizations (CSOs) and social movements: these included liberationist Catholics, feminist and Afro-Brazilian organizations, and LGBT groups, but most visibly the Central Única dos Trabalhadores (Unified Workers' Central – CUT) labor federation and the *Movimento dos Trabalhadores Rurais Sem Terra* (Landless Workers' Movement – MST). The PT enjoyed generally harmonious relations with these CSOs prior to 2002, but with Lula's accession to the presidency the party encountered the same problem endured by countless other socialist movements over the past century: once in government, the PT had to begin to say 'no' to historic constituencies. Disappointment with the Lula government quickly mounted within the labor movement, which objected to the social security reforms of 2003–04, and especially so in the MST, which rejected Lula's warm outreach to rural capitalists. The PT tried to grasp the best of both worlds, pursuing newly pragmatic policies while attempting to cultivate older left-leaning allies within civil society. Symptomatic of this approach was Lula's simultaneous appointments of Miguel Rossetto (a PT deputy close to the MST) to the Ministry of Agrarian Reform and Roberto Rodrigues (a wealthy agro-exporter) to the Ministry of Agriculture, with the latter ministry enjoying vastly more influence over agrarian policies. Tensions such as these led the MST and other progressive CSOs to withdraw into a position of *apoio crítico* (critical support), which consisted of voicing opposition to PT policies while simultaneously defending the Lula government against any potential comeback by the PSDB. These CSOs continue to construct their identities in the context of resistance to neoliberalism, and simply put, they defend the PT because they have 'nowhere else to go' in the contemporary Brazilian party system. The work of Kathryn Hochstetler (2008) has shown that *apoio crítico* has become the status quo since the mid-2000s, and that it is unlikely the PT will recover its previously symbiotic relationship with progressive CSOs as long as it remains in federal government.

A fourth and final lesson from the Lula era extends to the Cardoso period as well: *the marginalization of the federal opposition.* Under the recent Brazilian practice of coalitional presidentialism, opposition is hell. During the Cardoso administration (1995–2002), the PT was on the losing end of oversized coalitions: the pro-Cardoso alliance passed most of the key constitutional amendments of this period by huge margins, and the PT and its left-leaning allies were relegated to the role of bystanders. In the Lula period, the shoe was on the other foot: the PSDB-PFL opposition had very little influence over newly proposed legislation or policies. As discussed above, this marginalization effect is caused essentially by the migration of clientelistic and opportunistic parties to the government camp, which produces oversized coalitions and leaves only a small and ideologically unified bloc to serve as an open opposition to the president (the size of the 'clear' federal opposition since 1995 has been on the order of 25–35 percent of Congress). Long spells of exclusion from power have taught important lessons to the two main contending parties, the PT and the PSDB. For the PT, the lesson is to hang on to the presidency at all costs (even at the price of ideologically unwieldy coalitions) rather than to return to its backbench role of the 1990s. For the PSDB in the Dilma years, the lesson is likely to be to fight hard to retain subnational domains of power such as the governorships of São Paulo and Minas Gerais (which together are responsible for nearly half of Brazil's GDP). States and municipalities are essentially the only policy 'laboratories' available to the federal opposition.

Beyond the above four lessons of political practice, it is important to reemphasize a point made earlier: the Lula years have ingrained strong regional and class-based cleavages in *presidential* voting, as was abundantly apparent in 2006 and 2010. While this pattern does not emerge as obviously in other electoral contests, one can make the case that presidential politics is the 'centre of gravity' of the Brazilian political system (Amorim Neto, 2007), and that therefore patterns of presidential politics will reverberate throughout the political system writ large. This is essentially the logic behind Singer's (2012) claim of a progressive, New Deal-style realignment in the Lula era. A realignment, even if restricted only to presidential elections, would seem to imply a long period of continued PT dominance: a coalition implementing pro-poor policies in a country like Brazil is, mathematically speaking, a *majoritarian* coalition at the mass level. With adequate political management, a coalition like this one can expect electoral success as long as (1) equity-enhancing policies continue to constitute the signature initiative of the government; and (2) the social structure does not change so radically as to erode the electoral appeal of redistribution. The latter scenario is unlikely to manifest itself in Brazil even in the medium run.[9]

In 2010, the possibility of enduring PT hegemony seemed to focus the minds of conservative media outlets, which in the run-up to the presidential ballot evinced deep concerns about the potential for a third straight victory by the Lula alliance. A number of 'wedge issues' were deployed in an attempt to shake votes loose from Dilma and stymie the construction of a long-term political base along the lines described by Singer. These wedge issues included anti-welfarist discourse (for example, social policies were said to be electorally motivated, and/or to be creating a culture of dependency in Brazil), arguments against affirmative action policies in public employment and university admissions, claims that the Lula/Dilma camp were unwisely aligning Brazilian foreign policy with illiberal populist regimes in South America (Venezuela, Bolivia, Ecuador), politicization of debates about reproductive rights (including an Internet rumor campaign that Dilma would pursue decriminalization or legalization of abortion), and of course numerous references to Dilma's 1960s experiences in the armed resistance to military rule (throughout 2010, a 'Google bomb' automatically completed any search entry for 'Dilma Rousseff' with the word *terrorista*). However, the most interesting aspect of these wedge issues was that none of them gained any serious traction within the voting public in 2010 – they simply could not compete with the concept of upward social mobility that provided the master frame for Dilma's election campaign.

Concluding thoughts: the first two years of Dilma Rousseff

The chapters in this volume are linked together by their analyses of the legacy of Luiz Inácio Lula da Silva. Because Lula secured the election of Dilma Rousseff in 2010, her presidency will be counted among the most important elements of his legacy. What most observers have commented, and what Dilma hinted herself in her inauguration speech, is that Lula is a 'hard act to follow'. Yet taking a longer view of the Brazilian renaissance since 1994, both Lula and his predecessor have raised expectations about the transformative power of the Brazilian presidency, and Dilma will also be judged against various achievements of the previous 16 years. The legacy of Cardoso was economic stability while the legacy of Lula was social inclusion: Dilma will be expected to provide *both* economic stability and continued social inclusion. This is a tall order – and revealingly, her 2010 campaign slogan (see above) invoked only the latter objective.

As I write, Dilma Rousseff has completed only two years in power, and it is much too early to undertake a serious review of her government either in relative terms (compared to Lula) or in absolute terms (judged by her own initiatives). Nonetheless, it is possible to offer some initial observations about her early performance in office. I conclude this essay by remarking on three aspects of her early presidency: (1) her political maneuvers to move out from under Lula's shadow and establish 'ownership' of the Brazilian government; (2) her policy initiatives that suggest subtle differences from her predecessor; and (3) her astounding popularity with the mass public.

On the first point, the political front, Dilma faces the same basic challenge as did Cardoso and then Lula: she must manage an oversized, heterogeneous coalition of many parties. However, Dilma was not the original 'author' of this alliance: Lula was. Between 2006 and 2010 Lula created the basic format of the coalition, which now relies heavily on its two largest parties, the PT and PMDB, and which has ascribed a greater role to the latter as a support party (symbolized by the accession of Michel Temer, a wily PMDB-machine boss, to the vice presidency). In Dilma's inaugural cabinet of 37 ministers, no fewer than 16 were Lula holdovers – eight in the same jobs, and eight reshuffled to other portfolios. Lula's gift of a 'prefabricated' government to Dilma had both positive and negative aspects. On the positive side, Dilma was free to campaign unhindered in 2010 while Lula handled coalitional politics; on the negative side, not being the *formatrice* of the coalition, it was widely expected that Dilma would rely on Lula as a 'fixer' if the alliance should run into political trouble.

Yet the experience of the first two years has shown Dilma to be more than capable of sorting out coalitional management on her own. On nine occasions between June 2011 and February 2012, ministers were replaced by Dilma for reasons ranging from outspokenness (for example

Nelson Jobim at Defence) to unexplained wealth (for example Antônio Palocci, presidential chief of staff). Most were asked for their resignations almost immediately upon running into trouble, showing significant decisiveness on the part of the president (in sharp contrast to Lula, who was loath to sack allies and often dragged his feet in such situations). In eight of the nine cases, Dilma awarded the vacant portfolio to the same political party of the departing minister, showing respect for the principles of interparty power-sharing agreements. These reshuffles allowed Dilma to put her 'stamp' on the cabinet much earlier than most observers had anticipated: in the first year and half of her government, the 'Lula quotient' of the cabinet declined from 43 percent to under 20 percent of the portfolios.

On the second point, policy initiatives, Dilma has also signaled some departures from Lula. The year in which she was elected, 2010, was a massive boom year for the Brazilian economy: the growth rate of 7.5 percent was the best since 1986, but also generated some fears about a potentially overheated economy during the critical presidential transition. The perception of creeping inflation led Dilma to announce immediate federal spending cuts of 50 billion reals (approximately USD $30 billion) from Lula's projected layouts for 2011. Her new Central Bank president, Alexandre Tombini, raised interest rates twice in 2011, again showing caution and concern with regard to inflation (later, however, a rapid cooling of growth led to several consecutive rate cuts in 2011 and 2012). Dilma also resisted pressures to raise the minimum wage above the formula agreed in the Lula years, and she took a relatively hard line when in 2012 federal workers struck for higher wages, sternly reminding public sector unions that they had gained well above the rate of inflation under her generous predecessor. In these ways Dilma tried to project an aura of macroeconomic 'responsibility', though in a context very different from the way Lula had done so in 2003–04.

The most unambiguously original policy initiatives of the early Dilma presidency concerned an area in which Brazil had long been a laggard relative to its South American neighbors: transitional justice. Unlike other postauthoritarian societies, Brazil had never implemented a truth commission or engaged in punishment of leading state officials who abused human rights under the military regime (1964–85). The latter omission was due to the *Lei da Anistia*, the controversial 'two-way' amnesty passed by Congress in 1979 and upheld by the Supreme Court as recently as April2010, which prohibited punitive measures for 'political crimes' committed either by agents of the dictatorship or members of guerrilla groups. Despite the constraining effects of the *Lei da Anistia*, the debate on transitional justice had begun to shift notably prior to Dilma's election. One of the overlooked aspects of Brazil's renaissance since 1994 is that all three post-real presidents were prominent opponents of the dictatorship, each symbolizing a distinct faction of the opposition front: Cardoso was a key voice among pro-democracy intellectuals, Lula a major figure in the organization of unions and social movements, and Dilma a member of the armed resistance. Of the three, Dilma was by far the most directly impacted by the experience of dictatorship, having been arrested in 1970, tortured for 22 days, and sentenced to six years in prison (of which she served three). For this reason she has taken a strong and deeply personal interest in transitional justice, reviving the issue far beyond the tentative efforts of her two predecessors.

Notably, Dilma's first trip abroad was to Argentina in January 2011, where she made a public visit with Cristina Fernández de Kirchner to the Mothers and Grandmothers of the Plaza de Mayo, donning a white headscarf in solidarity with the relatives of the disappeared. This visit was clearly intended for Brazilian consumption, signalling Dilma's more dynamic approach to transitional justice and putting Brazil on notice that new policy initiatives were forthcoming. Shortly thereafter, she reintroduced legislation (originally drafted under Lula, but withdrawn after military complaints) proposing a National Truth Commission with investigatory but not punitive powers. The legislation was approved in November 2011. The Truth Commission was formally installed in May 2012 in an emotional ceremony in which Dilma was symbolically flanked by all four of her living predecessors (José Sarney, Fernando Collor, Cardoso, and Lula) in an eye-opening depiction of the increasing political maturity of Brazilian democracy. The Commission will have two years to complete its work and will report publicly while Dilma is still president. In her first year in office, Dilma already advanced transitional justice far beyond anything achieved in the first 25 years of the democratic regime.

On the third aspect of Dilma's young presidency – her support among ordinary Brazilians – analysts have been at a loss to explain the phenomenon. Her approval ratings have been nothing short of extraordinary, and have exceeded those of Cardoso and of Lula at similar moments in their respective presidencies. For example, in September 2012, some 62 percent of Brazilians rated her government as 'excellent' or 'good', and only 7 percent as 'poor' or 'terrible'.[10] Disapproval of the government has never climbed above 12 percent in any major opinion poll since Dilma's inauguration, thus defying the usual law of gravity that depresses presidential approval after a honeymoon period. Part of this is likely due to a Weberian 'charismatic transfer' insofar as Dilma was a key figure in the popular Lula government, and was his chosen successor in 2010. Part of it is certainly due to the decade-long decline in poverty and inequality, which continued even after the economy began to slow down in 2011 (IPEA, 2012a). Yet it is also reasonable to assume that Dilma's decisive management style – particularly her hard line on underperforming ministers and her impatience with any improbity in the government – has endeared her to a segment of the voting public that respects a 'managerial' presidency, especially one that has little patience for sleaze. Dilma's approach to day-to-day governance is very different from the extroverted, glad-handing style of Lula, who took a hands-off approach to detail while using the presidential office to communicate simple and easily understood principles to the mass public. In addition to her strong management skills, Dilma brings gravitas to the presidency in her multiple roles as a 'survivor' (both of torture and of cancer) and of course as the first female president of Brazil. Whereas Lula began his presidency with a reservoir of charisma, Dilma begins hers with a reservoir of respect.

As the classic work of Richard Neustadt (1990) demonstrated for the United States, presidential power derives equally from the president's standing with the public (popularity) and from her reputation within the political class (professional prestige). In her first two years in power, Dilma has enjoyed both. Yet, arguably, what she lacks so far is a 'signature policy' that will cement her legacy among ordinary voters in the same way that *Bolsa Família* did for Lula. Her stewardship of the multiyear *Programa de Aceleração do Crescimento* (PAC) occurred mostly under Lula and did not generate any one single *obra* (public work) that could be directly linked to Dilma. While transitional justice is a tremendously important moral issue for the future of Brazil, its impact among the general public is limited. And while the FIFA World Cup of 2014 is generating excitement among the Brazilian public, it was awarded back in 2007 and is not generally seen as an initiative emanating from the federal presidency. Arguably, what Dilma needs to secure the long-term New Deal-style realignment suggested by Singer (2012) is a major redistributive initiative that will link her more directly to the major legacy of Lula – social inclusion and upward mobility – and that will realize her campaign promise, 'that Brazil will continue to change'.

In conclusion, the transition from Lula to Dilma is an opportune moment to reflect on the increasing consolidation and maturity of Brazilian democracy. Dilma is more than just the successor of Lula, or even of the 16 years since the Plano Real – she is also the symbol of a democratic regime that has proven remarkably resilient, having rebounded from early setbacks to embark on a more creative and dynamic course since 1994. Her predecessors made impressive headway against traditional threats to sustainable democracy, such as hyperinflation and pervasive inequality, and commentators on the 'new Brazil' have focused largely on the good news on those two fronts. Yet significant challenges remain to test the regime, including corruption, violence, and an uneven rule of law. Notably, these are challenges not to the *survival* of democracy, but to the *quality* of democracy. Dilma is uniquely positioned to address these challenges: thanks to the achievements of her predecessors, no recent president has had a more favorable scenario in which to focus on persistent deficiencies of democratic quality. The democratic regime is secure for the present, but it cannot rest on its new laurels. The question for Dilma is whether she will continue to hoard political capital (for example, massive popularity and an oversized ruling coalition) as did her predecessor, or whether she will prove more willing to spend some of it on pressing social, political and economic reforms in the coming years.

Notes

The author is grateful to Cesar Zucco Jr. for allowing him to draw on their collaborative work on the Brazilian Legislative Survey, and to the co-editors of this volume for their helpful comments.

1. This occurred in the Palácio do Catete (today the Museu da República) in Rio de Janeiro on 31 January 1951, when Eurico Dutra transferred the presidency to Getúlio Vargas. Both Dutra and Vargas were members of the old *Partido Social Democático* (PSD). Five years later, the sash was passed once again from one member of the PSD to another (Nereu Ramos to Juscelino Kubitschek), but Ramos was an unelected interim president, one of three who combined to complete Vargas' term after his suicide in 1954.
2. An economic plan to control hyperinflation and stabilize the national economy implemented during the Itamar Franco government (1992–94) when Fernando Henrique Cardoso served as Finance Minister.
3. For a fuller elaboration of these five points of consensus, see Power (2010a).
4. The term is usually credited to Abranches (1988). For a discussion see Power (2010b).
5. For analysis of how this presidential duopoly developed after 1989, see Melo and Câmara (2012).
6. This was the sixth wave of the Brazilian Legislative Survey (BLS), implemented from March to July of 2009 in both houses of Congress (N=139). For details, see Power and Zucco (2011).
7. I thank Cesar Zucco for allowing me to reproduce Figures 1.1 and 1.2 from our ongoing collaboration on the BLS.

8. In this sense Lula is the historical inverse of Goulart. Goulart began his career as a product of a centrist coalition (the PSD-PTB alliance built by Vargas), but upon assuming the presidency came increasingly to rely on the left. Lula began his career as an icon of the left, but upon becoming president came increasingly to rely on a centrist coalition.

9. The 2011 national household survey (*Pesquisa Nacional de Amostra por Domicílios*, PNAD), released in September 2012, revealed that the Gini coefficient of income inequality had declined to 0.527– the lowest value recorded in Brazil since 1960, when it stood at 0.535. However, this value still leaves Brazil among the 15 most unequal societies in the world, signifying that redistribution will remain a central agenda item for decades to come. See IPEA (2012b).

10. This is from a national poll by IBOPE (www.ibope.com.br), on behalf of the Confederação Nacional de Indústria, conducted among 2000 adults and released on 26 September 2012. The margin of error is two percent.

References

Abranches, S. (1988) 'Presidencialismo de Coalizão: O Dilema Institucional Brasileiro', *Dados* 31: 5–38.

Amaral, O. (2010) *As Transformações na Organização Interna do Partido dos Trabalhadores entre 1995 e 2009*. Ph.D dissertation, University of Campinas.

Amorim Neto, O. (2007) 'O Poder Executivo, Centro de Gravidade do Sistema Político Brasileiro', in L. Avelar and A.O. Cintra (eds), *Sistema político brasileiro: Uma introdução*, 2nd revised edition (Rio de Janeiro: Fundação Konrad Adenauer).

Anderson, P. (2011) 'Lula's Brazil', *London Review of Books* 33(7): 3–12.

Braga, M. do Socorro Sousa and Pimentel, J. Jr. (2011) 'Os Partidos Políticos Brasileiros Realmente Não Importam?' *Opinião Pública* 17(2): 271–303.

Brazilian Legislative Survey. (2009) Brazilian Legislative Survey, Wave 6. http://thedata.harvard.edu/dvn/dv/zucco date accessed 7 July 2012.

Datafolha (2010) Pesquisa de Intenção de Voto, study no. PO3548, http://datafolha.folha.uol.com.br date accessed 7 December 2011.

Hagopian, F. and Mainwaring, S. (1987) 'Democracy in Brazil: Problems and Prospects', *World Policy Journal* 4 (Summer): 485–514.

Hall, A. (2006) 'From *Fome Zero* to *Bolsa Família*: Social Policies and Poverty Alleviation Under Lula', *Journal of Latin American Studies* 38(3): 689–709.

Hochstetler, K. (2008) 'Organized Civil Society in Lula's Brazil', in P.R. Kingstone and T.J. Power (eds), *Democratic Brazil Revisited* (Pittsburgh: University of Pittsburgh Press), pp. 33–53.

IBOPE. (2012) Pesquisa CNI-IBOPE: Avaliação do Governo (setembro 2012) http://www.ibope.com.br date accessed 3 October 2012.

IPEA. (Instituto de Pesquisa Econômica Aplicada) (2012a) *A Década Inclusiva (2001–2011): Desigualdade, Pobreza e Políticas de Renda*, Comunicado do IPEA no. 155 (Brasília: IPEA).

IPEA. (2012b) *Pesquisa Nacional de Amostra por Domicílios 2011*. http://www.ipea.gov.br (home page) date accessed 3 October 2012.

Lamounier, B. (1996) 'Brazil: The Hyperactive Paralysis Syndrome', in J.I. Domínguez and Lowenthal A. (eds), *Constructing Democratic Governance: Latin*

America and the Caribbean in the 1990s (Baltimore: Johns Hopkins University Press).

Martínez, J. and Santiso, J. (2003) 'Financial Markets and Politics: The Confidence Game in Latin American Emerging Economies', *International Political Science Review*, 24(3): 363–395.

Melo, C.R. and Câmara, R. (2012) 'Estrutura de Competição pela Presidência e Consolidação do Sistema Partidário no Brasil', *Dados* 55(1): 71–117.

Melo, M.A. (2008) 'Unexpected Successes, Unanticipated Failures: Social Policy from Cardoso to Lula', in P.R. Kingstone and T.J. Power (eds), *Democratic Brazil Revisited* (Pittsburgh: University of Pittsburgh Press).

Neri, M.C. (2012) *A Nova Classe Média: O Lado Brilhante da Base da Pirâmide* (São Paulo: Editora Saraiva).

Neustadt, R.E. (1990) *Presidential Power and the Modern Presidents: The Politics of Leadership from Roosevelt to Reagan* (New York: The Free Press).

Peixoto, V. and Rennó, L. (2011) 'Mobilidade Social Ascendente e Voto: As Eleições Presidenciais de 2010 no Brasil', *Opinião Pública* 17(2): 304–332.

Pereira, C., Power, T.J. and Raile, E.D. (2011) 'Presidentialism, Coalitions, and Accountability', in T.J. Power and M.M. Taylor (eds), *Corruption and Democracy in Brazil: The Struggle for Accountability* (Notre Dame: University of Notre Dame Press).

Power, T.J. (1991) 'Politicized Democracy: Competition, Institutions, and "Civic Fatigue" in Brazil', *Journal of Interamerican Studies and World Affairs* 33(3): 75–112.

Power, T.J. (2010a) 'Brazilian Democracy as a Late Bloomer: Reevaluating the Regime in the Cardoso-Lula Era', *Latin American Research Review* 45 (special issue): 218–237.

Power, T.J. (2010b) 'Optimism, Pessimism, and Coalitional Presidentialism: Debating the Institutional Design of Brazilian Democracy', *Bulletin of Latin American Research* 29(1): 18–33.

Power, T.J. and Zucco, C. Jr. (eds) (2011) *O Congresso por Ele Mesmo: Autopercepções da Classe Política Brasileira* (Belo Horizonte: Editora UFMG).

Rodden, J.A. (2003) 'Federalism and Bailouts in Brazil', in J.A. Rodden, G.S. Eskeland and J. Litvack (eds), *Fiscal Decentralization and the Challenge of Hard Budget Constraints* (Cambridge: MIT Press).

Samuels, D. and Abrucio, F. (2000) 'Federalism and Democratic Transitions: the "New" Politics of Governors in Brazil', *Publius: The Journal of Federalism* 30(2): 43–61.

Scolese, E. and Nossa, L. (2006) *Viagens com o Presidente* (Rio de Janeiro: Editora Record).

Singer, A. (2012) *Os Sentidos do Lulismo: Reforma Gradual e Pacto Conservador* (São Paulo: Companhia das Letras).

Spanakos, A. and Rennó, L. (2006) 'Elections and Economic Turbulence in Brazil: Candidates, Voters, and Investors', *Latin American Politics and Society* 48(4): 1–26.

2
Changing Repertoires of State-Society Interaction under Lula

Rebecca Abers, Lizandra Serafim, and Luciana Tatagiba

Introduction

During Luis Inácio Lula da Silva's two administrations as president of Brazil (2003–10), an entirely different kind of actor took over government decision-making. These are the conclusions of an innovative study by Maria Celina D'Araújo, who examined the social and political profile of upper-echelon federal government personnel during that period. She found that for the first time in Brazilian history, former union activists participated substantially in high levels of government, a fact that may not be that surprising considering that the Workers' Party, and especially the President, had strong links to that sector. Under Lula, D'Araújo found that 'about 26 percent of Ministers in the first term and 16 percent in the second came from labor unions' (2009, p. 117). The ministers were also closely connected to more broadly defined social movements: 43 percent in the first administration and 45 percent of those in the second participated in some way in movements, compared to around a quarter of ministers under the previous two presidencies (Ibid., p. 120). For D'Araújo, these numbers suggest that the Lula government represented a more diverse array of interests than seen in the past. Our argument in this chapter is that, in that context, social movements and state actors creatively experimented with historical patterns of state-society interaction and reinterpreted routines of communication and negotiation.

Activists who took office in the federal bureaucracy often transformed government agencies into militant spaces in which they continued to pursue claims developed previously in civil society.[1] In government, these activists sought to build and strengthen formal participatory institutions, which until then had been largely restricted to municipal governments. But they also experimented with other channels of communication, negotiation and collaboration between state and civil society, such as new forms of protest-based negotiation and less public, personal encounters between state and social movement actors.

When Lula took office in 2003, many supporters expected that his government would implement a broad democratic reform of the state, reproducing at the national level the local innovations such as participatory budgeting that had given Lula's Workers' Party (*Partido dos Trabalhadores – PT*) international renown during the 1990s (Cortês, 1998; Abers, 2000; Baierle, 2000; Navarro, 2003). Seeming to follow this legacy, the Lula government created a number of new *national councils* – permanent policy bodies with civil society members, usually elected by their peers – and strengthened those that had been created under previous administrations. It also promoted over 70 *national conferences* – large-scale participatory events, sometimes with local, state and national stages, for establishing broader policy goals – in areas as diverse as health care, human rights and public security.[2]

It would be wrong, however, to attribute these advances to a major pro-participation commitment by the president's office. They resulted less from the imposition of a new participatory approach to governing from on high and more from political dynamics within each policy sector. The presence of activists within many federal ministries allowed for experimentation, but the results varied from sector to sector depending on how civil society groups and state actors had historically engaged with each other. In some sectors, officially created, formal participatory institutions such as councils and conferences played a central role, while in others, less formal modes of interaction predominated. With allies in government jobs, social movements took to knocking on the doors of government officials and negotiating with them directly in meeting rooms and offices. Oftentimes, more and less institutionalized modes of interaction took place simultaneously. In this chapter, we show that these more personalized patterns of interaction did not necessarily undermine formal participatory arenas. The precise mix of personalized and institutionalized interactions varied tremendously.

We argue that this variation resulted from two factors. In the first place, the 'routines' of state-society interaction under Lula were profoundly influenced by past relationships between actors within the state and within movements – relationships that varied substantially across issue areas. In the second place, historical experience did not entirely dictate what actors would do after 2003. Instead, actors combined and transformed historical practices into new forms of interaction, often in response to momentary opportunities such as the nomination of movement activists to crucial decision-making positions. Under Lula, people who were committed to more participatory forms of government creatively combined different practices and routines, although each ministry did so in its own distinct way.

To deal with the idea that state-society interactions can grow out of both historical tradition and experimentalism, we draw on and adapt significantly Charles Tilly's concept of 'repertoire of contention'. Along with other social movement scholars, Tilly argued that when movements decide how to organize a collective action, they choose among a finite portfolio of techniques and practices with which they have experience and which have social and political legitimacy. Classic examples are the march, the petition and the barricade. Although the choice of how to organize is deeply influenced by past experiences and social norms, movement actors constantly modify their repertoire of collective action, experimenting and combining different practices in new ways of organizing, mobilizing support and expressing demands (Tilly, 1992; Clemens, 1993; Tarrow, 1998). In this chapter, we loosely adopt the concept of repertoire, originally conceived for the study of social movements, to think not only about *contention* but also about a broader range of *interactions* among state and civil society actors, that may include not only contentious relations but also collaborative ones.

Our analysis is based on an exploratory study conducted in 2010 in three policy sectors characterized by entirely different histories of state-society relations: (1) agrarian development, through the Ministry of Agrarian Development (Ministério do Desenvolvimento Agrário – MDA); urban policy, through the Ministry of Cities (Ministério das Cidades); and public security, through the National Secretariat of Public Security (Secretaria Nacional de Segurança Pública – SENASP). Each one is characterized by very different traditions of state-society interaction and underwent institutional changes under the Lula administrations that led to what, at least at first glance, looks like a similar outcome: the increased importance of formal participatory arenas, such as councils and conferences, in the policy-making process. We drew strongly on the secondary literature on each policy area, as well as on a brief field study conducted in November 2010, in which we interviewed six public officials involved in those policy processes. We emphasize the points of view of state actors in an attempt to invert the tendency of much of the literature to analyze participatory dynamics from the perspective of civil society actors.[3] One of the benefits of this approach is to help open up the black box of the state, presenting state actors as activists and not just cogs and wheels in bureaucracies, thereby contributing to the debate around the heterogeneity of the Brazilian State.

This chapter is based on three cases, in which new participatory institutions were built and strengthened, but with great differences with respect to their internal dynamics and external impacts. The literature on participation produced in recent decades has systematically examined variations among participatory experiences in terms of both their level of internal democracy and their impact on public decision-making. Explanations for variation refer to formal design, the level of organization of civil society, and the political and ideological commitments of the actors involved. This article draws on these insights and proposes the introduction of a new explanatory factor: the adaptation of historically constructed repertoires of interaction between social movements and the state.

Participation and repertoires of interaction

The relatively vast literature on participation in Brazil that has emerged in recent years approaches the topic from varied analytical and normative perspectives. Unlike countries where participatory experiments were imposed from above (e.g. development agencies), in Brazil extensive programs to ensure citizen participation in decision-making grew out of demands by civil society groups. Since the transition from military rule, left-wing parties with substantial social movement support – most notably the Workers' Party (PT) – took political office in local governments throughout the country and began to experiment with participatory governance. These local experiences produced new institutional models such as participatory budgeting and policy councils. Research on these new institutions has had a major impact on the debate about democracy within the Brazilian political science.

Early research largely involved in-depth case studies, especially on the Participatory Budget of Porto Alegre (Abers, 2000; Baierle, 2000; Baiocchi, 2005). Later works compared more and less successful cases of citizen participation. Participatory experiments varied both in terms of how much real power was devolved to participants and how open the experiments were to lower income, less educated citizens (Tatagiba, 2002; Fuks, Perissinotto and Souza, 2004). A number of authors concurred on the importance of three factors for explaining these differences: the design of the policies, local associational traditions, and the level of government of the programs (Avritzer, 2003; Wampler and Avritzer, 2004; Borba, Luchmann and Campo, 2007; Wampler, 2007). Recent studies have explored other aspects, such as the relationship between institutional design and citizen empowerment (Silva, 2001; Lubambo *et al.*, 2005), deliberative effectiveness (Avritzer, 2007; Cunha, 2007; Almeida and Cunha, 2009), the relationship between participation and representation (Gurza Lavalle *et al.*, 2006; Avritzer, 2007; Lüchmann, 2007; Abers and Keck, 2008), the question of scale (Silva, 2001; Faria, 2005) and the distributive impacts of participatory policies (Avritzer, 2010). Evelina Dagnino and her colleagues (Dagnino, 2002; Dagnino, Olvera and Panfichi, 2006) have explored what happens when government and civil society actors share political ideas and goals, drawing attention to the coexistence and tensions between the participatory and the neoliberal projects, both of which give priority to civil society, and to participation, though for very different reasons and with different implications.

All of these recent studies grow out of a common insight: new participatory institutions may look similar with respect to their legal and organizational structure, but the decision-making process within them can vary tremendously. We argue that looking at how these new arenas fit into broader traditions of state-society relations can help us explain such variation. For this purpose, we introduce the concept of repertoires of state-society interaction.

Charles Tilly (1992, p. 7; *apud* Tarrow, 1998, p. 30) defined *repertoires of contention* as 'a limited set of routines that are learned, shared, and acted out through a relatively deliberate process of choice'. Collective action, Tilly suggested, is influenced not only by the nature of existing problems, conflicts or demands, nor simply by the resources that are available to a group of actors, but also by the organizational know-how that actors learn both through past struggles and from their cultures. This practical experience and cultural knowledge influences the shape that collective action takes. As Tilly showed, repertoires are learned cultural creations that grow out of continual struggles and out of the response by powerful actors to those struggles (Tilly, 1995, p. 26). Such practices are reproduced for two reasons: because actors *learn* how to carry them out through previous experiences and because they perceive them to be morally legitimate ways of organizing, even when they involve legal transgressions. Circulating a petition, occupying a building and marching on the capital are actions that only occur because they have some degree of social and political legitimacy in contemporary political life, even when they occur outside of formal institutions.

If one central aspect of a repertoire is that it is learned from the past, on the other hand, Tilly and Tarrow both emphasize that social actors constantly create and transform the repertoires that guide them. Those involved in collective action cannot choose any organizational form: they work from the organizational formats with which they are familiar and that are politically and socially accepted. But repertoires can also be creatively constructed. In one of his last publications, Tilly (2008) gave emphasis to the idea that movements engage in what he called performances: at the same time that they reproduce old repertoires, they also improvise and reinterpret.

Although by combining the dimension of structure and agency, the notion of repertoire of contention is useful in allowing us to better understand how social movements operate, the concept has limits for understanding the Brazilian context. International literature on collective action has historically focused on relations between the state and social movements from the perspective of conflict, and for that reason protest is a central component of the social movement repertoire that authors such as Tilly and Tarrow describe (see e.g., Giugni and Passy, 1998; Hanagan, 1998; Goldstone, 2003). But as Abers and von Bülow (2011) have noted, the Brazilian case challenges this presumption to the extent that important movements were born out of alliances among state and non-state actors. This makes it necessary not only to 'theorize about how social movements collaboratively construct links with the state', but also 'how sometimes they seek to reach their goals by working within the state apparatus' (Abers and von Bülow, 2011, p. 78, our translation).

Despite the fact that Brazilian social movements often negotiate with the state (which would allow us to work with Tilly's original concept of repertoire), they have also invested heavily in action *within* state institutions, both through new participatory arenas and by strategically taking positions within the bureaucracy, transforming the state itself into a space for political activism. To incorporate this aspect of Brazilian politics, we suggest complementing Tilly's original notion of *repertoire of contention* with the concept of 'repertoire of interaction between state and civil society'. This addition allows us to incorporate the diversity of strategies used by Brazilian social movements and to examine how those strategies have been used, combined and transformed. The study identified at least four common routines of state-society interaction in Brazil: (1) protests and direct action, (2) institutionalized participation, (3) the politics of proximity, and (4) occupying positions in the bureaucracy. These are described below:

(1) *Protests and direct action:* Historically, social movements express demands and, in doing so, pressure state decision-makers to negotiate by demonstrating their mobilizing capacity. The exemplary

protest form is the march, but other methods similarly seek to make conflicts public, reinforce identities and commitments, and demonstrate the power of numbers. This sort of routine requires that actors express and sustain antagonisms, often by simplifying the terms and presenting them symbolically in ways that broaden their appeal to potential publics. The experience of the Lula administration suggests the need to go a bit further: when governments are seen as allies, protests do not necessarily disappear, but transform their meaning. We therefore identify two forms of protest and direct action routines: 'protest to initiate or reestablish negotiation', in the case of governments that are less permeable to movement demands; and 'protest as part of the ordinary negotiating cycle', more common in situations where government and movement actors are allied around shared political projects, as we will see in the case of the MDA (Ministry of Agrarian Development).

(2) *Institutionalized participation:* This form of interaction is characterized by the use of officially sanctioned channels of dialogue that are guided by previously defined rules, accepted by those involved (and in some cases established by law). Formal participatory arenas are characterized by public, documented meetings that have the explicit purpose of influencing particular policy decisions. Participation is usually indirect, involving different forms of representation (for example, civil society representatives are usually chosen in assemblies made up of other civil society groups active in the policy field). If in the first routine of interaction, social movement actors define the form, timing and agenda for both protest and for negotiations, this second routine is characterized by shared governance and by a central role of state actors in creating and running the process.

In Brazil, three models of institutionalized participation have become predominant. These are the participatory budget, policy councils, and conferences. The participatory budget brings together individual citizens at open meetings to discuss budget allocations, especially capital expenditures. They elect delegates to forums and councils that are re-elected each year and that are responsible for defining budget priorities. The policy councils are legally enacted decision-making bodies for particular policy sectors (such as health, social assistance, children's policy, environmental policy, water resources management and many others), with seats for state, civil society and service providers or the private sector. These permanent bodies, in which members usually hold two-year terms, are responsible for designing plans and regulations and for monitoring government actions. The conferences are meetings lasting no more than a few days, held every few years, in which larger numbers of people discuss general guidelines for a particular policy sector. Especially under Lula, the national conferences would usually start at the municipal or state level, where delegates are elected to participate in regional or state level meetings, and culminate in a national event. In all three of these models, state actors are protagonists because they have access to crucial resources – such as money and technical and human resources, not to mention the political authority to be delegated. However, the construction of these spaces is often negotiated in activist networks that cross the divide between state and civil society.

(3) *The politics of proximity:* This form of participation works through personal contacts between state and civil society actors. Particular actors obtain distinction or prestige through their location in a relational field, allowing them to circumvent institutional channels or rituals through which other actors must work to have access to decision-makers. The politics of proximity is characteristic of patron-client relationships. It should not, however, be reduced only to such patterns, since clientele relationships presuppose a personal exchange of favors, while direct contacts may also be a vehicle for making public demands and promoting the recognition of collective rights (Teixeira and Tatagiba, 2005). Activists often advance their goals by negotiating directly with decision-makers, within both the executive and legislative branches. This is made easier when direct ties between movements and the executive branch increase, as tends to be the case in left-wing governments when activists actually take positions within the state (see below). The resource that activists mobilize here are their statuses as recognized interlocutors. The reasons they may be able to 'speak directly' with public authorities can vary substantially, however, ranging from personal ties to the status of the organization to which they belong.

The politics of proximity is often referred to as *lobbying* and occurs not only in the executive branch, but also in the legislature. Studies of the relationship between social movements and the legislature are rare in Brazil, despite the fact that in various policy areas and at different historical moments, social movements have worked through political parties to try to get Congress to pass key laws or even articles in the Constitution. This gap in the literature likely results from the fact that such practices tend to be perceived as a less noble kind of politics. Yet important advances in Brazilian politics have resulted from lobbying by social movements, such as laws that reformed social policies and created systems of citizen participation in the first place (for example the Health Care and Social Assistance laws, the Children and Adolescent Rights Statute, The Statute of the City, among others).

(4) *Occupying positions in the bureaucracy*: For some Brazilian social movements, taking jobs in government is a common strategy for advancing movement goals. For the environmental movement, for example, the practice dates back to the military regime, when the first environmental agencies were headed by the activists who had fought for their creation (Alonso, Costa and Maciel, 2007; Hochstetler and Keck, 2007). When governments are perceived to be movement allies, this routine becomes more common. Occupying government positions has feedback effects on other routines of interaction. For example, social movements have greater opportunities to engage in the politics of proximity when their colleagues hold government jobs. When friends, allies, and co-activists become state employees, personalized connections between state and non-state actors are eased. Negotiations are much more likely to occur in unregistered meetings, not only in the ministry offices, but also over dinner, or in other spaces outside state institutions. Perhaps in most cases, activist bureaucrats began their social movement career outside the state. However, it is important to note that some social movements were formed by people who worked in the state from the beginning. The movement to reform Brazil's health system, for example, was founded in part by technical professionals and specialists in government positions (Dowbor, 2012).

In the next sections, we will present the three cases, emphasizing how different combinations of these practices and routines form the repertoire of state-society interaction in each policy area.

Case studies

Urban policy and the Ministry of Cities

Founded in 1985 to promote access to land and housing in Brazil's booming cities, the National Movement for Urban Reform (MNRU) involved shanty-town and tenement movements, progressive architects, planners, lawyers, NGOs and many other groups (Almeida, 2002). Initially focused on local politics, this diverse coalition made important advances on the national stage between the 1980s and the 2000s, such as the creation of municipal housing councils, the passage of federal urban planning legislation (the Statue of the City), and the creation of the Ministry of Cities in 2003. The repertoire of state-society interaction in this policy area was built over a 30-year period and included all four of the routines discussed above. During the early years of the Lula administration, activists involved in federal urban policy favored the strengthening of institutionalized participation, through the creation of the Council of Cities and the Conference of Cities. But they also directly engaged in policy design as government employees and consultants. The presence of movement activists within the state also made it easier for their movement colleagues on the outside to influence the design of urban policies.

Housing movements have been engaging in protests and land occupations since the 1970s, initially with a focus on publicizing demands and affirming autonomy from the state (Banck, 1986; Gay, 1990). By 1987, however, the MNRU targeted transforming national political institutions, starting with the new Constitution that was being drafted at the time. The movement rallied support around a proposal to include urban reform principles in the Constitution and was able to convince the Constitutional Assembly to approve guarantees (at least in principle) of the 'social function of property,' greater municipal autonomy and democratic urban government. These changes opened the door for civil society participation in city government through plebiscites, referendums, public hearings, councils, conferences and participation in the design of city plans. After the passage of the new Constitution, MNRU's name changed to National Forum for Urban Reform (Fórum Nacional da Reforma Urbana – FNRU), to express the idea that the organization had become an umbrella network.

The consolidation at the municipal level of these instruments became one of the FNRU's key goals in the 1990s. Although occupying positions and the politics of proximity were important routines of interaction between urban movements and local governments throughout the 1990s and 2000s, one of the main goals of these routines was the creation of new arenas for more institutionalized forms of participation. In the 1990s, the FNRU began to work with local governments – especially progressive ones – and their members often took political appointments in them to promote the creation of participatory budgets, conferences and councils. Once created, forum actors – especially those coming from popular movements – became actively involved in the new participatory institutions that they had helped build. By working to mobilize other civil society organizations to participate and by pressuring local governments to implement the decisions made, these actors helped to build knowledge and capacities within FNRU organizations. Over time, the FNRU gained legitimacy as a key actor in urban policy negotiations and came to be widely recognized for the sophistication of its policy proposals.

Urban reformers also gained experience in negotiating and pressuring the National Congress. Such lobbying efforts began with the Constitutional Assembly and continued in the 1990s, as urban movements attempted to pass complementary legislation that regulated the Constitution's chapter on urban policy, through bills such as the Statute of the City and the National Popular Housing Fund. The latter proposal was finally approved in 2005 as the National Fund for Social Housing (Fundo Nacional de Habitação de Interesse Social – FNHIS). Therefore, at the same time that urban movements had become experts at institutionalized participation, lobbying remained an important part of their repertoire of interaction with the state.

Despite this emphasis on institutional change, the FNRU's member organizations also engaged in the kind of protest routines that are commonly associated with contentious social movements, such as occupations and demonstrations. In general, these actions sought to pressure municipalities, states and the federal government to negotiate, especially when other channels for making claims were closed, as seemed to be the case during much of the 1990s as the Statute of the City stalled in congress. The approval of the law in 2001 breathed new life into the Urban Reform Movement's effort to transform state institutions, now with its sight on the federal bureaucracy.

In 2002, a group of urban reform activists participated in writing the urban policy component of Lula's presidential campaign platform. They called for the creation of a new agency that would integrate urban development, housing, sanitation, transportation and urban mobility policies. While they existed at the national level, all of these policies had been historically fragmented among ministries. Upon taking office in 2003, Lula immediately followed up on the proposal, creating the Ministry of Cities. The FNRU celebrated the decision as a major victory, made possible in part because decision-makers within the new government shared their ideals. The icing on the cake came when Lula named Olívio Dutra – the ex-mayor of Porto Alegre who had created the Participatory Budget – as minister. FNRU activists perceived this nomination to be a sign of Lula's commitment to the urban reform project.

A number of FNRU leaders and intellectuals were appointed to top-level ministry positions and the creation of two new participatory institutions quickly followed: the National Council of Cities and the Conference of Cities. According to interviews, however, state-society interaction was not limited to those arenas: movement activists worked as consultants for particular projects and informal meetings regularly occurred with representatives of the housing movement, NGOs, professional organizations and academics. The politics of proximity occurred alongside the expansion of institutionalized participation, both of which were propelled by an increased presence of movement activists within the bureaucracy.

During Olivio Dutra's period in the ministry, the Council and Conference became the central arenas within which urban policy was designed. The minister and FNRU leaders informally agreed that important decisions would be made jointly between the Ministry and the Council, following guidelines approved at the National Conference of Cities. The situation changed after 2005, when Márcio Fortes, of the Progressive Party (Partido Progressista – PP), replaced Dutra.[4] Fortes came from an entirely different political tradition, described by interviewees as largely based on personalistic, bilateral and even 'clientelistic' relationships. With Dutra's exit, most of the appointees who had come from the Urban Reform movement were replaced by a much more 'technocratic' staff. This reconfiguration within the ministry diminished the importance of institutionalized participation in decision-making, although the new arenas themselves remained in place.

Interviewees affirm that in this second stage, the Council of Cities lost momentum. Government officials – many of whom did not share a commitment to participatory forms of decision-making – were seen less often at the meetings. The minister had a new way of working with civil society and, according to one interviewee, civil society actors changed their behavior in response. 'When the pattern of dialogue changes, but the interlocutors in civil society remain the same, they change their pattern of interaction,' the interviewee noted. The politics of proximity now became the central routine of interaction. Movement activists began to 'play the minister's game', adapting to the new form of interaction. This suggests that changes in high level personnel within the state – with their particular political projects and practices – can make a huge difference in terms of the kinds of interaction that prevail.

Despite the decline in the centrality of institutionalized participation and the increase in a particular form of the politics of proximity, the repertoire of state-society interaction survived the Fortes administration, at least in part. Actors continued to engage each other through both of these historic routines. The Council continued to meet and conferences continued to be held every two years alongside regular informal contacts between civil society actors and state officials. This continuity suggests that, despite major changes in the political situation – likely to occur in any government – a relatively stable set of options, nourished by several decades of activism, remained in place, even if their content and capacity to influence policy decisions fluctuated over time.

Agrarian development policy

While urban social movements had a long history of working with governments to create institutionalized participatory arenas before Lula came to office in 2003, the history of rural social movements was dominated by routines of protest and direct action. This different history of state-society interaction influenced how participatory arenas were received within the agrarian development policy sector of the Lula administration. During Lula's first term, rural social movements were heavily involved in the design of policies promoting *family agriculture*. This did involve promoting strengthened policy councils, but negotiations between movements and the state mostly took place through an innovative adaptation of protest routines.

Most of the literature on rural social movements in Brazil has focused on the MST (Landless Workers Movement) and on land occupations aimed at pressuring the government to expropriate unproductive farms for land distribution. The MST was created in 1984, but the form of contentious actions for which it is most famous – the *encampment* – has a longer history. As Sigaud, Rosa and Macedo (2008) show, the transition from individualized land occupations to the *encampment* form of mobilization began to occur in the 1960s. From the beginning, state actors recognized that the encampments had a certain legitimacy. Indeed, the first ones occurred with the explicit support of state actors, such as a municipal mayor in one of the earliest episodes. Along similar lines, Wolford's study of an MST occupation of a regional office of the National Institute of Colonization and Agrarian Reform (INCRA) identified an almost symbiotic relationship between the movement and the government agency. Wolford notes that INCRA is 'arguably the least well-funded and most under-staffed agency in the Brazilian government' (Wolford, 2010a, p. 96). This fragility caused INCRA officials to depend on the organization's technical and organizational capacities to get their job done.

Another major rural movement organization in Brazil is CONTAG (Confederação Nacional dos Trabalhadores na Agricultura), a union organization created decades ago under a state-led corporatist regime. CONTAG was created in 1963, and although it was officially under government intervention for several years, the organization was able to continue operating legally during the military regime that lasted from 1964 to 1985. This made it possible for activists to use CONTAG's formal union structure to promote the organization of rural workers, despite a broader context of violent repression of social movements.[5] CONTAG's organizational structure is pyramidal, with local unions organizing in state-level Federations, which are members of the National Confederation. The result of this *bottom-up* structure is that lower level members do not necessarily follow orders from above (Ibid.).

In 1995, CONTAG held the first *Grito da Terra* (Shout of the Land), a huge march on Brasília, in which the organization demonstrated its capacity for mobilization and presented its main demands to the federal government. Since then, the organization has repeated the *Grito da Terra* annually. State federations also organized *Gritos* often to make demands on state governments. This routine of claims-making protest was also used by other rural movements. In 1997, the MST organized a march on Brasília that received much media attention. The first *Marcha das Margaridas* (March of the Daisies) – a term used to refer to women farmers and forest workers – occurred in 2000. In 2005, another rural organization was created, FETRAF (Federação Nacional de Trabalhadores e Trabalhadoras da Agricultura Familiar), and also began to hold annual marches.

Created under President Fernando Henrique Cardoso, the MDA (Ministry of Agrarian Development) has been influenced by protest, but has also tried to build more institutionalized routines of interaction: the policy councils. According to Wolford (2010b), the Cardoso government created an agrarian reform policy in response to international attention after massacres in Corumbiara (1995) and Eldorado dos Carajás (1996), where police killed landless peasants who were encamped in the region. Cardoso's main land reform policy was the National Program for Strengthening Family Agriculture (PRONAF), a market-based program whose priority was to create the economic conditions for small-scale agricultural production, rather than to distribute land (see also Branford, 2009). PRONAF funded infrastructure and services in municipalities that had created Municipal Rural Development Councils.

Rural movements thus associated the council model with the Cardoso administration's market approach to agrarian policy and looked on them with suspicion. Activists and academics who are sympathetic to the movements usually suggest that while councils are a good idea in principle, their implementation has had serious failings in practice because they tend to be created with the sole intention of allowing municipal governments to gain access to federal resources. A number of authors note that the rural poor tend to be under-represented in these bureaucratic and legalistic councils and that, in any case, they had little practical impact on local agricultural policies (Abramovay, 2001; Mattei, 2006; Schneider, Silva and Marques, 2009). In some places, rural social movements have explicitly refused to participate in the councils, concerned that doing so might diminish their capacity to criticize the government (Silva, Rocha and Alves, 2011).

The Lula administration invested in strengthening and politicizing the council model in the rural policy sector. The government restructured the National Rural Development Council (CONDRAF), which had been created during the Cardoso government. The council grew in size and now included a wider variety of civil society groups, such as those representing women farmers and environmentalists. The new government also created the National Council for Food and Nutrition Security (CONSEA) as part of Lula's Zero Hunger Project, the hallmark policy in his first year in office. CONSEA was directly connected to the presidency of the republic and also designed policies affecting family agriculture. Despite these changes, many rural social movement organizations still avoided relying only on the councils for channeling demands to government. According to an interviewee,

> the movements that are represented in CONDRAF oppose transferring all negotiations to that space. This is a good quality, because the mobilization is not just to make policy gains, but also to gain social power. If they channel everything through CONDRAF, institutionalization can become a mechanism of containment.

At the same time, after 2003, new patterns of direct negotiation between the ministry and the movements emerged. Under previous governments, rural movements regularly marched to Brasília, presented their demands to the government and then waited to receive an answer. After 2003, the government and the movement organizations began to interact much more intensely in what became an annual ritual. Between April and July, rural movements would initiate negotiations through a series of marches and other protest actions. The marches were timed so that they would occur in the months just before the government announced the following year's agricultural policies, which typically took place in July. Once marchers arrived in Brasília, they would present a detailed list of demands for the coming year and the movement and government would designate members to a joint negotiating team. The negotiators would agree on a schedule of meetings and a set of issues to be discussed. The process (repeated with each movement organization) would end with a presidential address, announcing that year's *Plano Safra* (Harvest Plan), which would incorporate the combined results of all of those negotiations. In sum, interactions between movements and government were molded by traditional repertoires of contention that looked very much like the protests in which movements had traditionally engaged to express demands to the national government. The difference was that with a *friendly* administration, those routines evolved in two ways. In the first place, under Lula, a more interactive process of negotiation took place, with the direct participation of the ministry as well as of the General Secretariat of the Republic, which coordinated negotiations when other ministries needed to get involved. In the second place, this negotiation process became routinized, occurring every year, always during the same period. Although the routine remained completely informal, as one interviewee noted, it had become a *noninstitutionalized institution.*[6]

The routinization of protest and negotiation did not necessarily diminish conflicts. The relationship between the government and the MST deteriorated during the first years of the Lula administration, after the organization concluded that the government had betrayed its campaign promise to carry out a broad-based agrarian reform (Branford, 2009). Although CONTAG is frequently considered to have been a government ally, the organization's decentralized structure meant that, while the national leadership tended to defend the government's position, local and state level unions often presented other positions and made demands that were off CONTAG's national agenda.

Indeed, the value that the MDA gave to protest routines was likely a result of the relative weakness of the ministry within the government. Wolford notes that, although the Lula government had ideological affinity with the agrarian reform project, the timing was not propitious for advancing agrarian reform. By 2004, the international pressure that existed after the massacres of the mid-1990s had dissipated and the price of rural land had gone up dramatically (2010b, pp. 214–215). Wolford shows that after a first year of increased investment in the MDA and in INCRA (the land reform agency subordinated to it), the financial and personnel situation quickly returned to the precarious state of the previous government. MDA officials saw the highly publicized protests of the rural social movements as a way to gain political support for their policy area and negotiate within the government: 'These mobilizations give force to [the MDA's] capacity to negotiate within the government.' This statement, by a government official we interviewed, suggests that repertoires of interaction are influenced not only by relationships *between* state and society, but also by internal relations *within* a heterogeneous government. This notion challenges the idea that such practices can be understood as simply a reflection of confrontation between state and society.

Public security policy

Efforts to build a national public security policy are still incipient in Brazil. The 1988 Constitution made state governments responsible for design and implementation of public security policy, without clearly defining the responsibilities of federal and municipal governments. In 1995, within the Ministry of Justice, the Cardoso administration created a secretariat responsible for Public Security, later named SENASP (Secretaria Nacional de Segurança Pública), whose mission was to work with state governments to implement a national policy (Carvalho and Silva, 2011). When a highly publicized bus hijacking in Rio de Janeiro mobilized national attention around the issue in 2000,[7] the government quickly published the National Public Security Plan that SENASP had been working on and announced the creation of a National Public Security Fund to finance it. Although considered to be important advances (Ibid.), these first steps toward building a national policy took place with little debate with what was at the time perceived to be a fragmented and weakly organized policy community.

A timid civil society debate on the issue began in the early 2000s, growing primarily out of denunciations of police violence against minorities and the poor (Pavez, Toledo and Gonçalves, 2010). Although the level of organization was nothing like what we saw in the two cases discussed earlier, the number of civic groups involved in policy debates around public security began to grow. While in the 1990s, the main protagonists were NGOs and research institutes, in the early 2000s, religious groups (especially a masonic group and the Brazilian Catholic Bishops' Council), human rights groups and organizations representing the urban poor began to organize campaigns, protests and other activities to call attention to the issue (Pavez, Toledo and Gonçalves, 2010). In 2000 the Brazilian Catholic Bishops' Council organized its annual Fraternity Campaign (a national program with strong impact on the catholic community) around the theme *Solidarity and Peace*. The national referendum on disarmament that took place in 2005 also mobilized public debates on the issue (Pavez, Toledo and Gonçalves, 2010).[8]

In 2002 the Citizenship Institute (Instituto da Cidadania), an organization affiliated with the Workers Party, wrote a proposal for a National Public Security Plan that would later be included in Lula's presidential platform. To design the proposal, the Institute held meetings with state officials, researchers, professionals and activists from various regions of the country (Soares, 2007). Beyond this effort, however, no significant advances took place in public security policy during the first Lula administration. The focus in those earlier years was on combating corruption through the federal police, rather than on urban violence (Ibid.). This began to change in the middle of Lula's second term, when the government announced a series of policies geared toward increasing federal government involvement and support for urban policing at the state and municipal levels (Pavez, Toledo and Gonçalves, 2010).

None of these policies, however, gave precedence to citizen participation, which only made the agenda after 2008. The proposal to create a policy council and to hold a national conference for public security policy came not from civil society, but rather from a group of public officials in SENASP who were personally committed to participatory approaches. A National Council of Public Security (Conselho Nacional de Segurança Pública – CONASP) had been created years earlier, in 1990, in the wake of the 1988 Constitution. But it was a dead letter, with no impact on policy-making (reflected in the fact that not a single academic study has been written about it after 20 years of operations). Reactivating the council and holding a national public security conference were demands neither of the government nor of civil society. Instead, those moves resulted from the work of a small number of state actors committed to a participatory agenda. The support of the Minister of Justice – Tarso Genro, another ex-mayor of Porto Alegre whose career was intimately associated with that city's participatory budget program – would also play an important role. However, the fact that only a small number of civil society organizations were involved in the issue, the lack of a tradition of state-society dialogue and a history of conflict between civic organizations and the police, as well as between upper and lower echelon police organizations, created an inhospitable terrain for experimentation with participatory dynamics.

While in the other two policy areas studied, institutionalized forms of participation were created in and had to adapt to a context where dense networks (among social movements and between them and the state) already existed; in this policy area, institutionalized participation was meant to *produce* relationships, activate connections and overcome distrust and hostility. In the absence of a historic repertoire of interaction, state actors sought to create one artificially, and to do so, relied on the models most cited by academic literature.

Overcoming resistance to participation required identifying key actors in civil society and in the state and getting them to commit to the process. The organizers started by creating a working group with the mission of preparing for the national conference. This national organizing commission included public security officials, civil society organizations and federal, state and municipal employees from all three branches of government. The commission devised a *conference methodology*, which included events throughout the country between July 2008 and August 2009. They also allowed for 'free conferences' on the initiative of civil society organizations to be held at any location, such as schools, prisons or churches (Pavez, Toledo and Gonçalves, 2010).[9]

Pavez, Toledo and Gonçalves's (2010) study used social network analysis to show that one of the main results of the year-long conference process was an increase in links among organizations in the policy area. The study showed that the network-building effect was greatest for public security labor unions, which were particularly likely to build new connections to other organizations over the course of the conference process. Pastoral groups and human rights organizations also increased their involvement in this emerging policy community.

After the first cycle of meetings, participants at the final national assembly in 2009 decided to extend the Commission's mandate an extra year so that it could organize elections for a revitalized national council (Soares, 2007). A year later the organizing commission fulfilled that charge by calling a general assembly, in which civil society organizations and public security labor unions chose amongst their peers to sit on the council for the 2010–12 term. There were 12 seats for civil society, nine for workers and nine for state officials (nominated by the government, rather than the assembly). Civil society organizations that mobilized actively for this election and the organizations that were elected held vastly diverse, if not conflicting, views of public security problems and policy priorities. The formation of the council meant that, for the first time, groups with extremely different positions in the debate would have to work together.

Conclusions

In this chapter we argue that two factors influenced changing state-society relations under Lula: (1) the migration of social movement activists and sympathizers into government and their creative transformation of exist-ing repertoires of state-society interaction in these new circumstances. When PT took over the national government, social movements con-nected to the party faced innumerable dilemmas and challenges as they interacted with a government seen to be an ally, most notably pressures to contain their criticisms or even moderate their demands. Nonetheless, the cases discussed here also suggest that the much closer ties between social movement actors inside and outside the state allowed for the crea-tive combination of historical traditions of state-society interaction in ways that promoted new forms of negotiation and dialogue.

Much of the literature on state-society relations under leftist govern-ments in Brazil emphasizes formal participatory institutions such as the participatory budget, councils and conferences. We argue, however, that those institutions should not be examined in isolation from other forms of interaction between movements and government. Understanding that broader context requires looking at the distinct history of state-society relationships in each policy area.

The very creation of the Ministry of Cities reflected decades of strug-gle by the National Urban Reform Movement to change municipal, state and federal government institutions. A key component of those struggles was the focus on creating formal arenas for civil society par-ticipation. By the time Lula came to office, housing movements had been working with such institutions for decades and, compared to the other two policy areas studied, had substantial faith in them. But these movements also knew how to engage in more personalistic forms of interaction, when necessary to reach their goals (Telles, 1987; Gay, 1990). When a new minister arrived on the scene, one who was skilled in such practices, social movements adapted to the new context, seek-ing to combine routines of interaction based on institutionalized par-ticipation in councils and conferences with a more personalized style of negotiation.

Rural social movements, on the other hand, largely considered the participatory institutions created before Lula to be an imposition of a 'neoliberal' government that lacked commitment to their interests. Those movements felt more comfortable with protest practices, a pref-erence they shared with officials from within the Ministry of Agrarian Development, many of whom came from the same movements. In this context, the main innovations in the repertoire of interaction did not occur in the area of institutionalized participation, but rather in the way protest occurred. State officials and movement activists reinterpreted traditions of claims-making through protest by creating a ritualized routine of negotiation marked by demonstrations of force and by the capacity of non-governmental actors to define the agenda for negotiations. This was made possible, to a large extent, because the politics of proximity and the occupation of public jobs by activists made it easier for the people inside and outside the state to build channels of communication and to trust each other. Those connections probably allowed them to modify a routine that benefitted both sides, since marches on Brasilia made it easier not only for the movements to push for their demands, but also for the Agrarian Development Ministry to lobby for support within the government.

Finally, in the absence of a history of national-level civil society mobilization in the field, changes in how state and society should negotiate federal public security policy occurred almost entirely by the initiative of government officials. The council/conference model of participation – broadly described in a large academic literature – was the form of interaction that those officials could most easily imagine. Not surprisingly, one of the key members of the group that proposed creating participatory institutions for public security had written a master's thesis on participatory councils. The fact that the Minister of Justice at the time was one of the main idealizers of Porto Alegre's participatory budget was also crucial for guaranteeing support for this more institutionalized participatory proposal.

Understanding the concrete construction of new routines of conflict, negotiation and participation requires examining how the networks that gained access to the state at particular moments of time worked with historical practices of state-society interaction in each policy area. The diversity of these experiences reaffirms our initial argument that the Lula government did not have a centralized and uniform project aimed at instituting participatory policies. Instead, participatory initiatives, capacities and experiences already existed in various policy sectors, long before Lula came to office. The fact that new routines seem to have proliferated during the Lula government should be understood as a result of the maturity and complexity of specific Brazilian social movements, combined with the opportunities provided by the presence of movement activists and allies within certain agencies.

One obvious direction for future research is to examine differences between the Lula government and the current one, under the presidency of Dilma Rousseff (2011–14). Rousseff was Lula's chosen successor and also notable for her militant past. When Brazil was under military rule (1964–85), she participated in an underground guerrilla organization and was imprisoned and brutally tortured. Her election thus seemed to reaffirm the idea that major transformations have occurred in Brazil: those once considered to be a threat to political and economic stability are now the dominant force in Brazilian politics. The election of a woman to govern the largest nation in Latin America also brings a sense of change: the old men of the traditional oligarchies seem to have been displaced.

Nonetheless, there are numerous signs that the Rousseff administration has distanced itself from social movements. The massive protests throughout Brazil of mid-2013 may reflect the fact that movements have found the new administration increasingly closed to dialogue. Rousseff's government still employs important activists in agencies such as the General Secretariat of the Presidency (SGPR), which continues to promote the strengthening of participatory arenas throughout the administration. However, the more fluid routines of negotiation that we described in family agriculture policy, for example, have broken down under the current government. Rousseff is often referred to as technocrat, less committed to the kind of open negotiations that Lula skillfully led. Yet the more constrained, formal arenas of institutionalized participation that her government still espouses are unlikely to be flexible enough to absorb what seems to be an increasingly mobilized, broader-based but more diffusely organized civil society. The question that remains is whether activists inside and outside the state will be able to invent new routines of interaction that can adapt to this new context.

Notes

This study was funded by Ford Foundation and the Brazilian Ministry of Science and Technology/CNPq and took place in the context of the 'Inter-University Consortium on the Americas in Comparative and Transnational Perspective. Interrogating the Civil Society Agenda: Social Movements, Civic Participation, and Democratic Innovation' coordinated by Sonia Alvarez, of the Center for Latin American, Caribbean, and Latino Studies (CLACLS), University of Massachusetts, Amherst (UMass).

The order of the authors' name is strictly alphabetical, not representing any differences in participation in writing this chapter, which was shared equally.

1. When we speak of the bureaucracy as a militant space, we are referring to the passionate commitment of many of the activists called upon to work in the Secretariats and Ministries of the government during the period. Acting with a strong sense of urgency, they tried to advance struggles that had been built and legitimized in the prior decades by militant networks within Brazilian civil society. This kind of bureaucratic activism was a theme that appeared in many of our interviews, but would require additional research to analyze in greater detail.

2. During the entire Lula government (2003–2010), 74 conferences occurred and 18 new national councils were created (www.secretariageral.gov.br). The General Secretariat of the Republic Presidency (Secretaria Geral da Presidência da República – SGPR), which is responsible for managing relationships between government and civil society, estimates that at least five million people participated in the conferences between 2003 and 2010 (personal communication). For evaluations of participation in the Lula Government, see Silva, 2009; Avritzer, 2009; Pogrebinschi, 2010.
3. The interviews were semi-structured and lasted on average 1 hour and 50 minutes. We would like to thank those interviewees for their time and contributions. In the area of Public Security (Policing), we interviewed the Office Head (Chefe de Gabinete) of SENASP (in that position between 2007 and 2010), and an Advisor to the Secretary of Public Security, who also served as Vice Secretary of the Public Security Conference and the Public Security Council between 2007 and 2010. In the MDA, we interviewed the Office Head (Chefe de Gabinete) of the Minister (in that position between 2005 and 2010). In the Ministry of Cities, we interviewed the Director of Urban Planning, who also served as National Secretary of Urban Programs (in those positions between 2003 and 2008) and the Area Coordinator of Urban Center Rehabilitation (2009–10). We also interviewed a former Vice National Secretary for National Articulation of the General Secretariat of the Presidency (in that office between 2006 and 2008), because of the importance of that agency as interlocutor between civil society and various sectors of the federal government during the Lula administration.
4. The switch resulted from a time of crisis in the Lula administration, when corruption scandals had weakened the president's coalition, thereby requiring him to redistribute offices in order to guarantee his majority in congress.
5. We thank João Elias Costa Sobrinho for sharing information on CONTAG, based on interviews he conducted in 2011.
6. Under Lula's successor, Dilma Rousseff, this routine no longer prevails. In 2012, for example, there was a breakdown in negotiations and the peaceful style of protest that occurred for years under Lula was interrupted when the MST occupied the MDA offices in Brasília, leading the government to suspend negotiations (Borba, 2012).
7. The story was even made into what became an internationally renowned documentary, *Bus 174*.
8. In this referendum, the proposal to make it illegal to own guns was rejected by voters.
9. According to interviewees, around 1500 free conferences took place during the preparation of the National Conference (CONSEG).

References

Abers, R. (2000) *Inventing Local Democracy: Grassroots Politics in Brazil* (Boulder: Lynne Rienner Publishers).

Abers, R. and Keck, M. (2008) 'Representando a Diversidade: Estado, Sociedade e Relações Fecundas nos Conselhos Gestores', *Caderno CRH* 21(52): 99–112.

Abers, R. and von Bulow, M. (2011) 'Movimentos Sociais na Teoria e na Prática: Como Estudar o Ativismo através da Fronteira entre Estado e Sociedade?', *Sociologias* 13(28): 52–84.

Abramovay, R. (2001) 'Conselhos além dos Limites', *Estudos Avançados* 15(43): 121–140.

Almeida Silva, C. (2002) 'Os Fóruns Temáticos da Sociedade Civil: Um Estudo sobre o Fórum Nacional de Reforma Urbana', in E. Dagnino (ed.), *Sociedade Civil e Espaços Públicos no Brasil* (São Paulo: Paz e Terra).

Almeida, D.R. and Cunha, E.S. (2009) 'A Produção de Conhecimento sobre os Conselhos de Políticas: Alguns Desafios Metodológicos', in L. Avritzer and E. Moreira da Silva (eds), *Metodologias e Participação* (Belo Horizonte: Faculdade de Filosofia e Ciências Humanas).

Alonso, A. Costa, V. and Maciel, D. (2007) 'Identidade e Estratégia na Formação do Movimento Ambientalista Brasileiro', *Novos Estudos CEBRAP* 79: 151–167.

Avritzer, L. (2003) 'O Orçamento Participativo e a Teoria Democrática: Um Balanço Crítico', in L. Avritzer and Z. Navarro (eds), *A Inovação Democrática no Brasil* (São Paulo: Cortez).

Avritzer, L. (2007) 'Sociedade Civil, Instituições Participativas e Representação: Da Autorização à Legitimidade da Ação', *Dados* 50(3): 443–464.

Avritzer, L. (2009) *Experiências Nacionais de Participação Social* (São Paulo: Cortez).

Avritzer, L. (ed.) (2010) *A Dinâmica da Participação Local no Brasil* (São Paulo: Cortez).

Baierle, S. (2000) 'A Explosão da Experiência: Emergência de um Novo Princípio Ético-Político nos Movimentos Populares Urbanos em Porto Alegre', in S. Alvarez, E. Dagnino and A. Escobar (eds), *Cultura e Política dos Movimentos Sociais Latino-Americanos* (Belo Horizonte: Ed. UFMG).

Baiocchi, G. (2005) *Militants and Citizens: The Politics of Participatory Democracy in Porto Alegre* (Palo Alto: Stanford University Press).

Banck, G.A. (1986) 'Poverty, Politics and the Shaping of Urban Space: A Brazilian Example', *International Journal of Urban and Regional Research* 10: 522–540.

Borba, J. (2012) 'Governo Suspende Negociações após MST Invadir Ministério', *Folha de São Paulo*. http://www1.folha.uol.com.br/poder/1076696-governo-suspende-negociacoes-apos-mst-invadir-ministerio.shtml, date accessed 25 April 2012.

Borba, J. Luchmann, L. and da Campo, A.M. (2007) *Orçamento Participativo: Análise das Experiências Desenvolvidas em Santa Catarina* (Florianópolis: Editora Insular).

Branford, S. (2009) 'Lidando com Governos: O MST e as Administrações de Cardoso e Lula', in M. Carter (ed.), *Combatendo a Desigualdade Social: O MST e a Reforma Agrária no Brasil* (São Paulo: Ed. UNESP).

Carvalho, V.A. and de F. Silva, M.R. (2011) 'Política de Segurança Pública no Brasil: Avanços, Limites e Desafios', *Revista Katálysis* 14(1): 59–67.

Clemens, E.S. (1993) 'Organizational Repertoires and Institutional Change: Women's Groups and the Transformation of U.S. Politics, 1890–1920', *American Journal of Sociology* 98(4): 755–798.

Cortês, S.M.V. (1998) 'Conselhos Municipais de Saúde: A Possibilidade dos Usuários Participarem e os Determinantes da Participação', *Ciência e Saúde Coletiva* II(1): 6–17.

Cunha, E.S.M. (2007) 'A Efetividade Deliberativa dos Conselhos Municipais de Saúde e de Criança e Adolescente no Nordeste', in L. Avritzer (ed.), *A Participação Social no Nordeste* (Belo Horizonte: Ed. UFMG).

Dagnino, E. (2002) *Sociedade Civil e Espaços Públicos no Brasil* (São Paulo: Paz e Terra).

Dagnino, E. Olvera, A. and Panfichi, A. (eds) (2006) *A Disputa pela Construção Democrática na América Latina* (São Paulo: Paz e Terra).

D'Araújo, M.C. (2009) *A Elite Dirigente do Governo Lula* (Rio de Janeiro: CPDOC).

da Silva, E.R.A. (2009) *Participação Social e as Conferências Nacionais de Políticas Públicas: Reflexões sobre os Avanços e Desafios no Período de 2003–2006* (Brasília: IPEA).

Dowbor, M. (2012) *A Arte da Institucionalização: Estratégias de Mobilização dos Sanitaristas (1974–2006)* (Doctorate Thesis: Sao Paulo: USP).

Faria, C.F. (2005) *O Estado em Movimento: Complexidade Social e Participação Política no Rio Grande do Sul*, Ph.D dissertation (Belo Horizonte: UFMG).

Fuks, M. Perissinotto, R. and Souza, N.R. (eds) (2004) *Democracia e Participação: Os Conselhos Gestores do Paraná* (Curitiba: Ed. UFPR).

Gay, R. (1990) 'Community Organization and Clientelist Politics in Contemporary Brazil: A Case Study from Suburban Rio de Janeiro', *International Journal of Urban and Regional Research* 14(4): 648–666.

Goldstone, J.A. (ed.) (2003) *State, Parties, and Social Movements* (Cambridge: Cambridge University Press).

Giugni, M.G. and Passy, F. (1998) 'Contentious Politics in Complex Societies: New Social Movements between Conflict and Cooperation', in M.G. Giugni, D. McAdam and C. Tilly (eds), *From Contention to Democracy* (Lanham: Rowman & Littlefield Publishers).

Gurza Lavalle, A. Houtzager, P.P. and Castello, G. (2006) 'Democracia, Pluralização da Representação e Sociedade Civil', *Lua Nova* 67: 49–104.

Hanagan, M. (1998) 'Social Movements, Incorporation, Disengagement, and Opportunities – A Long View', in M. Giugni, D. McAdam and C. Tilly (eds), *From Contention to Democracy* (Lanham: Rowman & Littlefield Publishers).

Hochstetler, K. and Keck, M.E. (2007) *Greening Brazil: Environmental Activism in State and Society* (Durham: Duke University Press).

Lubambo, C.W. Coelho, D.B. Abers, R. and Melo, M.A.B.C. (2005) *Desenho Institucional e Participação Política: Experiencias no Brasil Contemporaneo* (Petrópolis: Editora Vozes).

Luchmann, L. (2007) 'A Representação no Interior das Experiências de Participação', *Lua Nova* 70: 139–170.

Mattei, L. (2006) *Pronaf 10 Anos: Mapa da Produção Acadêmica* (Brasília: MDA).

Navarro, Z. (2003) 'O "Orçamento Participativo" de Porto Alegre (1989–2002): Um Conciso Comentário Crítico', in L. Avritzer and Z. Navarro (eds), *A Inovação Democrática no Brasil* (São Paulo: Cortez).

Pavez, T. de Toledo, D.G.C. and Gonçalves, R.R. (2010) *Redes Sociais, Políticas e Segurança Pública: Efeitos do Processo Preparatório para a 1ª CONSEG* (Brasilia: Ministerio da Justica).

Pogrebinschi, T. (2010) 'Participação como Representação: Conferências Nacionais e Políticas Públicas para Grupos Sociais Minoritários no Brasil', *ANPOCS Conference*.

Schneider, S. Silva, M.K. and Marques, P.E.M. (eds) (2009) *Políticas Públicas e Participação Social no Brasil Rural* (Porto Alegre: PGDR/UFRGS).

Sigaud, L. Rosa, M. and Macedo, E. (2008) 'Ocupações de Terra, Acampamentos e Demandas ao Estado: Uma Análise em Perspectiva Comparada', *DADOS – Revista de Ciências Sociais* 51(1): 107–142.

Silva, M.K. (2001) *Construção da 'Participação Popular': Análise Comparativa de Processos de Participação Social na Discussão Pública do Orçamento em Municípios da Região Metropolitana de Porto Alegre/RS* (Porto Alegre: Ed. UFRGS).

Silva, M.K. Rocha, A.G. and Alves, M. (2011) *Desenvolvimento Territorial e Associativismo: Uma Análise Comparativa* (Curitiba: XV Congresso Brasileiro de Sociologia).

Soares, L.E. (2007) 'A Política Nacional de Segurança: Histórico, Dilemas e Perspectivas', *Estudos Avançados* 21(61): 77–97.

Tarrow, S. G. (1998) *Power in Movement: Social Movements, Collective Action and Politics* (Cambridge: Cambridge Univ Press).

Tatagiba, L. (2002) 'Os Conselhos Gestores e a Democratização das Políticas Públicas no Brasil', in E. Dagnino (ed.), *Sociedade Civil e Espaços Públicos no Brasil* (São Paulo: Paz e Terra).

Teixeira, A.C. and Tatagiba, L. (2005) 'Movimentos Sociais e Sistema Político: Os Desafios da Participação', *Observatório dos Direitos do Cidadão* 25 (São Paulo: Instituto Pólis/PUC-SP).

Telles, V.S. (1987) 'Movimentos Sociais: Reflexões sobre a Experiência dos Anos 70', in I. Sherer-Warren and P.J. Krischke (eds), *Uma Revolução no Cotidiano: Os Novos Movimentos Sociais na America Latina* (São Paulo: Editora Brasiliense).

Tilly, C. (1992) 'How to Detect, Describe, and Explain Repertoires of Contention', *Working Paper150,* Center for the Study of Social Change, New School for Social Research.

Tilly, C. (1995) *Popular Contention in Great Britain, 1758–1834* (Cambridge: Harvard University Press).

Tilly, C. (2008) *Contentious Performances* (Cambridge: Cambridge University Press).

Wampler, B. (2007) *Participatory Budgeting in Brazil: Contestation, Cooperation, and Accountability* (University Park: Pennsylvania State University Press).

Wampler, B. and Avritzer, L. (2004) 'Participatory Publics: Civil Society and New Institutions in Democratic Brazil', *Comparative Politics* 36(3): 291–312.

Wolford, W. (2010a) 'Participatory Democracy by Default: Land Reform, Social Movements and the State in Brazil', *Journal of Peasant Studies* 37(1): 91–109.

Wolford, W. (2010b) *This Land Is Ours Now: Social Mobilization and the Meanings of Land in Brazil* (Durham: Duke University Press).

3
Brazil: From 'Sleeping Giant' to Emerging Power

Paulo Fagundes Visentini

Continuity in change or change in continuity?

Brazilian diplomatic aspirations, achievements and the pattern of the country's participation in world affairs are some of the most significant aspects of the Lula administration. At the turn of the twenty-first century, the multilateral dimension was a challenge to Brazilian foreign policies through two inflections. In the 1990s, it followed the medium powers, moving from resistance to the ongoing regime towards an acceptance of its bases and rules, putting them in harmony with the general principles of the system that emerged, along with their regimes and procedures. This move implied distancing itself from the Third World discourse and a perception based on the North-South divide. It involved instead the adoption of the international mainstream and the replacement, according to governmental discourse, of the 'autonomy through distance' model to the 'autonomy through participation' one.

Lula's foreign policy: an affirmative agenda

Lula's election in 2002 and the actions of his new government caused, initially, a great deal of apprehension inside and outside of Brazil. Most people expected the administration to demonstrate an ideological international behavior and for the president himself to be unprepared. However, diplomacy based on strategic and tactical insight and a long-range vision, both elements of which are going to be discussed, were noticed. Although the present course of Brazilian foreign policy started in the second half of Cardoso's government, there were no qualitative changes at that moment. The former President had possessed neither the will nor the political basis to implement modifications that could go far beyond timid critical rhetoric. Lula's inauguration has transformed this situation and, from the beginning of his administration, Brazilian foreign policy has witnessed remarkable development and leadership that surpassed expectations (Vizentini, 2008).

To fulfill his strategy, the International Relations department of Lula's administration was characterized by three dimensions: (1) an economic diplomacy, (2) an accompanying political diplomacy, and (3) a social agenda. The first dimension was realist, the second was aimed at offering resistance and assertiveness, whereas the third was propositive. They represent a project that was being matured for more than a decade and that is consistent with the balance of forces present in the country and the world; it was not a headstrong policy (Silva, Amorim and e Guimarães, 2003; Guimarães, 2006).

Considering the first point of view, it is necessary to keep the communication channels of the First World (OECD) open, attracting resources such as investments and technology, as well as negotiating Brazil's foreign debt and indicating that the government is willing to fulfill its international commitments, without any sudden break. On its own, the political diplomacy represents an opportunity for the reinforcement of national interests and of a true protagonism in international relations, with the clear intent of developing an *active and affirmative diplomacy*, ending a phase of relative stagnation and emptiness. Lula's government put Itamaraty (Ministry of External Relations) back to its former strategic position of formulating and implementing Brazilian foreign policy.

Finally, Lula's domestic governmental project also had a significant international impact, since its social projects were an answer to the need for an agenda that seeks to deal with the asymmetries that result from a globalization based only on free trade and investments. The campaign against hunger had a symbolic meaning that indicates the building of an alternative social-economic model in response to the neoliberal globalization crisis. Actions such as the stimulus of the internal market and savings of internal production, and the reform of domestic components that impede a more qualified international action (e.g., social inequality, unemployment, crime, weakness and administrative and fiscal disorder), represented the development of this project. The combination of social, energy, urban, agrarian and productive policies showed a real political will. At the same time, the president's charisma seemed to have embodied in his open and ordinary personality the characteristics that the world most admires in Brazil. This had allowed Lula to sustain an intense international agenda as the spokesperson for this project.

The regional dimension: South American integration

In practical terms, the Brazilian government had surpassed the limitations of its predecessor and searched for alliances outside the hemisphere as a means to improve its sphere of influence in the international arena, from the standpoint of an active and pragmatic attitude. The reinstitution of Mercosur and South American integration, creating room for Brazilian leadership, were the starting points and main priorities.

Therefore, within South American boundaries, Brazil offered its neighbors a much-needed partnership to regain their economic growth, an indispensable condition to make integration a concrete – not a virtual – reality, and to create the chance for a global strategic action to revert the growing marginalization in the region. Good governance and development for all of South America can only be guaranteed by regional integration, which is also an indispensable asset in Free Trade Area of the Americas (FTAA) talks (Vizentini and Wiesebron, 2004; Almeida, 2005).

This new reality has helped to reinforce the policy launched by South American countries to develop physical infrastructure (transport, communication and energy) as a means to re-start the integration process. President Toledo from Peru proposed that the international creditors of the countries from the region allocate 20 percent of their loan repayments to these infrastructure works. President Lula's Brazil viewed this initiative as an important strategic matter, advancing in substance policies put forward by Fernando Henrique Cardoso's (FHC's) government in its closure. In fact, the Brazilian Development Bank (BNDES) had already started to finance the works of South American integration (Faria, 2004; MRE, 2007; Cepik, 2008).

On the other hand, President Nestor Kirchner made clear Argentina's will to change the path the country's economic policies had followed in the previous 14 years, pushing neoliberalism aside and searching for a model sustained by public investments and the fight against poverty. In the international arena, however, the new president showed his intention to create a strategic alliance with Brazil, rescuing Mercosur and actively participating in the deepening of South American cooperation. What is noteworthy is the evolution of these new policies, from the era of close relations between Argentina and the US in the 1990s (humorously referred as *relaciones carnales* by Menem), to a posture of balanced distance between these two countries. For the White House, this movement was a cause of concern since it could have represented an autonomous Brazil-Argentina power pole.

It is worth mentioning that in December 2004, these initiatives gained momentum once more with a Mercosur-Andean community free trade treaty that was presented by the Brazilian government as a relevant step towards the consolidation of the South American Community of Nations (CASA, or 'home', later UNASUR, Union of South American Nations). In addition, Brazilian diplomacy continued to exercise an important role as a broker in the region, helping its South American neighbors to face their own internal crises. Bolivia, Ecuador, Colombia and the Venezuelan tensions are some examples of these stabilization actions.

Emerging actors: strategic partnerships and south-south cooperation

Solidarity towards Africa is a fundamental action, linking ethical values with national interest. The purpose of deepening relations (and creating a *strategic partnership*) with emerging powers such as China, India, Russia and South Africa, among others – as well as constructing a Mercosur-EU association and the appreciation of international organizations (mainly the UN) – added to economic advantages, indicating the will to contribute to the consolidation of a multi-polar international order. The democratization of international relations as a principle was clearly stated.

Considering Brazil's stance on multilateralism, the period between 2003 and 2010 was characterized by several initiatives. In the first year of Lula's presidency, one outstanding feature was his participation in the G8 Meeting in Evian, France. Attending the summit as a representative of South America, the President presented his plan to fight hunger and a proposal to convert 20 percent of the payment of Brazil's foreign debt interest into resources destined to finance infrastructure projects and development. Lula also addressed critically the recognized protectionism of rich countries and the need to reform multilateral institutions to better address the new realities of power of the post-Cold War world.

Faced by the difficulties of trying to preserve its advanced position and deal with the absence of attention by rich countries in regard to the needs and demands of Third World nations, Brazil deepened high-level diplomatic conversations and managed to create the Group of 3 (G3) with India and South Africa, also known as IBSA (India, Brazil and South Africa Dialogue Forum). Chancellors Celso Amorim, Yashwant Sinhá and Nkosazana Dlamini-Zuma made an announcement that the group would promote trilateral cooperation, mutual trade liberalization and a convergence and strengthening of agendas in multilateral forums.

The talks would involve Mercosur, the South African Customs Union (SACU) and possibly the South Asia Area of Regional Cooperation (SAARC). Also, these participants stressed their willingness to attract Russia and China to the group in the long run, creating a G5. (If this scenario becomes a reality, the group will represent the sum of almost half of the world's population and production, which has the potential to significantly affect multilateral talks). The creation of the G3 represented an opportune initiative, answering the need to mobilize the countries of the southern hemisphere to put forward their demands and change the course of the present international agenda.

Other initiatives that were part of Brazilian agenda between 2003 and 2005 and are worth mentioning were Lula's many trips to Arab countries of the Middle East and Africa. Lula traveled 11 times to Africa, visiting 29 countries and opening 17 new diplomatic missions there. The tours were important not only to the general scope of Brazilian-African relations, but also to the advancement of the creation of an institutional link between Mercosur and the South African Development Community (SADC), which has South Africa at its core in the Southern part of the continent.[1] Other outstanding results of these initiatives were the Africa-South America Summits (ASA) and South America-Arab Countries Summits (ASPA) that took place regularly in those regions and represented the consolidation of the political, strategic and economic links between those regions.

At the same time, the Lula administration started to exercise a strong hand in defense of Brazilian economic interests. As a global trader, the nation wished to keep its relations with different areas of the world, while at the same time giving priority to Mercosur and South American integration. By contradicting North American expectations that the government was going to be guided by leftist policies, Lula had effectively gained Washington's 'admiration'. It is important to note that, as soon as Brazilian diplomacy started to contest some guidelines of US hegemonic power and stress its autonomy, a certain amount of leverage was created. Therefore, it was possible to call attention to Brazil's social-economic demands and the country's infrastructure projects with neighboring nations. On the other hand, Brazilian diplomacy properly prepared itself to face this unavoidable and tough dialogue between opposites, by strengthening its stance in the world and in South America.

To summarize, Brazil developed an autonomous diplomacy, in accordance with the demands of globalization and its development projects. Alliances of *variable design* (*geometria variável*), such as G3, G4 and the so-called Commercial G20,[2] enabled the nation to exercise a worldwide presence and deepen its influence. Instead of an ideological diplomacy, Brazil built an active and pragmatic agenda that gained several allies in different arenas and that allowed the country to present its demands towards developed countries in a confident, but not confrontational, manner. At the same time, Brazil demonstrated considerable flexibility by respecting, without fully supporting, a number of problematic nations such as Cuba, Syria, Iran and Venezuela.

Lula's foreign policy represented the boldest field of action of his government and its success rested on the fact that it was run by Itamaraty (which regained its place) and on the support of governmental agencies that are concerned with the national issue, such as BNDES and the armed forces (Vizentini, 2008). However, these diplomatic initiatives generated some problems, leading to extremely high expectations. Internal and external adjustments were taken into account, but international variables remained important since the country still depended on a highly unstable world to try to make these projects work.

Dealing with the powerful: multilateral diplomacy

The multilateral space had been defined by Brazilian diplomacy in the 1990s as the best setting for the country's international power projection eagerly willing to participate in the building up of rules for the framing of a new world order. During Cardoso's administration, the country's development strategy was based not on a critique of the international system, but on the attempt to influence the construction of its rules by increasing the country's international insertion (Visentini and Silva, 2010).

With the change in government, and the swearing-in of President Luiz Inácio Lula da Silva, the multilateral policy kept its central position, despite the fact that its contents and strategies were profoundly reoriented. The new multilateral approach was based on a perception of the international system as having a multipolar tendency and power diffusion, but one that was still jeopardizing developing countries. As such, Brazil stood strong behind the need for increased representation in discussion forums as a means to democratize and augment the efficiency of organizations such as the UN; and it sought to explore new bargaining and negotiation spaces through the intense usage of articulation groups.

On the other hand, the multilateral agenda received a new makeover, adding the substantial issues of economic development and trade openness to the necessity of further democratizing the decision-making process (UN). As a result, an institutionalized coordination was established with other developing countries in forums such as IBSA and the Commercial G20.

An example of the ongoing power of the Brazilian government's diplomacy was the establishment of another alliance of variable design, the Commercial G20. This G20 had effectively taken part at the WTO Meeting in Cancun (which was preceded by President Bush's renowned and revealing phone call to Lula). Friendly but defiant, Brazilian diplomacy has created its alliances with developing countries that are affected by First World protectionism and agricultural subsidies. The G20 ignited the wrath of rich countries and led to the South voicing its discontent in the grand closure of the meeting. In spite of the success of the G20 since Cancun, its links to the G90 and other groups, countries and institutions have introduced some difficulties due to external pressures from developed countries and attitudes from some members of the alliance.

Nevertheless, Brazilian diplomacy was able to face these challenges. Active in supporting peace diplomacy, the country could contribute to the establishment of a multi-polar world governed by the United Nations system. In this sense, the reform of the UN Security Council (UNSC) is viewed as a priority by Brazilian foreign policy and, alongside G3, the country is also part of G4. Composed of Germany, Japan, India and Brazil, G4 promotes the expansion of UNSC to increase its legitimacy and openness, in accordance with the new power balance originated at the end of the Cold War. Brazil's command of Haiti's UN peacekeeping mission is also part of Brazil's diplomatic efforts to ascend to a permanent seat at UNSC. However, this reform is a highly sensitive issue and some setbacks are bound to happen, such as the opposition from Argentina and Mexico to Brazil's claim and other regional tensions regarding Japan, India and Germany.

As a result, Brazil's multilateral coalitions, bilateral strategic partnerships and South-South alliances are enabling the country and its partners to effectively and swiftly fill a power vacuum on the international stage. In this context, it is also relevant to examine the actions of other significant regional medium powers and their disputes, or talks, with the main representatives of these areas. For instance, G3 has a double impact on its members, strengthening their stance towards developed countries as well as possible regional adversaries (Rolland and Lessa, 2010).

Therefore, to continue to achieve its goals, Brazilian diplomacy will need to further increase its political capabilities to articulate alliances of variable design that answer to the demands, challenges and contradictions of North-South relations. Most of all, Brazilian diplomacy must continue to exercise a positive and stabilizing role in South America, deepening its political, economic and strategic integration, projecting the country and its partners in the international arena with renewed confidence and strength.

Back to the future: a sustainable foreign policy?

It is important to emphasize that some features in the current Brazilian foreign policy were instituted during Fernando Henrique Cardoso's term in office (Ricupero, 1995; Lafer, 1999; Lampreia, 1999; Cardoso, 2001; Cervo, 2002). Nevertheless, his vision was severely curbed due to internal difficulties and the international crisis underway at the time. Under Lula, Brazil started to work on an intense international agenda, transcending a subordinated approach to globalization and simple personal projection objectives. It tried to regain the country's capacity to negotiate concomitantly, breaking decisively from the North-Atlantic Liberal Consensus.

Brazil started to act with optimism and political will, constantly introducing political facts onto the international scene. Previously, it demonstrated a low self-esteem, as Collor and Cardoso had seen the country as less advanced in regard to the adjustments demanded by the rich countries. However, Brazil now sees itself as a leader capable of negotiating and as the beholder of a project that can even contribute to the insertion of a social agenda into globalization. Such a position makes the country eligible to pursue several initiatives such as its entrance into a reformed UN Security Council as a permanent member.

Instead of focusing on cooperation within large and saturated markets or with countries who see Brazil as secondary, Itamaraty has chosen to concentrate its efforts on unoccupied spaces. By coming closer together with its South American neighbors – particularly Andean ones – along with southern Africa, Arab countries, and international giants such as India, China, and Russia, Brazilian diplomacy was able to advance considerably and immediately, with astonishing business perspectives.

The presence of Argentinian guests and businessmen in the presidential delegation is an important manifestation of the new diplomacy's sensibility.

Furthermore, cooperation allowed for the construction of variable geometry alliances such as the G3 and the commercial G20, which are capable of exerting global influence. Rather than practising an ideologically strong diplomacy, Brazil developed an active and pragmatic posture, seeking allies for each problem and contesting them. However, Brazilian diplomacy avoided tackling the big issues (such as trade negotiations and disrespect toward the UN) and opted for respecting, but not supporting, the position of problematic countries such as Venezuela, Cuba and Iran.

The G3, as announced during its launch, could become a G5 with the inclusion of China and Russia (latter materialized as BRICS). Evidently, these two countries possess an important weight in the international system, and could form a group capable of exercising great influence in the alliance with Brazil, India and South Africa. As such, the G3 initiative also seeks to reinforce and engage less influential partners from the group of emerging powers, attempting to turn them into respectable protagonists. Therefore, the establishment of the G3 allowed Brazil to occupy an idle power space at a low cost, as can be surmised from the rapid advancement of the initiative.

On the other hand, the commercial G20 gave Brazil a large bargaining capacity as the leader of a group of countries with an important agricultural production, and instigated a change of focus in multilateral trade negotiations. However, it is necessary to enlarge and incorporate other actors, especially African ones. The G20 is still It not completely open to the poorer countries, and its action has been facing resistance from the African block of countries in agricultural liberalization negotiations in the WTO. To be able to reach its goals, Brazilian diplomacy will have to broaden its political capacity to articulate the variable geometries with North-South contradictions and demands.

Brazilian multilateral diplomacy with respect to environmental concerns has also put the country forward as a protagonist, not only through the presence of the Amazon rainforest, but also through initiatives to mitigate greenhouse gas emissions and to defend the environment against issues associated with development. Even though environmental policies in Brazil need to advance, the country is on its way to achieving the status of *environmental power* as a respectable interlocutor in mainstream forums and debates (see Castro this volume).

Through the reinforcement of multilateralism, taking into account a flexible perspective of alliances and the creation of coalition groups,

Brazil has developed a unique diplomacy that is appropriate in the era of globalization while still maintaining a development project for the country. However, this unique diplomacy can give rise to problems as huge expectations may be created, and it will only provide the expected results along with economic development and changes in the international system. In recent years, building a multilateral environment favorable to the defense of national interests has been one of the central elements for the defense of multi-polarity, development and democratization of international relations.

Finally, during the first decade of the 21st century Brazil has improved its economic and political position in world affairs, and it is maintaining its status through the global financial crisis (Sallum Jr, 2000; Sennes, 2003; Batista Jr, 2005). Despite some adjustments, President Dilma Rousseff, whose administration started in January 2011, is maintaining the main aspects of the development and foreign policies of former president Lula. Brazil's participation in the Financial G20 and in the BRICS (Brazil, Russia, China, India and now South Africa) are only some of the arrangements to deal with the increasing gap between economic and political order.

Dilma's foreign policy: rupture or continuity?

Dilma Rousseff is the first female president of Brazil and, importantly, follows the first 'worker' president of the country. Both belong to the Workers Party, but each has a quite different style. Dilma was engaged in an organization that was involved in armed struggle against the military regime and was incarcerated and tortured at the age of 19. She had a Marxist background, distinct from Lula's liberation theology and trade unionism. On the other hand, she is more technical, does not like to talk in public, is more centralistic and displays a more authoritarian personal behavior and a more executive profile than the former president. Lula, acting with political ability and seduction, opened many doors on the international stage and secured for Brazil the World Football Cup of 2014 and for Rio de Janeiro the Olympic Games of 2016.

As a result, Dilma faces a significant challenge as she attempts to improve the old Brazilian infrastructure: to choose the best opportunities within the large framework created by Lula's diplomacy in the context of an increasingly problematic world economic and political scenario. In this context, she is more concerned with domestic economic affairs, trying to maintain the PAC (Acceleration Growth Program), an initiative of public infrastructure works started by Lula. At the same time, Dilma replaced some ministers from Lula's government to improve efficacy and fight corruption.

In terms of foreign policy, Brazil intends to maintain its commitments, but in a more low profile style, and to try to show a more balanced approach between new and old partners (BRICS and USA/EU). At the same time, Dilma is making efforts to balance old fashion diplomats and those more loyal to Lula's approach to South-South cooperation and the enthusiasm to the emerging countries. The Minister of Foreign Relations, Antônio Patriota (replaced by Ambassador Luiz Alberto Figueiredo in August 2013), was very discreet and the current President prefers not to travel as much as Lula.

Another important aspect of Dilma's administration is the greater focus allocated to the Human Rights agenda. During the Arab Spring, Brazilian diplomacy was more careful with its support of Arab regimes, following the president's orders. But after some movements, Brazil's tendency was to follow the same pattern as the rest of the BRICS countries (including in the case of Syria). At the same time, it is possible to see an approach of improving the dialogue with the US. The pre-salt oil reserve is attracting Washington's attention, possibly building a new means of cooperation with Brazil. Meanwhile, the US State Department is putting some pressure on Brazil, trying to isolate the country from its other BRICS partners. One interesting incident is the Mercosur affair, when the Paraguayan Senate evicted the leftist President Lugo in a coup d'état. Ironically, this Senate was the only one opposed to Venezuela's entrance into Mercosur. The other three Presidents suspended Paraguay from the group and, finally, Venezuela became a full member of Mercosur.

As demonstrated above, there is continuity between Lula and Dilma's diplomacy, but their styles are remarkably different as a result of the international crisis and their personal characteristics. In spite of a more difficult international and domestic context, the ongoing priority of maintaining a sustainable economy and previous achievements remains strong.

The 2013 street demonstrations: is Brazil the weakest BRICS?

After almost a decade of intense international projection, economic growth and successful social policies, Brazil under Dilma's presidency was hit in June 2013 by a wave of unusual protests, characterized by contradictory motivations. Lula's achievement of making Brazil the host country for the 2014 FIFA World Cup and Rio de Janeiro the host city for the 2016 Olympic Games seemed suddenly at risk. What do these protests mean for Brazil's international position? Clearly, the protesters' demands for increased and improved public investments felt long overdue. The usual problems observed in megacities endure in Brazil. The investments for the World Cup and the Olympic Games could provide these urban areas with the long-needed infrastructure improvement. It is correct that all recent governments have been facilitating the acquisition of cars rather than the development and use of public transportation, which increases urban chaos. Car ownership has become part of a culture of consumerism, with broadened rights and no correspondent duties. The traditional Brazilian elite resent the increasing competition brought about by an ascendant middle class for an outdated infrastructure and a deficient service sector. A population depoliticized by opportunistic alliances of a coalition government and by the lack of distinction among party programs aggravates the situation. However, the scattered dissatisfaction per se is not able to produce such street rallies apparently out of the blue. To understand this, we need to take into account the potential of social media to facilitate rapid mobilization. This potential has not been adequately understood by most officials. The government thus demonstrated a lack of readiness, reacting in a faltering and erratic way that further fueled the protests. Not by chance, the building of the Ministry of Foreign Affairs in Brasília (Itamaraty) and other public institutions were the main targets of vandalism.

As for the other BRICS, China is maintaining its trajectory of development, sovereignty and stability, while Russia displays a renewed international political will, as in the case of Syria. India, on the other hand, is naturally socially and culturally unstable, and South Africa seems blocked by the contradictory post-apartheid political pact. It has lost its leading role even in Africa, where Angola emerges as an important player. As far as Brazil is concerned, the country seems to be losing its disposition to respond to challenges like the US electronic espionage and the international incident of the Bolivian presidential airplane holdup in Europe. A country that granted political asylum to former Paraguayan dictators and to the Italian far-left militant Battisti (perpetrator of many murders), Brazil now demonstrates fear of doing so for Edward Snowden. In the same vein, it vacillates regarding international selective criteria that weaken economic development in the areas of energy and infrastructure.

A BRICS member geographically distant from the Eurasian core, Brazil struggles with identity problems from the sociocultural predominance of miscegenation to the western project of nation-building. What is at stake in the external arena is the realignment of Brazilian diplomacy and the estrangement from other BRICS countries. In the domestic arena, it is the 2014 elections. Therefore, amidst an apparent *colored revolution*, what is in dispute is not a regime change (the Brazilian political class is well articulated), but the erosion of President Dilma's prestige, the revival of a weakened opposition and a possible change of the ruling coalition. Ironically, the name of President Lula reappears in opinion polls as the most preferred by the electorate. There is no corruption wave, but a struggle for the distribution of investment and public resources.

Therefore, the government is seeking to redress its excessive confidence and recover the clear decision-making that characterized the Lula administration. The economy, in spite of the lower rates of growth, maintains its stability, prosperity and vitality. This political crisis, which takes place in a democratic regime in full vigor, is losing strength due to the authorities' reaction to the protests and the self-criticism of political parties. Brazil, unlike other South American nations, managed to mitigate the most negative aspects bequeathed by the military regime and neoliberalism, and it also must overcome the present difficulties, in most part derived from the accelerated social transformations experienced during the past decade. To do that, Brazil has to reconsider certain aspects of its economic model and its political system.

Notes

1. South Africa is also a member of the G3 and a partner in other multilateral alliances and diplomatic talks
2. The commercial G20 was a coalition of developing nations from the South created by Brazil in 2003 to address the Worlds Trade Organization's talks in the Doha Round framework at the Cancun Ministerial Meeting. It represents a privileged forum of South-South cooperation. The text also makes reference to Financial G20, as another forum of debate, but in the economic and financial arena and with a broader South-South and North-South scope.

References

Almeida, P.R. (2005) *Relações Internacionais e Política Externa do Brasil* (Porto Alegre: Ed. UFRGS).

Batista, P.N. Jr. (2005) *O Brasil e a Economia Internacional: Recuperação e Defesa da Autonomia Nacional* (Rio de Janeiro: Campus/Elsevier).

Cardoso, F.H. (2001) 'A Política Externa do Brasil no Início de um Novo Século: Uma Mensagem do Presidente da República', *Revista Brasileira de Política Internacional* 44(1): 5–12.

Cepik, M. (Org.) (2008) *América do Sul: Economia e Política da Integração Regional* (Porto Alegre: UFRGS).

Cervo, A. (2002) 'Relações Internacionais do Brasil. Um balanço da era Cardoso', *Revista Brasileira de Política Internacional* 45(2): 5–35.

Faria, L.A.E. (2004) *A Chave do Tamanho: Desenvolvimento Econômico e Perspectivas do Mercosul* (Porto Alegre: UFRGS).

Guimarães, S.P. (2006) *Desafios do Brasil na Era dos Gigantes* (Rio de Janeiro: Contraponto).

Lafer, C. (1999) *Comércio, Desarmamento, Direitos Humanos: Reflexões sobre uma Experiência Diplomática* (São Paulo/Brasília: Paz e Terra/ FUNAG).

Lampreia, L.F. (1999) *Diplomacia Brasileira* (Rio de Janeiro: Lacerda Ed).

Ministério das Relações Exteriores – MRE (2007) *Obras de Integração Física na América do Sul* (Brasília: MRE).

Ricupero, R. (1995) *Visões do Brasil* (Rio de Janeiro: Record).

Rolland, D. and Lessa, A.C. (2010) *Les Relations Internationales du Brésil: Chemins de la Puissance* (L Harmattan: Paris).

Sallum, B. Jr. (2000) 'A Condição Periférica: O Brasil nos Quadros do Capitalismo Mundial (1945–1990)', in C.G. Mota, (org) *Viagem Incompleta: A Experiência Brasileira (1500–2000)* (São Paulo: SENAC).

Sennes, R. (2003) *As Mudanças da Política Externa Brasileira nos Anos 80: Uma Potência Média Recém Industrializada* (Porto Alegre: Ed. da UFRGS).

Silva, L.I.L. Amorim, C. and Guimarães, S.P. (2003) *A Política Externa do Brasil* (Brasília: FUNAG).

Visentini, P. and Silva, A.R. (2010) 'Brazil and the Economic, Political and Environmental Multilateralism', *Revista Brasileira de Política Internacional* 53 (special issue): 54–72.

Vizentini, P. (2008) *Relações Internacionais do Brasil: De Vargas à Lula* (São Paulo: Editora Fundação Perseu Abramo).

Vizentini, P. and Wiesebron, M. (eds) (2004) *Free Trade for the Americas? FTAA and the US Push for Integration* (London/New York: Zed Books).

4

Trade-offs and Choices of Economic Policy in Brazil: The Lula Years and the New Directions toward Development after 2010

Hélio Henkin

Introduction

In the liberal democracies of the western world since the Second World War, there have been a number of examples of politically sensitive moments during which a progressive party came into power and tried to introduce new directions in economic policy. At such times, there has been an escalation of economic and political tension, as the implicit or explicit promises in the political discourse and in the government plans have been interpreted as urgent welfare improvements by the lower classes and as threats of wealth confiscation, or at least lower income, by the upper and middle classes. Often, these ambitious programs of economic reformism could not be sustained. In France, for instance, the first term of the socialist Mitterrand government, which began in 1981, took a sudden turn toward austerity in 1983.The record of the current president of the United States, Barack Obama, who began his government in 2009 in the midst of a severe economic crisis, provides another example of economic difficulties and political tensions faced by reform-minded administrations. When Lula won his first presidential election in Brazil, in 2002, a remarkable moment of political and economic tension was also reached. The demographic and economic weight of Brazil, as well as its problems of social and regional inequalities, contributed to increased uncertainty about the policy changes that could be implemented.

Economic policy is often central to these changes, because it carries the expectations of new goals and instruments to achieve enhanced economic growth, income distribution and inflation control. In many other countries, progressive policies were frustrated or resulted in severe economic instability. In some cases, these progressive policies were soon followed by orthodox policies, even in developed countries, as mentioned above.

Against this background, this chapter aims not only to evaluate the economic policies and achievements of Lula's two terms, with a dynamic and evolutionary approach, but also to analyze the sustainability of economic and social transformation in Brazil, focusing on the challenges faced by Lula's successor, the current president Dilma Rousseff, a fellow representative of the *Partido dos Trabalhadores* (PT, Workers' Party). Of course, the analysis must be contextualized in the dynamics of the Brazilian economy after two decades of economic, monetary and political stability since 1994. The trajectory of economic policy during the two terms of Lula's government was the result of strategic choices that took into account the political and economic scene, both at the national and international level.

The second section contains a brief overview of how the contradictions of a dynamic but unstable economy led to the social and economic context within which the election of Lula brought the promise of economic change, social welfare improvement and a faster response to the long-term problem of social exclusion in Brazil. Although the overview considers the trajectory of the Brazilian economy since the 1950s, it is mostly focused on the economic framework that was built during the presidency of Fernando Henrique Cardoso (1995–2002), and in particular the ingenious Plano Real (1994) as a successful stabilization program[1] and the external vulnerability that resulted in the so-called Samba crisis of 1998. This crisis caused a shift towards fluctuating exchange rates, which implied the adoption of new anchors in the stabilization efforts. This will be the starting point of the analysis of the years under the Workers' Party rule, from 2003 onwards. These strategic choices were also conditioned by specific trade-offs that confronted the Brazilian economy. In this chapter, the economic policies (and their effects on the process of economic development) will be analyzed as strategic choices regarding such trade-offs.

The evolution of economic policy under the Lula administration (2003–10) was strongly influenced by the international economic landscape. The nature and dimension of this influence will therefore be the object of the present analysis. In the third section of this chapter, the initial policy choices will be discussed in the context of the effort of stabilizing the Brazilian economy, especially in view of controlled inflation rates and the preservation of the macroeconomic management model that was adopted during Fernando Henrique Cardoso's second presidential term. As far as the Lula government was concerned, these antecedents had the logical result of a more conservative approach, adopted in Lula's first term, followed – in the second term – by a gradual movement toward more progressive and less orthodox policies.

Two important economic achievements will be highlighted in my analysis: the decreasing external vulnerability of the Brazilian economy and the increasing purchasing power of the Brazilian populace, especially that of the lower classes. The relatively low level of Brazil's exposure to the international financial crisis, in its 2008–09 opening stage, was a result of these achievements. Indeed, levels of productive activity in Brazil started to recover in the last quarter of 2009, in contrast with the depressed economic performance in the United States and Europe. The political and electoral effect of this performance should not be underestimated, as it contributed to the election of Dilma Rousseff in 2010.

The third section analyzes what might be called the 'big pay-off' of stabilization: increased room for income distribution, industrial policies and growth during Lula's second term. Economic growth allowed for public spending growth without bringing inflationary pressure or a high debt-to-GDP ratio. In turn, the expansion of public spending helped to support more ambitious poverty alleviation and income redistribution programs, without worsening the fiscal deficit.

The fourth section discusses the consequences of both the international landscape and macroeconomic policies for the structure of production and investment in the Brazilian economy. Brazil has become an emerging power specialized in the export of primary products but with a strong domestic market dominated by transnational companies in its more dynamic industries. This last section contains a brief discussion of the development challenges that Dilma Rousseff's government has been facing, among them the problem of de-industrialization in some Brazilian industrial sectors and regions. This has become an issue of particular concern in view of the slowdown of economic growth in Brazil after 2011.

Contradictions of a dynamic but unstable economy: Brazil from the 1950s to the 1990s

From 1950 to 1990, Brazil's Gross Domestic Product (GDP) growth rate systematically surpassed the average growth rate of the world economy, except during brief periods of strong austerity policies in the opening and closing years of the military regime (1964–85), as shown in Table 4.1.[2] After 1990, Brazil's growth rate fell below global economic

Table 4.1   Brazil and the world economy – average annual real rate of GDP growth (%)

Time period	Brazil	World economy
1950–1970	6.70	4.09
1970–1990	5.03	4.16
1990–2000	2.48	4.06
2000–2010	3.61	4.97

Source: IPEADATA

growth rates, but in the 2000s there has been a recovery of the growth performance of the country.

Brazil's economic growth from the second half of the 1970s through the mid-1990s occurred in spite of high and chronic inflation rates, continuous external vulnerability (due to current account imbalances) and the absence of stable and binding 'rules of the game' (see Table 4.2).[3] However, good growth performance until the 1990s hasn't brought a proportional alleviation of key social problems that have been keeping Brazil out of the group of more developed countries: high levels of social and regional inequalities and high levels of (extreme) poverty. Table 4.3 shows that personal income distribution (measured by the Gini coefficient) and the incidence of poverty and extreme poverty (as a proportion of total households) deteriorated from 1981 to 1990.

In more general terms, the long period of growth has not produced the desired catching-up process: neither making Brazil a globally competitive and integrated economy, nor providing a developed-world-pattern of equity and social welfare.

Towards the end of the 1980s a consensus was being built based on the diagnosis that both the Brazilian model of industrial development and the management of macroeconomic problems had become inefficient. Not only did the protectionist incentives to industrialization face tough challenges brought about by the fast pace of global technological and economic transformation, but also the debt burden carried by the public sector did not allow for the necessary investment in infrastructure. Moreover, it became more difficult to cope with high and chronic inflation with the 'Brazilian tools' of indexation.[4] At that time, the limits to social welfare improvement could be seen not only as a result of historical and structural problems, but also as a result of a set of restrictive conditions that had directly or indirectly made any public policy unviable and inefficient. First, there was the so-called 'socialization' of the foreign debt

Table 4.2 Growth, inflation, and current transactions balances in Brazil

Year	GDP growth (%)	Rate of inflation* (%)	Current transactions Balance (USD millions)
1970	10.40	19.26	−838.74
1971	11.34	19.47	−1,629.70
1972	11.94	15.72	−1,687.95
1973	13.97	15.54	−2,085.43
1974	8.15	34.55	−7,504.12
1975	5.17	29.35	−6,999.50
1976	10.26	46.26	−6,425.84
1977	4.93	38.78	−4,826.22
1978	4.97	40.81	−6,983.39
1979	6.76	77.25	−10,708.23
1980	9.20	110.24	−12,739.19
1981	−4.25	95.2	−11,705.87
1982	0.83	99.72	−16,273.20
1983	−2.93	210.99	−6,773.03
1984	5.40	223.81	94.91
1985	7.85	235.11	−248.34
1986	7.49	65.03	−5,323.26
1987	3.53	415.83	−1,437.92
1988	−0.06	1,037.56	4,179.77
1989	3.16	1,782.89	1,031.89
1990	−4.35	1,476.70	−3,783.72

Source: IPEADATA
* General Price Index (IGP-DI), as calculated by the Getulio Vargas Foundation

Table 4.3 Social indicators in Brazil

Year	Gini coefficient	Extreme poverty (% of households)	Poverty (% of households)
1981	0.584	12.9	33.35
1982	0.591	13.13	33.34
1983	0.596	17.53	40.95
1984	0.589	16.54	40.93
1985	0.598	13.56	34.72
1986	0.588	6.37	20.93
1987	0.601	13.25	32.92
1988	0.616	16.16	37.13
1989	0.636	14.83	34.96
1990	0.614	15.59	36.04

Source: Instituto Brasileiro de Geografia (IBGE).

crisis, through which the public sector had absorbed the burden of the adjustments and incentives needed to solve the problems of the balance of payments. This 'socialization' resulted in increasing levels of fiscal deficit and public debt and, as a consequence, less room for spending on social programs. Second, by the mid-1980s, the adjustment process had brought recession and lower rates of growth, without ending high inflation (see Table 4.2),and also produced a volatile exchange rate. The local currency had been strongly devaluated in some years (especially in the beginning and in the end of the 1980s). In spite of the heterodox plans of stabilization that had been adopted after the return to civilian government in 1985, the overall outcome of this process was a diminishing purchasing power that affected mainly the lower classes (Table 4.4).

Towards the end of the 1980s and the first years of the 1990s, there was not only a perception that the long-term social inequalities would not be overcome in the prevailing economic environment, but also that what had been seen as successful in relative terms – the industrialization process of the previous decades – was fundamentally threatened by this enduringly unstable environment. This perception led to a new set of successive stabilization programs that culminated in the Plano Real, in 1994. This package was successful in overcoming the problem of so-called *inertial inflation*, a combination of chronic increases of consumer prices and the automatic adjustment of the price index (Table 4.5). However, a more comprehensive macroeconomic stabilization was not reached. Brazil was still highly vulnerable on the external side of the

Table 4.4 Real effective exchange rate (EER) and real minimum wage (MW) in Brazil

Year	EER	MW
1980	104.8016	554.58
1981	89.8188	552.65
1982	76.8635	560.10
1983	98.2438	505.79
1984	108.2503	462.03
1985	111.9423	479.25
1986	113.4302	495.96
1987	107.6896	405.75
1988	105.6934	419.96
1989	81.8922	419.97
1990	69.7255	315.30

Source: IPEADATA

Table 4.5 Inflation rate and the *Plano Real* (%) in Brazil (index: IPCA)

Year	Inflation rate
1988	980.21
1989	1972.91
1990	1620.97
1991	472.70
1992	1119.10
1993	2477.15
1994	916.46
1995	22.41
1996	9.56
1997	5.22
1998	1.65
1999	8.94
2000	5.97
2001	7.67
2002	12.53

Source: IPEADATA

economy and the fiscal deficit (as a proportion of GDP) was growing. After the 1998 financial crisis in Russia and Asia, and on the eve of the re-election of Fernando Henrique Cardoso in 1998, the Plano Real was under pressure because the 'exchange rate anchor' had become less credible. Indeed, the Samba crisis had ended the supposed fixed parity between the Real and the US dollar.[5]

At the beginning of 1999, already in the second term of president Fernando Henrique Cardoso's administration, confidence in the sustainability of Brazil's external balance of payments had deteriorated. As a consequence, an important change in the macroeconomic regime was introduced. Instead of an exchange rate anchor, the government adopted a mix of inflation rate targeting, fiscal equilibrium and monetary stability as the main control instruments. The exchange rate was allowed to fluctuate as an endogenous variable. A devaluation of the Real was therefore unavoidable. Nevertheless, this new macroeconomic regime required a strong fiscal adjustment; otherwise, the only way to achieve the inflation rate targets would be to increase interest rates even more, which was economically and politically unviable.[6]

In the course of Cardoso's second term, economic policy efforts were directed toward the consolidation of the structural and institutional reforms that aimed to, first, reduce the presence of the state as a producer (through privatization and the end of state monopolies in oil and telecommunications); second, put a limit on the spending of the government at all levels (local, states and federal); and third, reduce the presence of public financial institutions at the state level (through new forms of financial regulation and privatization).

Although some social programs (like *Bolsa Escola* and *Bolsa Alimentação*, see Wiesebron this volume) had been adopted or improved, and in spite of the effort to consolidate a social protection network, the emphasis during the Cardoso years was put on the stabilization process and, more broadly, on the improvement of some basic systemic conditions on which the competitiveness of the economy depended (infrastructure, macroeconomic stability, legal improvements concerning property rights and intellectual property). This emphasis on horizontal policies (in contrast with the traditional vertical or sectorial industrial policies) was seen as a neoliberal agenda[7] because these horizontal policies included – in the Brazilian case – privatization and other policies that aimed to reduce the role of the state as an economic actor. In addition, as the government focused on economic openness and trade liberalization, industrialization as a public policy goal was abandoned, which was also seen as a sign of neoliberal principles.

However, it is useful to critically review the economic policy performance during the Cardoso years, because it can help not only to identify the challenges that would be faced by Luís Inácio Lula da Silva after taking office in January 2001, but also to discuss broader assumptions about issues of economic development, especially as part of the appraisal of the so-called Washington Consensus and the neoliberal agenda that had been the policy guide in many countries in the 1990s.

As a stabilization policy against the complex institutional apparatus of indexation and against high and chronic inflation, the Real was successful (Table 4.5). Furthermore, the privatization program was a necessary step toward the increase in infrastructural investment, given the high level of public debt. As already argued as early as the late 1970s by Ignácio Rangel (1978), the public services concessions and the privatization of the traditional state-owned infrastructure and public utility companies were a necessary condition to improve investment and capital formation in Brazil.[8]

Nevertheless, in spite of these crucial efforts, the results in terms of economic growth performance after eight years of stabilization was not substantial. The average annual growth rate in Cardoso's second term (1999–2002) dropped to 2.1 percent, from 2.6 percent in his first term. The unemployment rate was 7.8 percent at the end of the first term, and was not substantially reduced in the course of the second term (although the rate of job creation had increased, as compared to the first term). The rate of gross fixed-capital formation, a variable that depends on both private and state investment, decreased as a proportion of the GDP (from 19.8 percent in the first term to 19 percent in the second term).[9] The average annual growth rate of family consumption, a sensitive political and electoral variable, decreased during the second term (from 3.6 to 0.9 percent). The contraction of imports (due to the external sector adjustment and currency devaluation) contributed to this low performance. In addition, other development-related issues started to be discussed.[10] These issues had to do with interest rates and financial policy, the sectorial and structural impact of economic liberalization, industrial policy, poverty and equity, and the overall role of the state in the economy.

These issues belonged to the broader remit of development economics. According to Ocampo (2005, p.11), the promises of the neoliberal agenda were not fulfilled and instead brought, especially for Latin American countries, '(...) variable mixes of macroeconomic vulnerability, low investment ratios, increasing international and domestic technological gaps and distributive tensions.' In the particular case of Brazil, increasingly considered to be an emerging power, the trajectory of the economy during the Cardoso years had brought to the forefront debates about the limits of market reforms and the role of the State from a broader perspective, namely the economic and social dimensions of the development challenge. As for the latter, democratization and the adoption of the *Constituição Cidadã* (the citizens' constitution) in 1988, broadened the spectrum of political and social rights and created an increasing demand for social improvement, for more efficient public services to the poor and the lower middle classes, and for a better income distribution.

When Lula won the 2002 presidential election, it was clear that his first term would require hard decisions related to these debates. In a more synthetic view, the challenges faced by Lula were as follows: first, how (and to what extent) to maintain the compromise on stabilization and systemic competitive factor improvement, while at the same time reducing the rate of unemployment? Second, how could industrial development and the sectorial composition of production be an important and manageable issue?[11] Third, what would be the role of the state in a more globalized and competitive economic landscape? Fourth, how to promote the transformation of production structures combined with macroeconomic stability, to allow for sustainable and higher growth rates, as well as for a more rapid catching up process?[12] Finally, how to pay the so-called 'social debt', which involved not only improving income distribution, but also reducing the number of people below the extreme poverty line? The next section deals with the trade-offs faced by Lula at the start of his presidency in 2003. These trade-offs were very important. Although the social and economic balance of the previous eight years did not include a substantially positive change in socioeconomic conditions, it was clear that monetary stabilization was a substantial asset. To lose it would be catastrophic to the project of Lula and to the Workers' Party.

Price stabilization priority in Lula's first term

The historical commitment of Lula and his Workers' Party to progressive policies, on one hand, and the well-known problems of a transition from conservative to progressive policies, on the other hand, presented an array of choices to be made as soon as Lula was inaugurated as the new president of Brazil in January 2003: fiscal austerity or public spending-led growth? Conventional monetary policy or administrative control of the interest rate? Public pension reform or a passive policy regarding the cumulative deficits on social security issues? Maintaining the Plano Real agenda or immediately fulfilling social and distributive demands? Unlike progressive governments elsewhere, Lula's government made a clear choice of starting with a strong commitment to the stabilization policies and the macroeconomic management model adopted by his predecessor Fernando Henrique Cardoso. This choice implied an emphasis on controlling the inflation rate and on a set of policies that was more aligned with an orthodox economic view than with a progressive approach.[13] Therefore, the new government maintained the high interest rate-based monetary policy, the free influx of short-term capital, and the primary fiscal surplus target (Table 4.6). Thus, Lula initially kept up the hierarchy of the macroeconomic goals and the macroeconomic regime inherited from the Cardoso government. These policies focused on price stabilization through the definitive elimination of the long memory of high inflation expectations as well as the practice of high level indexation. The basic macroeconomic instruments to achieve this were inflation targeting through higher interest rates, free movement of short-term capital flows, maintaining a primary fiscal surplus, and a floating exchange rate.

It is important to remark that this choice was also an important campaign commitment that aimed to build domestic and international credibility, inside and out. Besides, there was a good reason to make

Table 4.6   Inflation and interest rates in Brazil

Year	Inflation rate (% annual) – IPVA index variation	Average basic interest rate (% annual)
2000	5.97	17.43
2001	7.67	17.32
2002	12.53	19.17
2003	9.30	23.35
2004	7.60	16.25
2005	5.69	19.05
2006	3.14	15.08
2007	4.46	11.88
2008	5.90	12.48
2009	4.31	9.93
2010	5.91	9.76
2011	6.50	11.62
2012	5.84	8.49

Source: IPEADATA

this choice, as there was a serious problem to solve in the short term. According to Table 4.6, in the last year of Fernando Henrique Cardoso's term, the inflation rate reached a two-digit level. This was perceived as a threat that could bring back the high inflation rates and inertial indexation practices that characterized Brazilian monetary policy during the last decade of the 1980s.

However, in 2003 the inflation rate returned to one-digit level. During the two terms of President Lula, inflation was kept at a level that was compatible with monetary stability and the preservation of the purchasing power of the workers. As is shown in Table 4.6, from an annual rate of 12 percent in 2002, the inflation reached its lowest level in 2006 and thereafter it has fluctuated within the limits of the inflation target range. The economic policy instruments were effective and inflation was kept under control.

Meanwhile, the robust growth of both the world and the Brazilian economies pushed up international prices of commodities and energy inputs between 2000 and 2008. Due to this pressure, inflation sped up in Brazil, but was not hard to control after 2008 because international prices of inputs fell sharply due to the deepening financial crisis. As a result, during the two terms of Lula's presidency, the control of inflation helped to preserve the gains of purchasing power that benefited working-class wage earners (and consumers in general).

The successful stabilization policy stopped the depreciation of the national currency, the Real. The exchange rate of the Real to the Dollar (BRL/USD) reached a high level in 2003 (BRL/USD 3.08 annual average). Since 2003, the exchange rate has fallen continuously and reached a level below (BL/USD 2.00). At the end of Lula's second term, in 2010, there was a 180 degree shift in the currency market: the Real had by then become one of the most overvalued currencies of the world (Table 4.7). This trend of currency appreciation was the result of the following factors: first, price stabilization, which increased the trust in and credibility of the Real; second, attractive risk-adjusted interest rates in the domestic bonds market; third, the growth of Brazilian exports and the corresponding foreign currency influx; and fourth, the expansion of global liquidity during the 2000s, which pushed up the influx of short-term capital in the Brazilian financial market.

The macroeconomic policies of Lula's first term produced another important result on the external front: the Central Bank of Brazil's international reserve holdings increased significantly, as is also shown in Table 4.7. Brazil's position in the global credit market shifted from an external debtor to an external creditor. Undoubtedly, the improvement of the external sector of the Brazilian economy during this period

Table 4.7 Real effective exchange rate and foreign accounts in Brazil

Year	Real effective exchange rate (annual average)	Current transactions account (USD million)	International reserves (USD million)
2000	104.89	−24,224.53	33.011.49
2001	124.23	−23,214.53	35,866.41
2002	121.22	−7,636.63	37,823.45
2003	120.51	4,177.29	49,296.20
2004	117.78	11,679.24	52,934.84
2005	99.93	13,984.66	53,799.28
2006	91.15	13,642.60	85,838.86
2007	86.15	1,550.73	180,333.60
2008	90.38	−28,192.02	206,806.04
2009	90.65	−24,302.26	239,054.10
2010	81.19	−47,273.10	288,574.60
2011	88.39	−52,472.62	352,012.07
2012	101.00	−54,246.41	377,836.52

Source: IPEADATA.

was due to the increasing international demand for natural resource-intensive products. But it is also true that, if the economy had not been stable and the positive expectations within the business community had not been present, the international stimulus would not have been as beneficial as it was. Nevertheless, the emphasis on the stabilization process implied – again from a trade-off perspective – not only high interest rates, but also low levels of spending in public investment. As a result, there were weak incentives for private investment (Carvalho, 2010; Ferrari Filho, 2004).[14]

It is true that in Lula's first term the government tried to reintroduce industrial policy, which in itself was something of an inflexion in the development policy. During the 1990s, following the neoliberal agenda, even the term industrial policy had become synonymous with bad policy or to 'protecting the inefficient'. The fashionable policy was the 'horizontal' approach: instead of trying to identify and support strategic sectors or companies, the neoliberal agenda proposed to concentrate on the systemic competitive factors that horizontally affect entire sectors of the productive system (for example, price stability and binding and stable 'rules of the game' are seen as important systemic factors that are beneficial to the competitiveness of all sectors in the economy).

The limits of this horizontal approach (not only in Brazil, but in other Latin American countries), and the success of more sector-oriented and state-interventionist policies in the Asian countries, impelled Lula's government to adopt a 'vertical' policy. This industrial policy of Lula's first term was called PITCE (Política Industrial, Tecnológica e de Comércio Exterior). It had a narrow scope in sectorial terms: only four industries were targeted (semiconductors, pharmaceuticals, capital goods, software). But even with this small set of industries as a target, both efficiency and effectiveness of the new industrial policy were limited. A more complete discussion about the reasons of the low performance of this new industrial policy cannot be attempted here. Organizational failures were probably one important reason, as many of the initiatives announced were not even implemented. It is important to mention, in this regard, that organizational failures may be a 'natural' consequence of the previous abandonment of industrial policies by the state and its agencies.[15] As stabilization was ensured, the focus of the economic policies could shift: *increasing economic growth* and *income distribution* came to the center stage as Lula won his second term in the 2006 elections.

Pay-off on stabilization: income distribution, industrial policies and growth in Lula's second term

Both continuing growth of the world economy and domestic macroeconomic policies resulted in a kind of virtuous cycle throughout the two terms of Lula's presidency. Growth induced increasing fiscal revenues. Increasing fiscal revenues generated the capacity to spend without failing to maintain the primary fiscal surplus. Increasing social transfers stimulated consumer spending. Economic growth allowed for the continuing increase of the real minimum wage, because companies could still operate and expand without 'profit squeezing'.

Table 4.8 shows that even the 2008–09 financial and economic crisis in the developed countries did not, initially, alter the growth trend during the closing years of Lula's second term. Even 2011 – the first year of Dilma Rousseff's government – showed growth, albeit at a more modest rate. Economic growth created the basic conditions for income redistribution policies. The continuing increase of the real minimum wage (and its effects on social security payments) and the cash transfer-based social programs could be implemented without having adverse effects on the management of internal public debt, at least in the short run.

As suggested in the previous section, the sequential choice of Lula's government was to implement first an orthodox stabilization policy

Table 4.8 Annual GDP growth rate (%)

Year	Brazil	World economy
2000	4.31	4.7
2001	1.31	2.4
2002	2.66	2.9
2003	1.15	3.7
2004	5.71	4.9
2005	3.16	4.5
2006	3.96	5.2
2007	6.09	5.4
2008	5.17	2.8
2009	−0.33	−0.6
2010	7.53	5.3
2011	2.73	3.9
2012	1.6*	2.3*

Source: IPEADATA.
* estimates

and subsequently to hold up to the expectations and promises that accompanied the rule of the Workers' Party. The efforts in this direction were made through economic and social development policies, mainly during Lula's second term.

There has been a strong increase in the number of families included in social programs that are based on direct conditional cash transfers aimed at fighting poverty.[16] Besides these income transfer policies, the economic growth rate and the legally determined real growth rate of the minimum wage have contributed to a labor market more favorable to the purchasing power of the lower and lower-middle classes. Table 4.9 shows the steady decrease of unemployment and the extreme poverty rate, as well as the steady increase of the real minimum wage.

While in Lula's first term the similarities to the Cardoso administration were highlighted because the emphasis was put on stabilization, in Lula's second term the emphasis on economic growth brought about important differences. First of all, the government took on a stronger role in investment coordination (mainly in producer goods industries, infrastructure and long-term financing). Public companies increased their size to help the government in some areas, such as petroleum and petrochemical (Petrobrás), electricity (Eletrobrás) and long-term financing (BNDES). The government has also tried to improve the coordination and speed of implementation of investment in infrastructure, through the Growth Acceleration Program (*Programa de Aceleração do Crescimento*, PAC).

Table 4.9 Selected socioeconomic welfare indicators in Brazil

Year	Rate of unemployment	Real minimum wage	Extreme poverty rate
2000	Not available	339.06	Not available
2001	Not available	369.86	15.28
2002	11.7	379.30	13.99
2003	12.3	381.94	15.2
2004	11.5	396.16	13.2
2005	9.8	423.74	11.49
2006	10.0	483.30	9.44
2007	9.3	512.51	8.65
2008	7.9	528.28	7.57
2009	8.1	566.43	7.28
2010	6.7	596.52	Not Available
2011	6.0	597.05	6.32

Source: IPEADATA.

Although the industrial policy launched during Lula's first term did not result in an important shift in terms of production structure and international performance of the manufacturing sector, it did establish a different perspective for the second term. Under this much broader perspective, industrial development policy had to deal with tough challenges. In the first place, how to avoid or attenuate a premature and harmful process of de-industrialization in more vulnerable regions and productive sectors? Second, how to coordinate investments along productive chains where the price system is not efficient enough to do it and where uncertainty is especially high? Third, how to deal with the protectionism and subsidies deployed by some trade partners (notably Argentina)? Finally, how to make those policies that have been shown to be very useful –at least in theoretical studies and through empirical evidence in some countries – concrete and effective?[17]

This led to efforts to implement a new industrial policy, dubbed *Política de Desenvolvimento Produtivo* (Productive Development Policy, PDP) during Lula's second term, which was characterized by more federal spending, more industries to be supported, a more nationalistic approach (in select supply chains), and export promotion in more technology-intensive industries (or, at least, products that are more 'value-added').At this point it is interesting to note that two important economic goals were interrelated in the agenda of Lula's second term. On the one hand, there was economic growth itself, as a macroeconomic goal that had to be balanced with the stabilization goal, as we have already seen above. On the other hand, there was the industrial policy agenda, as a structural policy that aimed at an improvement in the composition of the productive system and a better external insertion of the industrial sectors. These two goals were meant to be mutually reinforcing, although neither of them is a sufficient condition for the other. Flexible fiscal and monetary policies facilitate economic growth, at least in the short term. If fiscal spending includes increasing investment in public infrastructure, it will help to achieve growth and also to make some investments that support the goal of industrial development viable.

Because the initial stabilization policy was successful, the second term could adopt a bolder approach, increasing public investment and stimulating economic growth. During Lula's second term, the PAC was conceived as the main program for the goal of economic growth.[18]

As for industrial policy, as an introductory evaluation it can be said that it was more successful in government-led supply chains (such as petroleum, gas and naval industries) than in export diversification. The remarkable example here is PROMINP (Programa de Mobilização da Indústria Nacional de Petróleo e Gás Natural), a federal program that aims to promote national companies in the oil and gas supply chain. However, the manufacturing sector was still facing a complicated scenario at the end of Lula's second term. These pressures have been seen as powerful threats both in the internal and external markets. The share of manufacturing in total GDP didn't stop diminishing during the last decade. This trend may be attributed to the following key factors: the overvaluation of the Real as a result of the macroeconomic policy regime and of the structural features of public debt-financing in Brazil; the strong competitiveness of China and other Asian countries; Brazil's role as a big international supplier of commodities (natural resource-intensive products), which is shown by the export performance of Brazil being much better in primary products than in manufacturing from 2000 to 2010 (Figure 4.1).

At this point it is useful to interpret the shift in industrial policy towards a more coordinated and vertically focused set of instruments in the context of Latin American and especially Brazilian development models of the early twentieth century. Surely, the development policies implemented during the eight years of Lula's presidency have been neither a return to the import substitution model based on protectionist trade policies, which had been abandoned in the late 1980s, nor an export-led growth model of building competitive advantages, along the lines of Japan and other Asian countries in the second half of the

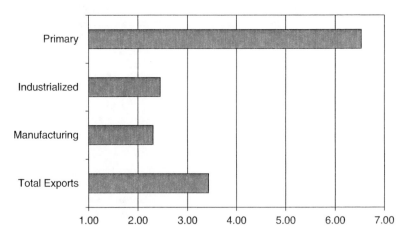

Figure 4.1   Export index by groups of products in Brazil, 2000–10

twentieth century. In my view, recent Brazilian industrial policy aims to preserve the level of diversification of the industrial system, based on the large size of the domestic market in combination with exploration of foreign market opportunities and niches, especially (but not exclusively) in developing and emerging countries. It is not completely a question of choice, because Brazil had lost other opportunities to become a more competitive industrial power, both during the first wave of 'Asian tigers' in the 1960s and 1970s, and in the 1990s when China was leading the catching up process in global manufacturing.

Following the approach adopted since the Plano Real, in 1994, the dimension of the Brazilian domestic market has been used as an advantage to attract foreign direct investment and to build a platform for the regional activities of multinational corporations. Such a policy is expected to produce effects of productivity spillovers from multinationals to domestic firms throughout the production system. In the terms used by Ocampo (2005), as already seen in the previous section, these spillovers could attenuate the gap between high productivity and low productivity sectors. On the other hand, the industrial development policy seeks to increase and improve the production capacity of national firms, mainly in industries in which the comparative advantages help international insertion, as well in industries in which small and medium sized firms can satisfy the domestic demand with quality and efficiency.

It is true that Lula's government sought to support the exporting effort of Brazilian manufacturing companies, through the projects and initiatives of the Brazilian Trade and Investment Promotion Agency (APEX). However, as export performance depended on a lengthy learning process, the results have not been impressive. Indeed, due to the negative systemic factors already analyzed in the previous section, manufacturing exports showed a relatively low performance during the 2000s (Figure 4.1).

How have the challenges faced by the long-term process of industrialization been related to the economic growth results under Lula and subsequently at the beginning of Dilma Rousseff's term? To understand the evolution of this issue, it is useful to analyze the long-term dynamics of GDP composition, both on the demand side and the supply side. On the demand side, the main trends of the past 20 years (after the adoption of the Plano Real in 1994) are, first, an increasing aggregate consumption (by families and government) from 77 percent of GDP in 1994 to 83 percent of GDP in 2009. Both family and government consumption increased as a share of GDP. Secondly, we observe decreasing gross fixed capital formation (which corresponds to investments), from 22 percent of GDP in 1994 to 16.5 percent in 2009. Thirdly, there was the increasing share of exports (mainly natural resources intensive-products) and imports (mainly manufacturing products). These developments correspond to the political and economic changes in Brazil. Increasing imports are related to trade liberalization during the 1990s. Increasing consumption (including government) is related to the social welfare policies, which derive from political pressures that resulted in increasing real wages and increasing social transfers, as discussed above.

Because a low level of gross fixed capital formation (as a share of GDP) is not compatible with high levels of GDP growth, this is one important trade-off that was to be faced by Dilma Rousseff's government when it took office in January 2011. With a slowdown of world economic growth, meaning that exports would not behave as dynamically as in the previous decade, Brazil's economic growth came to depend on solving an equation that can be expressed as follows: how to maintain social improvement, leading to increasing consumption, in combination with a higher rate of investment, which implies capital goods having a higher share of GDP? On the supply side, the share of manufacturing in GDP has been steadily decreasing since 1994 (from 23.5 percent in 1994 to 15.5 percent in 2009).[19] In contrast, the share of commerce and services (except financial services) in GDP has been increasing in the same period: total services (including commerce) had a 68 percent share of GDP in 2009, compared to 56 percent in 1994.

The new economic landscape and the old organizational failures: development challenges faced under the government of Dilma Rousseff

It has become clear that the link between macroeconomic conditions and the problem of the production structure of the Brazilian economy makes it hard to prevent the risk of de-industrialization in some industries. Public spending growth and public debt management put pressure on interest rates (to maintain capital inflows and the capacity to finance the deficit and refinance the debt). This is a kind of low exchange rate–high interest rate trap. The risk this brings is to diminish incentives to invest in manufacturing industries with negative long-term effects on production, employment and technological development. As a long-run consequence, the current account balance could further deteriorate, as the country may become more vulnerable to the volatility of the prices of primary products in global markets. It is important to note that Brazil has already incurred current account deficits every year since 2008 (see Table 4.7). The persistence of this deficit in the long run might cause high currency devaluation, with negative effects on inflation and real wages (and, consequently, on income distribution).

In addition, some of the good results of Brazilian socioeconomic performance in the 2000s may have a lack of competitiveness as a collateral effect, at least in some industries (for example, the increase in the real minimum wage, the shortage of qualified workers, the increase in relative prices of strategic inputs, etc.).

These bottlenecks and shortages of qualified workers subsist even in the context of a low economic growth rate, which was what was happening in 2012. The government has reacted to slow economic growth. The Central Bank has begun to substantially reduce interest rates. The federal government has tried to really expedite the implementation of PAC 2 (its growth acceleration plan), trying to overcome the regulatory and bureaucratic rules faced by the program.[20] Nevertheless, the economic growth recovery equation in Brazil had still not been solved by the end of 2012.

Besides the currency overvaluation problem and the lack of systemic competitiveness, the government of Dilma Rousseff faced yet another economic development challenge that is not unknown to Brazil: how to create a more effective national system of innovation? How to build a better international insertion in the global value chain? How to manage this as an issue of international relations policy?

The attempt to expand the domestic market and diversify exports was limited by the growth of exports of primary products and the capital inflow attracted by the rate of return on the Brazilian bonds market. Paradoxically, the period in which Brazil began to be seen as an emerging economic power has been marked by an increased concentration of exports of primary products and commodities. The exports of primary products as a proportion of total exports grew from 22 percent in 2000 to 43 percent in 2010 (MDIC, 2010).

Is the specialization in natural resource-intensive production and exports a kind of backward movement to the primary export model of the colonial, monarchical and early republic times, which would imply a strong de-industrialization process? The answer is certainly no. The present specialization coexists with a strong domestic market that not only attracts foreign direct investment in manufacturing but also creates opportunities for investment in the services and retail industries. Besides, Brazilian agricultural production is much more technologically advanced, integrated across branches, and efficient than it was during the 1950s and 1960s, when the structuralist school blamed the primary export specialization for the underdevelopment of Latin American countries.

Furthermore, there is no strong evidence of de-industrialization in Brazil in the short run (neither a broad fall in aggregate employment levels, nor extraordinary firm closures). It is true that the currency over-valuation affects the sales and the financial conditions of companies in some sectors of manufacturing industry (mainly national small and medium sized companies). Indeed, some industrialized regions have already suffered job losses and firm closures (although some of these losses are related to internal migration of companies from the southeast to the northeast of the country). Moreover, manufacturing imports are growing at a higher rate and exports are slowing down. But this is not an evidence of a strong de-industrialization process.

However, at the end of Lula's second term and the beginning of Dilma's government, the de-industrialization debate was reinforced, not only by academics, but also by businessmen and union leaders.[21] This was a result of an increase in the import coefficient in many manufac-turing industries, which does not mean de-industrialization but does mean a loss of the domestic market share of Brazilian companies. This could cause a long-term loss of manufacturing employment and dete-rioration in the financial health of domestic firms.

The euro zone crisis has worsened since 2011 and the recovery of the US economy was still at a slow pace in the two first years of Dilma's term. In this context, competition became fiercer, both in the inter-national and domestic markets. The reaction of Dilma's government consisted of two main policy lines: an anti-cyclical macroeconomic policy, based on monetary policy (which means lower interest rates); and a broader industrial development program, called 'Programa Brasil Maior' (PBM), that was embryonically launched in 2011 and was fully designed in 2012. The PBM aims to deal both with systemic competitive bottlenecks (for example, reducing the labor-related tax burden of the labor-intensive manufacturing industries, improving the institutional structure of trade defense) and with sector-specific goals and policy instruments.

Can a broader industrial development program be implemented in such an unfriendly environment, that is to say, that of international fierce competition and the systemic domestic bottlenecks? There has been a lack of implementation of industrial policies adopted during both terms of Lula's government, as many propositions were not turned into concrete actions. As a consequence, the PBM has been viewed with some skepticism. But one thing appears to be certain: the effectiveness of this new program would depend on the improved performance of governmental initiatives and instruments, which means improvement in the state structure and in the organizational and coordination capabilities of public agencies. These capabilities will also be needed to reconcile the distributive and social welfare goals with the economic growth goal. If it is true that Brazilian economic policies have recovered the developmental approach, with a more democratic and equalitarian public spending and a more prominent role of the state in coordinating economic development, it is also true that the concrete limits and tradeoffs confronting the economic and social goals will require a more sophisticated and efficient state apparatus.

This analysis does not intend to fully discuss the different views on the so-called new developmentalism (in contrast with the old developmentalism of the structuralist school at CEPAL (Comissão Econômica para a América Latina e o Caribe)). Given the limited scope of this chapter, it is also not possible to enter the debate on the developmentalist state.[22] What can be said about Lula's and Dilma's administrations, as a continuous strategy of a progressive party, is that a developmentalist agenda has been introduced. This agenda includes a more interventionist state, either in terms of leadership in infrastructure investment or of public-private partnership. It also includes an effort to reconcile economic growth and social equity goals, despite the difficulties involved in this process. But this agenda does not necessarily imply a permanent adoption of either an orthodox macroeconomic approach or a post-Keynesian approach. The choices here, as we tried to show, are more dynamically and politically determined, depending on the international and national conjuncture.

Conclusion

This chapter aimed to evaluate the economic policies and achievements while the Workers' Party has been in charge of the federal government in Brazil. I analyzed the two consecutive terms of the Lula presidency (2003–10) and the sustainability of economic and social transformation in Brazil, focusing on the challenges faced by the government of Dilma Rousseff, which took office in 2011. I showed that the trajectory of economic policy during the two terms of Lula's government was the result of strategic choices that took into account the political and economic scene, both at the national and international levels. Such strategic choices were successful. In the first term, the stabilization process was guaranteed and basic structural reforms were maintained and were also deepened. Growth-oriented and income distribution policies were implemented in the second term. Poverty has been reduced and income distribution has been improved. However, the sustainability of social transformation also depends on the development of the production structure and manufacturing performance. It is hard to figure out a country with a large population and good social indicators but without a strong and diversified industrial economy. In addition, there is a need to improve gross fixed capital formation to sustain the increasing levels of consumption. In this sense, Brazil needs an improvement in the capacity of the state (through structural upgrading and better organizational and coordination capabilities) to implement industrial development policies and infrastructure investment. This is clearly the main challenge faced by the economic agenda of Dilma's government.

Notes

1. The Plano Real was adopted during the Itamar Franco government (1992–94), in which Fernando Henrique Cardoso served as finance minister.
2. See Jayme Jr and Mattos (2011).
3. For a broader description of this period of macroeconomic turbulence in Brazil, see Baer (2007) and Fishlow (2011).
4. There is a broad literature on the origins and dissemination of the macroeconomic and structural problems that affected the Brazilian economy throughout the 1980s. See, for example, Castro and Souza (1985), Coutinho and Belluzzo (1984), Bier *et al.* (1987), Carneiro and Modiano (1990), Modiano (1990).
5. Along the rules of the Plano Real, there was not a guarantee of fixed parity exchange rate of the BRL and the USD (or any other strong currency). The exchange rate 'anchor' was more tacit than based on a legal rule.
6. In 1998, the basic interest rate was 29 percent (annual base), while the inflation rate was 1.65 percent (annual base). This difference results in a very high real interest rate, which implies high transference of income to the financial owners and a strong inhibitor of the productive investment.
7. However, the adoption of horizontal policies (or even the emphasis on it) is not necessarily a neoliberal agenda), because these policies can be compatible with a stronger role of the state (see Possas, 1996).
8. Rangel's (1978) argument was different from (but not incompatible with) the so-called 'efficiency motive', according to which incentives to efficiency are higher in private-owned companies than in state-owned ones.
9. The data described in this paragraph were elaborated by Giambiagi (2005), in which there is a broader analysis of the Brazilian economic performance in FHC years.
10. The economic debate in the first years of FHC rule were more concentrated in the monetary policy and its relation with the problem of currency

overvaluation, especially between orthodox economists and, on the other side, post-Keynesians. But as the main lines of FHC were consolidated, the debate began to involve structuralist economists and other heterodox economists, which challenged the ideas and policies that guided FHC government in the fields of industrial development, namely the role of the state and social welfare issues.

11. As the debate on industrial development became more superposed with arguments around the de-industrialization threat, this question could also be put in this way: is the risk of deindustrialization important and does it imply a more robust industrial policy? See Palma (2005) for a cross-countries analysis and perspective. For a seminal study, see Rowthorn and Wells (1987).

12. Ocampo's (2005, p.32) central argument is that sustainable growth in developing countries depends on breaking the dualism between high productivity sectoral enclaves and low productivity sectors across the production structure. This would require innovation, entrepreneurship, small firms services support, linkages along supply chains (and not only macroeconomic stability).

13. This choice was controversial and drew criticism from those economists who had expected a more heterodox policy. A strong debate was instigated in the academic field. See Ferrari Filho (2004).

14. These authors share a heterodox and post-Keynesian view on and critique of Lula's first term.

15. See Suzigan and Furtado (2006) for a discussion of these institutional and organizational failures. These issues have not been discussed for a long time in Brazil but are now beginning to be treated as relevant to the question of how to implement a feasible industrial policy once more.

16. *Bolsa Família* and other social welfare programs to support urban and rural families: from less than three million families in 2003 to more than 12 million families in 2010. See Wiesebron (Chapter 6); Buainain *et al.* (Chapter 9).

17. Both on the theoretical and the empirical level there has been a wider literature that supports the idea of industrial development policies, although different approaches and visions of how to operationalize it. See Rodrik (2004), Pack and Saggy (2006), Cimoli (2009), Aghion et al. (2011). For the Brazilian experience and debate, see Suzigan (1996), Pinheiro Pessoa and Schymura (2006) and Cano and Gonçalves (2010).

18. The first version of PAC, which was implemented in Lula's second terms, is known as PAC 1, in contrast with PAC 2, the second edition of the program, which has been implemented during Dilma Rousseff's mandate from 2011 onward.

19. Agriculture and Real State has also decreased as a share of GDP, but a lower rate. The data employed in this analysis are based on the statistics of IBGE ('Instituto Brasileiro de Geografia e Estatística').

20. By September 2012, it had been spent only 40 percent of BRL 900 billion (USD 450 billion) allocated for PAC 2.

21. See, for example, Nassif (2006), Bresser-Pereira (2008) and Barros (2011).

22. For a discussion of the new-developmentalist view, see Bresser-Pereira (2006) and Sicsú and Renaut, (2004).

References

Aghion, P. Dewatripont, M. Du, L. Harrison, A. and Legros, P. (2011) 'Industrial Policy and Competition', *GRASP Working Paper* 17.

Baer, W. (2007) *Brazilian Economy: Growth and Development*6th edition. (Bolder: Lynne Rienner Publishers).

Barros, L.C.M. (2011) 'A Questão da Desindustrialização', *Jornal Valor Economico* p. A15.

Bier, A. Paulani, L. and Messenberg, R.L. (1987) *O Heterodoxo e o Pós-Moderno: O Cruzado em Conflito* (São Paulo: Paz e Terra).

Bresser-Pereira, L.C. (2006) 'O Novo Desenvolvimentismo e a Ortodoxia Convencional', *São Paulo em Perspectiva* 20(3): 5–24.

Bresser-Pereira, L.C. (2008) 'Dutch Disease and Its Neutralization: A Ricardian Approach', *Brazilian Journal of Political Economy* 28(1): 47–71.

Cano, W. and Gonçalves, A.L. (2010) 'Política Industrial do Governo Lula', *Texto para Discussão*IE/UNICAMPn. 181.

Carneiro, D. and Modiano, E. (1990) 'Ajuste Externo e Desequilíbrio Interno: 1980–1984', in M.P. Abreu (org), *A Ordem do Progresso: Cem Anos de Política Econômica Republicana–1889–1989* (Rio de Janeiro: Campus).

Carvalho, F.J.C. (2010) 'Crescimento Econômico e Financiamentono Brasil', in L.C. Bresser-Pereira (org), *Doença Holandesa e Indústria* (Rio de Janeiro: Editora FGV).

Castro, A.B. and Souza, F.P.A. (1985) *Economia Brasileira em Marcha Forçada* (Rio de Janeiro: Paz e Terra).

Cimoli, M., Dosi, G. and Stiglitz, J. (eds) (2009) *Industrial Policy and Development: The Political Economy of Capabilities Accumulation* (Oxford: Oxford University Press).

Coutinho, L. (1996) 'A Fragilidade do Brasil em Face da Globalização', in R. Baumann (org.),*O Brasil e a Economia Global* (Rio de Janeiro: Campus).

Coutinho, L. and Belluzzo, L.G.M. (1984) 'Política Econômica, Inflexões e Crise: 1974–81', in L.G.M. Belluzzo and L. Coutinho (org), *Desenvolvimento Capitalista no Brasil* (São Paulo: Brasiliense).

Ferrari Filho, F. Corazza, G. (2004) 'A Política Econômica do Governo Lula no Primeiro Ano de Mandato: Perplexidade, Dilemas, Resultados e Alternativas', *Indicadores Econômicos*FEE 32(1): 243–251.

Fishlow. (2011) *Starting Over: Brazil Since 1985* (Washington, DC: Brookings Institution Press).

Giambiagi, F., Villela, A., Castro, L.B. and Herman, J. (org) (2005) *Economia Brasileira Contemporânea (1945–2004)* (Rio de Janeiro: Elsevier).

Jayme, F.G. Jr, and Matos, F.A.M. (2011) 'Ganhos Sociais, Inflexões na Política Econômica e Restrição Externa: Novidades e Continuidades no Governo Lula', *Revista Economia & Tecnologia* 7: 35–48.

MDIC. (2010) 'Exportações Brasileiras por Fator Agregado: 1964 a 2012'. http://www.mdic.gov.br/sitio/interna/interna.php?area=5&menu=608

Modiano, E. (1990) 'A Ópera dos Três Cruzados: 1985–1989', in M.P. Abreu (org.), *A Ordem do Progresso: Cem Anos de Política Econômica Republicana – 1889–1989* (Rio de Janeiro: Campus).

Nassif, A. (2006) 'Há Evidências de Desindustrialização no Brasil?' *Texto para Discussão do BNDES*n.108:22.

Ocampo, J.A. (2005) 'The Quest for Dynamic Efficiency: Structural Dynamics and Economic Growth in Developing Countries', in J.A. Ocampo (ed.), *Beyond Reforms: Structural Dynamics and Macroeconomic Vulnerability* (Stanford: Stanford University Press).

Pack, H. and Saggy, K. (2006) 'The Case for Industrial Policy: A Critical Survey', *World Bank Policy Research Working Paper Series* Washington.

Palma, G. (2005) 'Four Sources of "Deindustrialization" and a New Concept of Dutch Disease', in J.A. Ocampo (ed.), *Beyond Reforms: Structural Dynamics and Macroeconomic Vulnerability* (Stanford: Stanford University Press).

Pinheiro, M. Pessoa, S. and Schymura, L.G. (2006) 'O Brasil Precisa de Politica Industrial? De que tipo?' *Ensaios EPGE, Rio de Janeiro* 627.

Possas, M.L. (1996) 'Competitividade: Fatores Sistêmicos e Política Industrial: Implicações para o Brasil', in A.B. Castro, M.L. Possas and A. Proença (eds), *Estratégias Empresariais na Indústria Brasileira: Discutindo Mudanças* (Rio de Janeiro: Forense Universtitária).

Rangel, I.M. (1978) 'Posfácio à 3a edição', in I.M. Rangel (ed.), *AInflação Brasileira* (São Paulo: Brasiliense).

Rodrik, D. (2004) Industrial Policy for the Twenty-First Century *Paper prepared for UNIDO.* www.ksg.harvard.edu/rodrik/

Rowthorn, R. and Wells, J. (1987) *De-Industrialization and Foreign Trade* (Cambridge: Cambridge University Press).

Sicsú, J.L.F.P. and Renaut, M. (orgs)(2004) *Novo-Desenvolvimentismo: Um Projeto Nacional de Crescimento com Eqüidade Social* (Barueri/SP: Monole/Fundação Konrad Adenauer).

Suzigan, W. (1996) 'Experiência Histórica de Politica Industrial no Brasil', *Revista de Economia Política* 16(1): 5–20.

Suzigan, W. and Furtado, J. (2006) 'Política Industrial e Desenvolvimento', *Revista de Economia Política* 26(2): 163–185.

5
Poverty Reduction and Well-Being: Lula's Real

Marcelo Cortes Neri

Introduction

A study by the Center for Social Policies at the Fundação Getulio Vargas (CPS/FGV) launched in 2007 has shown two marked changes in poverty levels in Brazil: one in the period from 1993 to 1995, in which the proportion of people below the poverty line fell 18.5 percent, and another one from 2003 to 2005, in which it dropped 19.2 percent.[1] The first period is associated with the impacts of the so-called Real Plan, a successful stabilization policy that brought down inflation rates from more than 2,000 percent per year to more civilized single digit rates. Ten years apart, these two episodes were separated by a period of relative stability in poverty levels.

The remainder of the Lula administration gives a year-by-year sequence of the achievements observed in the two exceptional periods mentioned above. As a result, 22.9 million Brazilians rose out of poverty between 2003 and 2011, reducing the observed number of poor people from 50 million in 2003 to 26.4 million in the last year of this period. In the meantime, during the Lula administration, Brazil achieved the first and most important target of its earlier 25-year Millennium Development Goals (MDGs): the reduction of poverty rates by half. This means that Brazil reduced poverty at a pace more than three times faster than the United Nations agreement had predicted. This marked poverty reduction, which plays as important a role as stabilization did in the Cardoso era, is what we call in this paper, *Lula´s Real*.[2]

The fall of inequality combined with the resumption of economic growth after the end of the recession in 2003 are the direct determinants of poverty reduction during President Lula's years in office. Behind the fall in inequality is the creation and expansion of the Conditional Cash Transfer Program *Bolsa Família* (see Wiesebron, this volume), following long-established but not always successful traditional Brazilian income policies. However, the key ingredient in the recipe behind the Workers' Party's social boom is labor income. In particular, formal employment generation increased 50 percent on a permanent basis after the 2003 recession. In this chapter, I show that behind the growth of formal employment and reductions in poverty and inequality, there are signs of an improvement in education and also a confidence shock that was translated into the reduction of widespread uncertainties. All of these effects were inherited from the Cardoso administration but gained momentum during Lula's term in office.

A key consequence of the continuous movement towards a more prosperous, equitable and predicable society is the improvement of well-being among Brazilians. We believe that, besides income-based social statistics, direct subjective questions about people's quality of life are useful for capturing the full extent of the transformations experienced in Brazil during the Lula years, as well as some of their political implications.

This chapter analyzes the evolution of poverty and the well-being of Brazilians during the period of Lula's Real. We also aim to compare social changes during Lula's two presidential terms with those observed during the administrations of Fernando Henrique Cardoso and Dilma Rousseff, while discussing their main determinants and some of their consequences. It synthesizes and extends the findings of various researches that I have conducted over the last 15 years, most of which are implemented with freshly harvested microdata. The chapter is organized in eight sections. The next section provides a historic analytic background to the main changes observed during the Lula years. Next, the evolution of poverty and its direct determinants, namely growth and inequality, are discussed based on primary data from the Brazilian National Household Survey (*Pesquisa Nacional de Amostra por Domicílio*, PNAD) from 2003 to 2011. The following section takes advantage of the richness of the PNAD questionnaire to address the role played by different policies such as education, minimum wage and official income transfer sources as the main determinants of the evolution of income. The two next sections use *Pesquisa Mensal de Emprego* (PME) data to complement the analysis. First, it takes advantage of higher frequency PME data collection to trace the divisive points between the Lula administration and those of his predecessor and his successor. It then updates this discussion to grasp changes in poverty and income distribution during the first two years of Dilma Rousseff's term. I also use the PME to analyze the role played by education and the evolution of individual family earnings risk. A further section addresses the subjective dimension of well-being. It uses the Gallup international surveys data on life satisfaction with respect to the past, the present and the future. Finally, the last section presents a summary of social changes observed during Lula´s years and their possible determinants.

Historic overview

During the last 30 years, changes in Brazilian social indicators based on per capita income such as inequality and poverty have reflected the marked volatility of the macroeconomic environment: until 1994 the source of instability was the rise and failure of successive attempts to stabilize inflation, while after this period the main source of instability was the arrival (and the departure) of external crisis. This chapter argues that to understand the mechanics of these sharp macroeconomic fluctuations, as well as their consequences on income-based social indicators, is key to understanding the role played by various state-sponsored income policies. During the period of inflationary instability, up until 1995, income policies were at the core of both chronic inflation and stabilization attempts. That is to say, they were part of both the problem and the solutions offered. Anti-inflation plans, such as the Cruzado, Collor and the Plano Real just to mention the main plans, tried to interfere directly with the process of price formation – and income determination – through various ingredients such as price freezes, exchange rate policies, wage de-indexation rules and currency changes. Only the Plano Real was successful in controlling inflation.

Similarly, besides price stabilization, state-sponsored regressive income transfers are also key to understanding the causes behind high inequality and the attempts to fight it in Brazil. More recently, anti-inequality policies, which are other types of income policies, have been used; such as the transferring of incomes by the state directly from the public budget. At this point there is considerable evidence of the changing short-run income inequality role played by specific income policies.

We show here that this role offers a diversity of results, depending on which specific policies we are talking about (i.e. CCTs (Conditional Cash Transfers) or social security benefits linked to the minimum wage). These impacts may also change over time given the developments observed in the coverage and values of the policy parameters and the economic circumstances.

This redistributive movement is noteworthy since Brazil has been notorious as one of the countries with the highest income inequality in the world. After a steep rise in the 1960s, Brazilian income inequality was high and stable from 1970 through 2000, with a Gini coefficient per capita income around 0.6. From 2001 to 2011, however, inequality was in decline. The drop in inequality observed in this ten-year period is comparable to the rise observed in the 1960s (Fishlow, 1972; Langoni, 2005; Bacha and Taylor, 1978), as a sort of mirror image. This change reflects the combination of improvements in the labor market performance of low-skilled workers, increasing their respective education attainment and the adoption of increasingly targeted official income policies.

The fact is that Brazilian inflation is the lowest it has been in decades and the inequality of per capita income is at its lowest level since 1960, when household survey statistics on income started to be available. In both cases – stability of prices and equity of results – the so-called income policies have played an instrumental role. A common name, *income policy*, is shared by redistributive programs and anti-inflation plans. They attempt to target the problem, be it price stability or income equality. The common aspect is the speed at which they seek to impose their objectives. Maybe because of their potential to make rapid impacts, both types of income policies were used in fine-tuning with the electoral cycle.

The role of the stabilization plan is now played by redistributive income policies. Obviously, stabilization and redistribution are sides of the same coin, since there is no way to obtain a permanent reduction in inequality with high inflation, although we are talking about necessary conditions, not sufficient ones. President Cardoso stabilized the currency; President Lula continued this process and redistributed this stable currency through social programs. In the same way that Brazilian society has taken a long time to learn the importance of macroeconomic fundamentals in the achievement of lasting stability, the achievement of a sustained decrease in inequality depends on other fundamentals – most notably equality of opportunities – represented by access to stocks of productive assets such as education and their impactful outcomes.

A final word has to be said on the impact of keeping to macroeconomic fundamentals and on the role played by the confidence shock that occurred during Lula's administration. This reinforced stability played a crucial role for growth and for generating formal employment prospects, plus it had a direct impact on individual well-being.

Income-based indicators from PNAD

This section discusses the evolution of poverty and its direct determinants, namely growth and inequality movements, in using PNAD during the 2003 to 2011 period.

Analyzing income-based social indicator trends over different horizons requires the use of complementary databases. The data from the national household survey (*Pesquisa Nacional de Amostra por Domicílio*, PNAD), mentioned above, is the main source for the analysis of income in Brazil due to its annual frequency, multiplicity of questions and, above all, the constancy of the income questionnaire since 1992. However, there were no PNAD-surveys in the key years 1994, 2000 and 2010, which are crucial for drawing distinctions between the presidencies of Fernando Henrique Cardoso (1994–2002), Lula (2003–10) and Dilma (since 2011).

To fill in these gaps, the PNAD data is complemented with data from the monthly employment surveys (*Pesquisa Mensal do Emprego*, PME). PME surveys are more restricted in their geographical coverage and use a different concept of income. PMEs only collect data on labor income in the six main metropolitan areas. Labor income, however, accounts for three-quarters of people's income and its form of inequality almost uniformly corresponds to total income inequality. To make PME and PNAD data more comparable, PNAD (which are collected during the month of September) are compared to September data taken from the PME monthly surveys.

Poverty

Brazilian Poverty series, based on the new PNAD data starting in 1992, show two marked changes in poverty levels in Brazil: one started in 1993 and the other in 2003. The first one is more concentrated in time and is associated with the impacts of the Plano Real (Neri and

Considera, 1996). It was followed by a period of relative stability in poverty levels, interrupted only in 1998 and 2002. The fluctuations of poverty that occurred during presidential election years (1994, 1998, 2002, 2006 and 2010) can be seen in Figure 5.1 below:

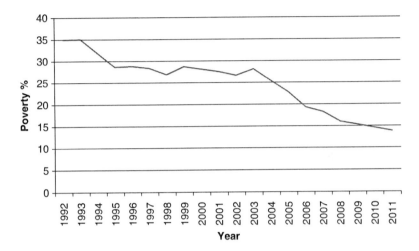

Figure 5.1 Percentage of population with per capita household income below poverty line

Poverty has maintained a continual downward trajectory since the 2003 recession, regardless of the poverty line and measure used. Looking at the period from 2003 to 2011 as a whole, whether we use the measure utilized by *Fundação Getúlio Vargas* (FGV), in real terms, or the international lines of the Millennium Development targets of poverty (USD 2 a day purchasing power parity, [PPP]) or extreme poverty lines (USD 1.25 a day PPP), all fell more than 55 percent between 2003 and 2011. Therefore, Brazil met a quarter century's commitment in less than one decade; more than was anticipated for 25 years was accomplished in eight years.

Of the 56.5 percent of FGV poverty-line decrease shown on Figure 5.1, a little less than half of the decline[3] (42 percent) was caused by changes in income inequality, while the remaining 58 percent is explained purely by growth effects. Without the reduction in inequality, average income would have had to increase almost 89 percent between 2001 and 2011, for poverty to have fallen that much. The immediate causes of the poverty reduction do not change much depending on the poverty lines that we use.

Growth

Looking at the immediate causes of the poverty fall, one should notice that there is a markedly high disproportion between the per capita GDP growth rates and the ones found by PNAD for per capita household income during Lula's term. This means that, not even taking into account inequality changes, the performance of Brazil in this period differs a lot depending on how you look at it. Between 2003-11, per capita household income growth averaged 4.4 percent per year while per capita GDP growth rates rose 3.1 percent. In cumulative terms PNAD growth was 40.6 percent against 27.8 percent of GDP (Figure 5.2). In other words, between 2003 and 2011, PNAD's average income increased 50 percent higher than GDP (41 percent against 28 percent), which indicates that average lifestyle standards were improving more than GDP suggests. In most other countries the opposite has happened: their respective National Household Surveys indicate lower income growth rates than GDP growth rates.

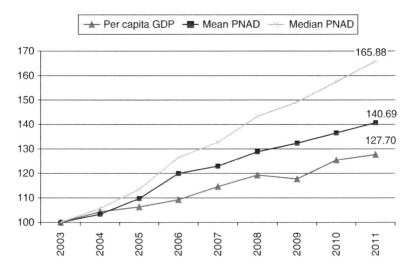

Figure 5.2 Increase of per capita GDP, income mean PNAD, and income median PNAD between 2003 (standardized at 100) and 2010
Source: Microdata from PNAD/IBGE and national accounts/IBGE.

A new aspect addressed here is identifying the main cause of this recent divergence between the average GDP and PNAD growth: the discrepancy between their respective deflators (i.e. inflation measured by the GDP deflator and the National Consumer Price Index, INPC). The former increased 1.9 percent per year more than the latter. Recalculating the real GDP performance by people's cost of living would give an average GDP growth of 5 percent per year instead of the 3.1 percent noted for the period from 2003 to 2011. Stiglitz, Sen and Fitousi (2011) emphasize that growth indicators based on the Gross Domestic Product (GDP) should be complemented with household income surveys and consumption data to gauge the evolution of average material life standards. While in the long-term the evolution of aggregates such as the GDP of national accounts and income from PNAD may present similar tendencies, they were seriously detached from each other during Lula's terms as president.

Inequality[4]

The 2000s can be referred to as the decade of the fall in income inequality. After 2001 inequality measured by the Gini coefficient decreased in all successive years. If we take the per capita household income as measured by the PNAD, group the households into deciles according to size of income and compare the changes in income over the years, we get a clear picture of the reduction of inequality. Between 2003 and 2011,[5] the per capita income of the poorest 10 percent of households increased by 80.8 percent whereas the income of the wealthiest 10 percent of households increased only by 26.9 percent, nearly one-third of what was observed (see Figure 5.3).

How does the income inequality development in the first decade of 2000 compare with previous decades? Fortunately, we now have studies on income inequality in Brazil for half a century. They started with the 1960 Census, the first representative household survey to ask direct questions about income. The data from the 1960 Census cannot be applied directly, as it is impossible to deduce the per capita income from the individual income of each household. Because of such limitations, we compare changes of different measures.[6]

Figure 5.4 depicts the development of the Gini coefficient between 1960 and 2011, following the inverted U-shaped process proposed by Simon Kuznets, but with different time spans observed on the rise and fall. The peak of inequality was in 1990. It is interesting to note that inequality levels observed 11 years before and after this date, in 1979 and 2001, are roughly similar while the inequality levels in 1970

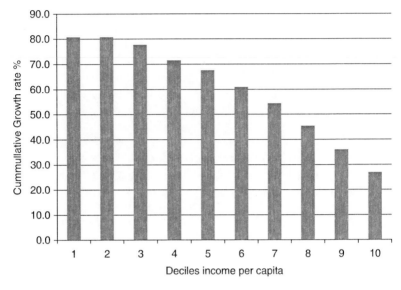

Figure 5.3 Growth of per capita income per PNAD income decile, 2003–11
Source: Microdata from PNAD/IBGE.

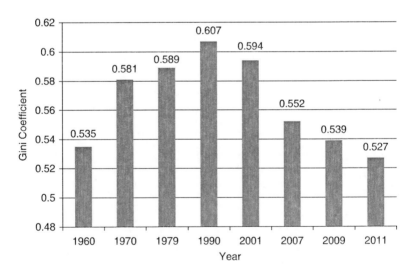

Figure 5.4 Long run perspective on inequality (Gini coefficient)
Source: Census/IBGE and Langoni (1973) and microdata from PNAD.

and 2003 are exactly the same. In other words, the rise observed in the 1970s was similar to the fall observed in the period between 2001 and 2003. Similarly, the rise of inequality in the first decade of its measurement in the country (1960–70) is similar to the one observed in the six year period between 2003 and 2009. We can call this a 360° revolution. At the end of last decade, we went back in inequality terms to where we were half a century before. From 2009 onwards we observe inequality measures lower than the ones observed 50 years earlier.

In short, income measurements must be accompanied by indicators reflecting their distributions. From 2001 to 2011, real per capita income growth, according to PNAD, was that the poorest 10 percent grew 550 percent faster than the wealthiest 10 percent of Brazilians (91 percent versus 16 percent). Brazil has experienced growth rates comparable to those of China but only for the poor. In developed countries like the USA or UK, or emerging countries like China and India, we observe the opposite: inequality is on the rise. In the period from 2003 to 2011, median income in PNAD grew 65 percent versus 41 percent in the mean and 28 percent of GDP.

Poverty and growth across different political administrations

Brazilian poverty reduction during the period from 1994 to 2010 has been significant. The country underwent social transformations under both the Fernando Henrique Cardoso (1 January 1995 to 31 December 2002) and Luis Inácio Lula da Silva (1 January 2003 to 31 December 2010) administrations. Indeed Brazil in 2010 looks quite different from Brazil in 1994.

Linking the beginning of the Cardoso period to its later years creates some difficulties; Brazil was faced with a hyperinflation that was ended with the introduction of the Real as the country's new currency on 1 July 1994, during the presidency of Itamar Franco and under the authority of Fernando Henrique Cardoso as the Minister of Finance. Comparing the September 1993 or 1994 PME data with the first PNAD income data collection in 1995 ignores seasonal factors and does not fully reflect the distributional impact of hyperinflation and the introduction of the Real during these months.[7]

The greatest poverty decrease (13.9 percent), between 1993 and 1995, occurred during Fernando Henrique Cardoso's administration. This was followed by a period of international crises, during which poverty fell an additional 7 percent until the end of the Cardoso era, totaling a 20 percent decrease. If we calculate from when the Plano Real was implemented (July 1994) until 2002, there was a 31.9 percent decrease in what we consider to be the Cardoso era.

To assess the impact of Lula's presidency on poverty, we must take PME results from December 2002 to December 2009, by which poverty decreased by 50.6 percent, and add the findings from the PNAD surveys. Combining PME and PNAD results, poverty decreased by 51.9 percent during the Lula era.

Income policies and education roles[8]

What were the means and policies that led to the reduction of income inequality in the period from 2003 to 2011? This section identifies the effects on the reduction of income inequality. We look at the role of official social transfers, as well as labor income and related issues such as minimum wage and education.

Transfers

Regarding non-labor income, special attention must be paid to incomes directly affected by social policies, such as social security benefits, and other non-labor income that includes cash transfers from social programs and capital income.

Social security is the main component of social income in Brazil, and second only to labor earnings among all income sources collected by PNAD. In 2011, it amounted to 18.3 percent of all income sources. Social security benefits include a contributory pay-as-you-go old age pension system and non-contributory benefits, both subject to discretionary income policies from the government. Today, Brazil is the country in the Latin American region with the highest transfers of income to the elderly, relative to its GDP. One key policy variable is the progressive differentiation of social security adjustments, meaning higher income groups receive lower real gains.

Referring to the short-term aspect of fighting inequality, there is in Brazil a new generation of social policies that are better focused on and more capable of redistributing income than the policies implemented in the past. This includes state-sponsored income transfer policies such as the *Bolsa Família* and minimum wage adjustments. However, the problem is that Brazil maintains other less effective official income transfer policies when tackling inequality and trying to improve welfare. The government has opted for expanding both new and old policies, both targeted and less targeted, policies.

How was inequality reduced? By applying a methodology of decomposition of Gini variations into different income sources to the 2003–11 period, we find that 55.5 percent of the reduction in inequality in that period is due to changes in labor incomes, followed by social security benefits at 21.6 percent and social programs – especially *Bolsa Família* and transfers (non-social security related) – at 12.4 percent. Then follows the Continual Installment Benefit (*Benefício de Prestação Continuada*, BPC[9]) at 4.8 percent and other income, such as rent and interest, at 5.8 percent. That is to say, the lion's share of the decreasing inequality was due to the observed effects of labor market expansion, which confers stability on the assumed redistributive process. Without the redistributive policies sponsored by the Brazilian state, inequality would have fallen 38.8 percent less in Lula's years.

The sources of income listed above, categorized by relative role in observed inequality reduction in the decade, may also be evaluated in terms of their impact on mean income. As a result, we can assess the amount of money involved in each: labor (79 percent), social security (17.4 percent), *Bolsa Família* (2.2 percent), continual installment benefit (BPC 1.75 percent) and other income (–0.47 percent).

Note that because public transfers, such as BPC, *Bolsa Família* and social security, correspond to funds derived from the federal coffers, relative effectiveness can be evaluated in terms of the impact of each Real on the decrease in inequality obtained – or, alternatively, vice versa. From the viewpoint of public policy, a combination of the two viewpoints mentioned above (the importance of each source of income for income and for inequality) enables us to generate a useful measure for analysis of the fiscal cost versus social benefit ratio in terms of the observed equity gains. The ratio varies by source of income. Each percentage point of reduced inequality in the 2003 to 2011 period cost 100.7 percent more via increases in social security than via BPC. If all the funds could be channeled to BPC (instead of social security) with the same distributive impact, inequality would have fallen twice more than it did via the chosen allocation.[10]

Likewise, the fiscal cost versus distributive benefit ratio of *Bolsa Familia*, which is a little less than half that of the BPC for the 2003–11 period, would imply a doubling of the effect were it the channel utilized and its relative performance maintained. In other words, by transitivity, *Bolsa Família* would produce impacts 345.5 percent greater than social security, provided that the same technical relationship could be maintained throughout the period.

From this analysis we can also calculate the differences in the cost-benefit ratio between the two sets of programs. While social security has had somewhat higher effects on the reduction of income inequality than *Bolsa Familia*, public financing of social security benefits has been six to seven times the amount of payments through *Bolsa Familia*. Overall the additional cost for the fiscal budget of each percentage point of inequality fall was 345.5 percent more expensive for social security than for *Bolsa Familia* in the 2003 to 2011 period ().

Labor

The labor market provided the main means for reducing income inequality (56 percent of the inequality fall and 79 percent of the income growth observed from 2003 to 2011). This is due to various reasons, such as expanding employment, moving labor from informal to formal employment and reducing inequality within labor by increasing minimum wages (see Figure 5.5), which also affects social security payments as a floor for benefits distributed.

Neri (1997) shows that minimum wage rises had a major impact on labor market-based poverty and inequality measures in the mid-1990s. However, as minimum wage increases progressed, these effects faded away (Neri, 2007). The most important contribution of minimum wage

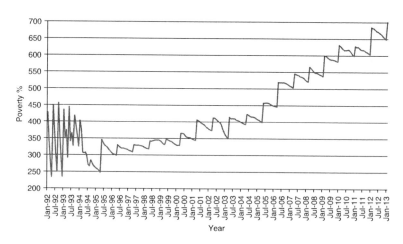

Figure 5.5 Real minimum wage trends, 1992–2013
Source: Labour ministry and INPC/IBGE.

increases in Brazil was its effect on non-labor income through its linkage to social security contributions.

Education

Besides the short run impacts of income policies, such as *Bolsa Familia* and minimum wage, the key public policy to consider when seeking to understand the long-run changes observed in income distribution (both inequality and growth) is educational policy. The educational level of a Brazilian citizen ranks low on an international scale. In 1990, 16 percent of children between seven and 14 years of age were out of school, in 2000 they constituted 4 percent and today less than 2 percent. Translating advances in flows into stocks of schooling took a while but education attainment has been rising in recent years; in 1992 individuals aged 25 years or over had completed just 4.98 years of schooling but in 2011 this was 7.46 years. Figure 5.6 below demonstrates:

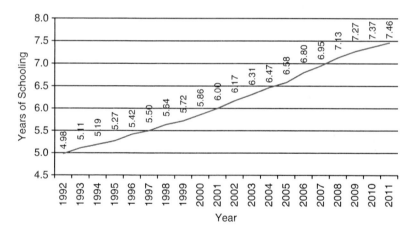

Figure 5.6 Mean years of schooling among 25 years of age or higher, 1992–2011
Source: Microdata from PNAD/IBGE.

An analysis of the forces driving the recent rise in mean income in Brazil shows that, everything else being equal, the increase in learning translates into a 2.2 percent annual gain in income per capita. In turn, the poorest 20 percent should gain 5.5 percent in income. Such an increase could be considered the educational bonus earned when schools are no longer underdeveloped. As a matter of comparison, the bonus from demographic transition (referring to the expected increase in the population at an active age) was considered today to be around 0.5 percentage points by 2024.

This gain would be even greater for Brazil's poorest, presented with better educational opportunities. We must also consider the benefits of obtaining quality of education. From this perspective, the average PISA rating[11] applied to 15-year-old students is discouraging. In a group of 64 countries, Brazil ranks 54 in all educational requirements. However, Brazil was among the top three countries with the highest rates of change in educational proficiency during the period from 2000 to 2009.

Researchers are seeking to better understand how much students truly learn, as well as the factors that determine their educational successes. Proficiency test scores – such as those from *Prova Brasil*, Enem and Enade[12] – help to provide stakeholders in the educational market with information on how students are performing. Educational targets, such as the Index of Educational Development (IDEB), help to identify what the country wishes to achieve, and what the role of each stakeholder is in this aggregated educational effort. The use of these tests as part of educational targets holds the promise of supporting motivation and transparency on the way to achieving excellence in learning.

The good news is that, lately, citizens have been prioritizing education. Until recently, opinion polls ranked education seventh in the priority list of public policies. However, they now suggest that education has moved up to second place, behind only health.

Subjective well-being

Brazilian Household surveys such as the PNAD and PME allow us to gauge the performance of various aspects of Brazilian society over the years, and to analyze performance distribution among different groups defined by income, socio-demographic or spatial characteristics. However, the PNAD does not give an idea of Brazilian differences as compared to other countries. Furthermore, the PNAD is a survey that provides measures of objective variables, as they are informed by individuals. If we really want to know particular Brazilian traits compared to other nations, we have to look at international data. Subjective measures of living conditions, such as those explored in the emerging literature on happiness, do not yet belong to the IBGE (Brazilian Institute of Geography and Statistics) tradition.

Combining objective measures on subjective welfare, based on questions asked during the evaluations people make of their own lives, helps to obtain a broader picture of quality of life in different countries. That is to say, it is not enough to improve life objectively: people have to notice the improvement. Since Brazilian household surveys do not typically garner information about people's perceptions, we used Gallup's Global Life Satisfaction Index World Poll from 2006, in which Brazil was ranked 22nd out of 132 countries. Just before Lula´s first term in 2001, (seen retrospectively from 2006) Brazil was ranked in 44th place among 132 countries. As we have seen, Brazil was in 22nd place in 2006. In 2011 (seen prospectively from 2006), Brazil was ranked 1st. Looking at the progression throughout the last decade, we observe a sense of improvement throughout the Lula years.

Did the apparent increase in life satisfaction of Brazilians remain until the end of Lula's years as president? In all surveys analyzed, with an increasing number of countries surveyed – reaching 158 countries in 2010 – Brazilians were still ranked as number one in future life satisfaction. On a scale from 0 to 10, Brazilians give an average rating of 8.6 for expectation of life satisfaction in 2015, above that of all other 157 countries in the sample (Neri, 2011). Given that the world average is 6.7, Brazilians seem to have ended the Lula Era as optimistic as possible given other countries' parameters.

Sustainability of changes under Dilma[13]

Monthly Employment Survey (PME) allows us to test how much of Lula's Real trends were kept during the first half of the Dilma administration. In addition, based on labor earnings, it is a proxy for the more permanent aspect of income changes. In this section, we use PME to gauge four types of effects, namely: (1) the temporal evolution of mean and median labor earnings gross trends; (2) net growth trends, keeping socio-demographic characteristics constant in order to assess the role played by year, as varied by the net labor performance observed; (3) the evolution of returns to education over earnings across years in order to grasp the permanent role played by education; and (4) the use of the longitudinal aspect of PME to capture the evolution of per capita earnings risk observed at the individual level.

Mini GDP x PME

From 2003 to 2011 the discrepancy between cumulative growth rates of GDP with respect to PNAD household income, as mentioned earlier (GDP 27.7 percent, PNAD mean 40.5 percent and PNAD median

65.5 percent), is also observed with respect to PME. PME mean and median per capita in labor earnings in the 2003 to 2011 period grew 45.1 percent and 66.1 percent, respectively. This difference is even higher using data collected by the PME for the two first years of the Dilma administration. Working separately with 2011, per capita GDP grew at 1.7 percent while mean and median PME real per capita earnings grew 3.7 percent and 6.5 percent respectively. The fact that the median is growing faster than the mean suggests that inequality continued its downward trend.

During 2012, while GDP showed a 0.9 percent increase and per capita GDP had a near zero growth, the per capita work income of households had an increase of 5.1 percent in comparison with the same period the year before. On the other hand, the median rose 1.45 percentage points and, using the same comparison, reached 6.5 percent. This means that the per capita average and median labor earnings reported by households in the PME increased by around five and 6.5 percentage points, respectively, more than the observed per capita GDP growth rates. The growth in labor earnings-based statistics indicates that the growth and equality trends initiated in the Lula years have been maintained by Dilma in her first two years.

If PME data is limited in its income concept and geographical coverage, all main shifts in Brazilian income distribution over the past 30 years were first anticipated by it. These include the booms that resulted from launching the Cruzado and Real stabilization plans, *Lula's Real* after 2003, the effects of the 1997, 1999 and 2008 foreign crises and so on. According to PNAD, labor income corresponds to 77 percent of household income in national terms and 81 percent in the six main metropolitan areas covered by PME. Furthermore, social security income was boosted by the 14 percent nominal minimum wage increase in January 2012 and by the expansion of the *Bolsa Familia*, when the *Brasil Carinhoso* program was launched in May 2012. From October 2011 to October 2012, with inflation already deducted by INPC, the total sum of benefits paid by the National Social Security Institute (INSS) increased 7.1 percent and the family allowance by 13.2 percent . In other words, growth estimates restricted to labor income are somewhat conservative.

Year effect

With the PME microdata from 2003 to 2012, we conducted a per capita household income Mincer regression controlled by socio-demographic features – namely gender, age, skin color, metropolitan area, position in

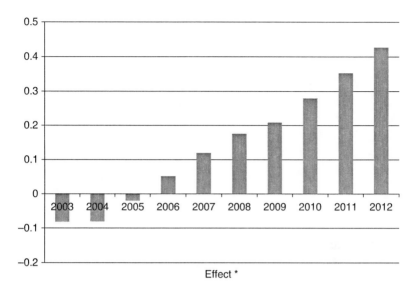

Figure 5.7 Per capita income equation – year effect (* cumulative gain with respect to year 2002)
Source: Microdata from PME/IBGE.

the family and education –to separate time effects from changes in the observable characteristics in question. The data shows that controlled income has been growing each year and the largest leaps occurred in fact between the two last years of the series (Figure 5.7). That is, even comparing the same type of people in different years, 2011 and 2012 cannot be considered anything but favorable years in terms of per capita earnings growth. The cumulative gain up to 2012 was 42.7 percent, indicating an increase of little more than seven percentage points with respect to the previous year.

Returns of education effect

Another temporal effect that we analyzed incorporates into the Mincerian equation framework mentioned the year variable interacting with the one referring to completed years of schooling brackets. The objective is to capture the effect of changes in returns to schooling. If we analyze the highest category, of 11 or more years of schooling, compared with people with one year or less of schooling used as the reference basis (omitted variable), we find a drop in the higher education premium from 2004

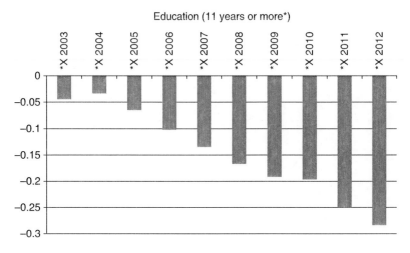

Figure 5.8 Falling school premium – per capita income equation – interactive dummies, 2003–12 (* cumulative change of earnings since 2002, of those with 11 or more years of study in relation to those with zero years of schooling)
Source: Microdata from PME/IBGE.

onwards. In 2012, the accumulated drop of the education premium compared to 2002 is 28.4 percent. Between 2011–12, the drop is 3.4 percentage points, a sign that there are still reductions in inequality in education in that period, no less than any other year in the series (Figure 5.8).

Family earnings risks

Another possibility arising from the longitudinal structure of the PME, which accompanies the same families across time, is to measure the income risks associated with the newly acquired living standards. In particular, we verified the proportion of people crossing the median per capita income line.

The likelihood of crossing the income median in an upward direction, in this period, generally increased between 2002 and 2012. It moved up from 18.4 percent in the period 2002–03 to 22 percent in the period 2007–08, slightly dropping during the 2008–09 crisis and rising sharply ever since: 25.8 percent (2009–10), 27.7 percent (2010–11), culminating at 30.1 percent in the period 2011–12 (Figure 5.9).

The risk of downgrade, measured by the probability of moving downward through the median, is weakening as time goes by. It has halved

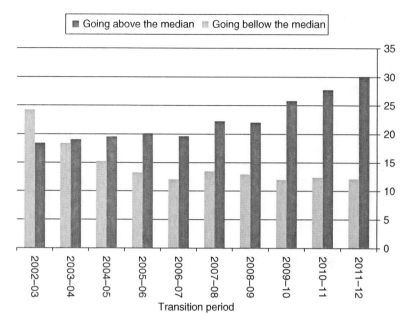

Figure 5.9 Income risk over the years – probability of dropping below and rising above the median
Source: Microdata from PME/IBGE.

from the 24.2 percent observed during the 2002–03 recession to the 13.4 percent registered in 2007–08, on the eve of the crisis. Even after the crisis, such statistics flat-lined to around 12 percent, achieving 12.1 percent between 2011 and 2012.

Similar to the income level analysis based on the PME longitudinal data, we examined the per capita household income analysis above and below the median, controlled by socio-demographic characteristics such as gender, age, skin color, metropolitan region, position in the household and education, to separate the time effects of these changes from those in the observed socio-demographic characteristics. The controlled results demonstrate even more strongly than the uncontrolled results that the transitions to below the median reached their lowest in the periods 2010–11 and 2011–12, while the upward transitions peaked during the last two-year period.

In short, considering the median as a benchmark, the probability of a drop in income has flat-lined in recent years at the bottom line of the PME series, while the probability of rising has never been so high.

In addition to being a period of relative stability of reported income for each individual, 2012 has been characterized by people having the best chance of moving upwards.

Conclusions

Figure 5.10 synthesizes the main elements of the social transformations that occurred during President Lula's years in office.

The scheme divides the different public policy channels into growth and equality effects and their final outcomes on poverty and well-being (Kakwani, Neri and Son, 2010), starting with inequality channels, where income policies such as *Bolsa Família* and minimum wage played important roles in explaining the observed changes. However, our results show that the fiscal cost incurred for each percentage point fall in the Gini coefficient was around 362 percent higher with social security transfers than with *Bolsa Família*, which denotes larger effects of the latter on the binomial social justice and macroeconomic stability.

The education bonus, keeping other variables constant, explains the 2.2 percent mean income growth per year, while the same statistic for the 20 percent poorest is 5.5 percent. Besides the significant effect of education on inequality, the price of education also fell (as shown by PME data) and thereby reinforced the impact. In addition to education impacts through redistributive and growth channels,

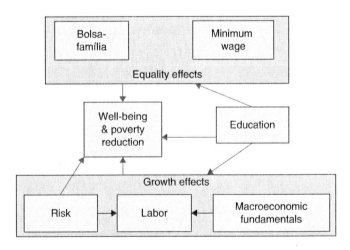

Figure 5.10   Lula's Real – analytical framework

there is also a direct effect on well-being through the empowerment of individuals. Finally, a sort of confidence boost was given during the start of Lula's administration. This confidence boost played a crucial role promoting growth and formal employment generation prospects, plus it had a direct impact on individual well-being derived from the individuals' increased ability to look ahead to the future.

To sum up, we may say that Brazilian economic progress in the significant feature of the Lula era is not growth in terms of GDP but rather growth of household income and especially spread of income distribution. Not only can this movement be seen objectively, it is also felt subjectively by Brazilians in terms of their own lives. Among all countries, in 2010 Brazilians reported the highest level of expectation with respect to their individual life satisfaction. To understand Lula's success in creating his legacy and passing the baton to his successor, one may paraphrase Carville on Brazil: 'It is the social, companion'.

Notes

This chapter summarizes some of my previous work on poverty and income inequality in Brazil (see www.fgv.br/cps). I would like to thank the excellent assistance provided by Luisa Carvalhaes and Samanta Reis. I would also like to thank the editors of this book for their very careful comments.

1. Defined as the share of the population with an income below 155 reais in September 2011. Average Brazil prices adjusted for regional differences in the costs of living. See Ferreira, Lanjouw and Neri (2003).
2. While Cardoso's original Real started in 1994 (before his presidential term) with the launch of the Plano Real under his supervision as Finance Minister, Lula's Real started after a confidence shock and macroeconomic adjustments were implemented in the first months of his first term. The division between administrations is cumbersome given PNAD's limitations; it is conducted in a single week in September. PNAD restrictions in 1994 and 2010 in the year before Cardoso first presidential mandate and also in the last year of Lula's second mandate.
3. The definition of poverty developed by Ferreira, Lanjouw and Neri (2003) and by the Center for Social Policies at Fundação Getulio Vargas (CPS/FGV) is used here. It incorporates updated regional differences in costs of living that affect purchasing power. The highest criterion for access to *Bolsa Família* 2011 per family each month (with average Brazil prices adjusted for regional differences in the costs of living) is relatively close to the CPS/FGV regionally adjusted poverty line.
4. Neri and Ferreira (2012).
5. PNAD did not make field trips in the Census years 2000 and 2010. Therefore, we are only able to know, according to PNAD data, what happened in eight of the ten years of the decade.

6. The concept that Carlos Langoni used in his seminal work was individual income. Langoni's work is still surprisingly up-do-date in its methodology to cover the most recent data and conclusions, if the deciles order are inverted.

7. According to PME data, poverty increased 6.6 percent from September 1993 to September 1994 and decreased 16.9 percent from September 1994 to September 1995. If we incorporate the instant reduction effect the implementation of the Real imposed by vanishing the 'inflation tax' which particularly affected the poor, it shows that poverty decreased by 22 percent between September 1994 and September 1995.

8. Neri (2009) and Campello and Neri (2013).

9. The BPC program is directed at older people (over 65 years of age) and people with disabilities, both low income, with a criterion of *per capita* family income below one fourth of the monthly minimum wage. The transferred amount corresponds to one monthly minimum wage and, unlike *Bolsa Família*, can be cumulative among the members of a single family. Thus the BPC is another channel of impact related to the policy of minimum wage readjustments.

10. This type of analysis assumes zero administrative costs, and is merely retrospective. To apply it in a prospective manner would imply maintaining an unchanging ratio, not taking into consideration broader interactions in the general equilibrium.

11. Program for International Student Assessment.

12. Enem (Exame Nacional de Ensino Medio) and Enade (Exame Nacional de Desempenho dos Estudantes) are national exams which evaluate high school and undergraduate students, respectively.

13. Neri (2012).

References

Bacha, E.L. and Taylor, L. (1978) 'Brazilian Income Distribution in the 1960s: Facts, Model Results and the Controversy', *Journal of Development Studies* 14(3): 271–297.

Campello, T. and Neri, M.C. (org.) (2013) *Programa Bolsa Família: Uma Década de Inclusão e Cidadania* (Brasília IPEA-MDA).

Ferreira, F. Lanjouw, P. and Neri, M. (2003) 'A Robust Poverty Profile for Brazil Using Multiple Data Sources', *Revista Brasileira de Economia* 57(1): 59–92.

Fishlow, A. (1972) 'Brazilian Size Distribution of Income', *American Economic Review* 62(2): 391–402.

Kakwani, N. Neri, M.C. and Son, H. (2010) 'Linkages Between Pro-poor Growth, Social Programmes and the Labour Market: The Recent Brazilian Experience', *World Development* 38(6): 881–894.

Langoni, C. (2005) *Distribuição da Renda e Desenvolvimento Econômico do Brasil* 3rd edition (Rio de Janeiro: Fundação Getúlio Vargas – FGV)

Neri, M.C. (1997) 'O Reajuste do Salário Mínimo de Maio de 1995', *Anais do XIX Encontro da Sociedade Brasileira de Econometria* 2: 645–666.

Neri, M.C. (2007) 'A Dinâmica da Redistribuição Trabalhista', in R. Paes de Barros, M.N. Foguel and G. Ulyssea (orgs) *Desigualdade de Renda no Brasil: Uma Análise da Queda Recente* (Brasilia: Ipea).

Neri, M.C. (2009) 'Income Policies, Income Distribution, and the Distribution of Opportunities in Brazil', in L. Brainard and L. Martinez-Diaz (eds), *Brazil as an Economic Superpower: Understanding Brazil's Changing Role in the Global Economy* (Washington, DC: Brookings Institution Press).

Neri, M.C. (2011) *A Nova Classe Média: O Lado Brilhante da Base da Pirâmide* (São Paulo: Editora Saraiva).

Neri, M.C. (2012) '2012: Desenvolvimento Inclusivo Sustentável?' *Comunicados do Ipea* 158 (Brasília: Ipea).

Neri, M.C. and Considera, C.P. (1996) 'Crescimento, Desigualdade e Pobreza: O Impacto da Estabilização', *Economia Brasileira em Perspectiva* 1:49–82.

Neri, M.C. and Ferreira, P.H. (2012) 'A Década Inclusiva (2001–2011): Desigualdade, Pobreza e Políticas de Renda', *Comunicados Ipea* 155 (Brasília: Ipea).

Stiglitz, J. Sen, A. and Fitousi, J.P. (2011) *Mismeasuring Our Lives* (New York: The New Press).

6
Social Policies during the Lula Administration: The Conditional Cash Transfer Program *Bolsa Família*

Marianne Wiesebron

During his first inaugural speech as President of Brazil, on 1 January 2003, Luiz Inácio Lula da Silva (Lula) stated that his first priority was to combat hunger. He regarded it as shameful that in a country as rich as Brazil people go hungry. This led to the establishment of a program of food security, *Fome Zero* (Zero Hunger). Lula stated that if – at the end of his term – all Brazilians had the possibility of eating three meals a day, he would have accomplished the mission of his life (Silva, 2003). His other 'obsession', as he stated in the same speech, was creating jobs focusing particularly on first jobs in his *Projeto Primeiro Emprego* (First Job Project; Silva, 2003). This would entail a number of economic and financial measures. He has dedicated significant resources to promoting economic growth and investing in energy diversification. Creating jobs (increasing formal employment) was one of his campaign promises, as he firmly believed that having formal employment is one of the best ways to combat poverty and create security (Singer, 2009). While five million jobs had been created during the administration of his predecessor, Fernando Henrique Cardoso (1995–2002), that number increased threefold during Lula's term (2003–10), to 15.3 million jobs. In ten years, unemployment decreased by 6.8 percent, from 12.3 percent in 2002 to 5.5 percent in 2012. These numbers include the first two years of the Dilma administration, which started on 1 January 2011 (Sicsú, 2013).

Lula's fundamental aims were to reduce hunger and poverty, to diminish deficiencies such as illiteracy and to make it generally possible for Brazilians to live with dignity. Lula's focus on these specific issues may be, in part, due to his own background. President Lula is the first Brazilian president who does not come from the Brazilian elite. He has experienced hunger. He did not finish primary school. He was a manual laborer and lost part of one finger while working in a factory. He was one of the foremost and most active trade union leaders during the harshest years of the military regime and is responsible for organizing some major strikes. Although the strikes were somewhat successful, they also made trade union leaders aware that working through a trade union has limitations, and that workers needed real political organization (Keck, 1992, pp. 64–66). So when, in 1979, it became possible to set up political parties and Brazil became a multiparty nation again, the *Partido dos Trabalhadores* (PT, Workers' Party) emerged as one of the first parties and was formally established in 1980. Lula was one of its most important founding fathers. When democracy and direct elections were re-established, he ran for president.[1] He was runner-up three times but only succeeded in 2002, when he was elected with a very comfortable margin.[2]

Lula immediately acted on the promises of his 2002 campaign, starting to develop social projects on his first day in office. The aim of this study is to get a closer look at Lula's social policies and evaluate their impacts on Brazilian society. Furthermore, as the election of president Dilma has been seen as the option for continuity – the first time there has been real political continuity in Brazil – this study will also look at the social policies of her administration and will point out the implementation of policies that are the same, those that have been transformed, and those that are entirely new. This will be done on a policy-by-policy basis. The focus will be on the *Bolsa Família* program (BFP, Family Allowance or Grant), as it is the main social program, encompasses many sub programs, and is considered to be the most significant and representative of the Lula administration's social policies. A number of other social programs are discussed in different chapters of this volume such as housing (Bonduki, Chapter 8) and small-scale farming (Buainain *et al.*, Chapter 9), but the BFP has grown and has had an impact on about one quarter of the Brazilian population. This study will start with a historical background. The empowerment of women through this program will receive specific attention as this topic is widely discussed in programs of conditional cash transfer (CCT) in different countries. A third part will be dedicated to an evaluation of the BFP, followed by a conclusion.

Attention to education became another major social issue for Lula, especially from his second term onwards. As he stated in his second inaugural speech on 1 January 2007:

It is to be certain that your children will study in a school of quality and that the children of poor families can dream of having the same access to the same universities as the richest son of the country, because this is the way we will build a strong democracy, a solid democracy.

(Silva, 2007)[3]

Some of his critics wondered why Lula was investing in higher education, as he himself had never finished primary school. Perhaps exactly for this reason he, more than others, understood the importance of education. However, his investments in education, in terms of quality, quantity and finances, have been so enormous and so diverse that a whole different study should be dedicated solely to this topic. It should analyze what has been done in the area of education, from elementary to higher education in general, and specifically the improved access to the best universities by students of (very) reduced financial means. Inequality in education in Brazil is a huge problem, but access to higher education for poor students has certainly improved considerably since 2007. To give one example, since 2012, the Quota's Law (n. 12.711) reserves 50 percent of all places at federal universities and institutions for students from public (state) schools, specifically those who come from families with an income equal to or less than one and a half times the minimum salary per capita. Furthermore, besides social criteria, this 50 percent also includes skin color as a criterion and gives priority to students who are or consider themselves to be black, brown (*pardo*) or indigenous, proportionally to the number of people of color per state, according to the 2010 census. In Brazil, ethnicity is self-declared (Moehlecke, 2009, pp. 461–487).[4] In this study, education will be limited to *Bolsa Escola* (School Allowance), as part of the BFP.

Lula did not invent or start all of the social programs that he set up; one of the many criticisms that he and his government received in the media and by politicians of opposition parties. He used existing programs, but transformed them quite substantially and consolidated the different policies in one big coherent program, and made it his priority.[5] The changes that Lula made were crucial for a highly improved implementation of these social programs. The financial investment also increased considerably.

Historical background

The social programs that were initiated in the 1990s are the result of the amplification of social rights in the Brazilian Constitution of 1988. This Constitution, which is known as the Citizens' Constitution because of all the civil rights it incorporates to prevent another military regime, also includes quite an extensive system of social protection, which has social well-being and social justice as its general objectives. This is developed in articles about social security, health, education, culture, children, adolescents, the elderly and the indigenous (Companhole and Companhole 1992, pp. 98–112). The Constitution states clearly in its different sections that those in need have a right to receive assistance and that the State has to provide, free of charge, an education, a health system and social security benefits for all of its citizens. The Constitution also guarantees a minimum salary for the elderly and those with a handicap, who cannot provide for themselves (Ibid. art. 203, V). The protection of weaker citizens was reinforced during the Itamar Franco administration (1992–94) through the Organic Law of Social Assistance of 1993 (Law n. 8742, 1993), where the problem of poverty is addressed in detail. For the elderly and those with a handicap, the Continued Benefit (*Benefício de Prestação Continuada*) was instituted. For the first time, the necessity to do something about poverty was recognized within a legal framework.

Meanwhile, in 1990, Senator Eduardo Suplicy proposed a program of guaranteed minimum income, without any conditions, which was only approved by the Senate. From 1995 onwards, many programs of conditional cash transfer (CCT) were instituted, mostly at a municipal level or in the federal district. These CCT programs had two objectives: to provide either (1) a minimum income for the whole family or (2) a grant for education, both with specific conditions. In 1995, first the municipalities of Campinas and Ribeirão Preto started with programs of guaranteed minimum income, under certain conditions. Another CCT program was established in Brasília, providing a family grant for education. Many other municipalities followed suit, the majority opting for the education program and the remainder for the minimum income program. Two federal programs of CCT were also set up. The first, set up by the State Secretary of Social Assistance in 1996, was the Program for the Eradication of Child Labor (*Programa de Erradicação do Trabalho Infantil* – PETI) for children between seven and fourteen years of age who were working or were about to start working, especially in dangerous, unhealthy or degrading jobs. These children received a monetary benefit for going to school instead of working, with the condition of a minimum attendance at 75 percent of the classes. In 2001 a second federal CCT program was introduced, the *Bolsa Escola Federal* (Federal School Allowance), based on the Brasília program. In this case, children from age six to fifteen had to go to school with at least an 85 percent rate of attendance. The Ministry of Education transferred money for up to three children, from 15 to a maximum of 45 reais. The Ministry of Health introduced the third CCT program, *Bolsa Alimentação* (Food Grant), which established a series of conditions linked to health: medical exams for pregnant and breast-feeding women, and vaccinations for children. Also in this case, the maximum benefit was the same for the number of children per family, from 15 to a maximum of 45 reais (Soares and Sátyro, 2009, pp. 8–9).[6] These three CCT programs were developed during the Fernando Henrique Cardoso administrations (1995–2002). The next CCT program was created in 2003 under the Lula administration: the *Cartão Alimentação* (Food Card), through which families whose income was under half the minimum salary per person received a sum of 50 reais, which had to be spent solely on food. These federal programs were under the responsibility of four different ministries. While the coordination between the ministries was quite difficult, there was no communication between the different administrations about the CCT programs existing at municipal or state level. As a result, some families could get transfers from different programs, while other families – in similar conditions – did not receive anything at all, for no clear reasons. The only common denominator of all these different programs, which often worked with different criteria and different transfers, was their objective to fight poverty. The inconsistency between proliferation of programs was finally recognized as a problem that had to be dealt with, but all of these federal, state and municipal social programs did not cover the whole Brazilian territory. The creation in 2003 of a program – the *Bolsa Família* – at the federal level under the responsibility of only one Ministry was a huge improvement, as was the use of the *Cadastro Único*, also called *CadÚnico* (Unified Register), where poor families were registered along with detailed data (Soares and Sátyro, 2009, pp. 9–10; Cacciamali, Tatei and Batista, 2010, pp. 272–275).

Lula was hardly starting from scratch, as the project *Fome Zero* had already been formulated by him in 2001, when a very detailed analysis was published in a study by the *Instituto Cidadania* (Citizenship Institute), giving a historical background to the world food problem (Programa Fome Zero, 2001). According to this report, the fact that people go hungry is neither due to a lack of food nor to the size of the population. There is enough food for the whole world, but its distribution is very unequal, as is caloric intake across the globe (Projeto Fome Zero, 2001, pp. 16–22). Furthermore, healthy nutrition is also decreasing in the whole world. This is a general pattern, not only related to hunger. In Brazil the same pattern is seen: there is enough food for all Brazilians, but with unequal distribution and unequal caloric intake. Moreover, hunger and poverty are not concentrated in the Northeast but are also a major metropolitan problem. For instance, in four years, poverty has increased by 45 percent in the metropolitan area of São Paulo, from 26 percent in 1995 to 39 percent in 1999 (Ibid.). All of the existing programs related to food in Brazil are then studied in detail: food production, food distribution and access to food, all of which are compared with other countries (Ibid., pp. 23–78). Finally, the study contains a series of proposals on how to solve the problem of hunger and poverty in Brazil with a series of social policies. The proposals are partly based on existing policies, some of which need improvement, and on a number of new ones. A detailed budget is included (Ibid., pp. 79–118).

Lula wrote the preface to the study *Projeto Fome Zero* and signed it. He states that, 'quality nutrition is an inalienable right of every citizen' (Projeto Fome Zero, 2001, p. 5). When he wrote in 2001, Lula saw a society confronted with growing problems such as increasing unemployment, amongst other things. The number of families he believed should benefit from the program was 9.3 million, or 44 million individuals. Lula indicated that this information is available to everybody, and may be used by any interested political party (Ibid.). A couple of things emerged from his words and from this publication: that eradicating hunger and poverty is really fundamental to him; that he had thought about this for quite some time; and, at that point in time, he was not yet sure that he would be the one implementing the program. Once president, though, he did so and he started immediately.

On his very first day in office, with the Provisional Measure n. 103 (01 January 2003), Lula set up an Extraordinary Ministry of Food Security and Fight Against Hunger. This led immediately to criticisms, including that a new ministry would not solve the problem of hunger and that this would imply that existing programs would have to be expanded and that more funds were necessary. Questions were asked about how efficient and effective this project was. Setting up a pilot project in the semi-arid climate of the Northeast led to other criticisms, as much of the poverty is urban, not rural, and is a problem that especially plagues big metropolitan areas. In practice, some relatively useful measures were taken in the 20 municipalities chosen for the pilot: the building of cisterns, inclusion of initiatives, digital inclusion, microcredit, incentives for family agriculture and literacy programs. These last programs were also implemented from the beginning of the Lula administration. One program, *Programa Brasil Alfabetizado* (Brazil Literacy Program), was instituted in 2003 by the Ministry of Education and was set up for youngsters, adults and the elderly throughout the entire country. However, it focuses mostly on municipalities with the highest percentage of illiteracy, most of which are found in the Northeast.[7] Another important action was creating the possibility to obtain documents at the civil registry, free of charge (Yasbek, 2004, pp. 110–111). Getting the correct documents is absolutely essential for citizens for a wide range of processes, from entering the formal job market to becoming a beneficiary of a social program.

The *Bolsa Família* Program – BFP

Although an impressive number of actions had already been taken in his first months in office, to increase the efficiency of the various existing programs, the Lula administration instituted the *Bolsa Família* (Family Grant) Program. The *Bolsa Família* was established on 20 October 2003 by Provisional Measure n. 132, effective immediately. It unified the following five programs, one of his administration and four set up at the end of the second term of the Cardoso administration: (1) the *Bolsa Escola* Program, set up by law in 2001 (Law n. 10.219, 2001), (2) the National Food Access Program (Law n. 10.689, 2003), (3) the National Program of Minimum Income linked to health (*Bolsa Alimentação*, Provisional Measure n. 2. 206–1, 2001), (4) the Gas Subsidy (*Auxílio-Gás*, Decree n. 4102, 2002) and (5) the CadÚnico from the Federal Government (Decree n. 3877, 2001).[8] The Provisional Measure setting up the *Bolsa Família* program (BFP) became Law in 2004 (Law n. 10.836, 2004). The BFP has as its objectives to ensure the human right to adequate food, to promote food security and a balanced healthy diet, to eradicate extreme poverty, and to promote access to citizenship for the most vulnerable part of the population. It also fosters health, education and social assistance. To ensure that these objectives are met, the BFP works with conditions.

To receive the BFP, children and adolescents have to be sent to school, children must get vaccinated, pregnant women must get prenatal care, and young mothers (especially when they are breastfeeding) must also seek medical care. In short, children up to fifteen years old have to go to school, young children up to seven years old must be medically monitored, and women must seek pre-natal and post-natal care. According to some authors, the conditions are as important, or even more important, than the financial benefit that families receive. These conditions represent an investment in human capital. For others, however, social protection should be a right without strings attached (Bichir, 2010, pp. 123–125). The amount that the families get depends on the economic situation of each individual family, not only on its income but also on its family composition, on the number of children and whether or not they are of school-going age. Families are considered poor if they live on less than half the minimum wage, while those who are extremely poor live on less than a quarter of the minimum wage (MDS, 2007).[9] The difference between poverty and extreme poverty is worked out in the different programs. Therefore, children who get the school grant (*Bolsa Escola*) have to be vaccinated before going to school and also get one healthy meal per day at school, which has a positive effect on the family budget. In cases of extreme poverty, the cash transfer for the family is larger, and the children get two balanced school meals per day. In 2006 an Organic Law on Food and Nutrition Security fortified the importance of healthy nutrition and food security in ensuring the human right to proper food and in sufficient quantity (Law, n. 11.346, 2006). In that same year, PETI was also incorporated into the BFP. It is quite successful, as it has developed a number of activities in culture, sport and digital inclusion to prevent children from working when they are not studying (Cacciamali, Tatei and Batista, 2010; Morais *et al.*, 2007). In 2008 up to two adolescents, aged 16 or 17, could also be included in the BFP. The condition was going to school with a minimum attendance rate of 75 percent.

Meanwhile, unifying these various programs of social benefits in only one program has a couple of advantages: a better overview of the needs of the different families, making adequate payment easier, less bureaucracy and more transparency (Moreira *et al.*, 2010, p. 202). Shortly after the BFP became law, on 23 January 2004, the Extraordinary Ministry of Food Security and Fight Against Hunger was incorporated into the Ministry of Social Development, which became the Ministry of Social Development and Fight Against Hunger (MDS). That way, one ministry would be dealing with all of the different programs brought together in the BFP, thereby making the management of social programs much more coherent and efficient, and also much easier to monitor.

The *Bolsa Família* law did not only unify the previous programs, it was also a tremendous improvement. Just to give one example: the CadÚnico was established under Cardoso in 2001. Under Lula, it was expanded and one very important element was added, namely the payment is made preferentially to women (§14 of Law n. 10.836, 2004). In practice, 94 percent of the recipients are women (Holmes *et al.*, 2010, p. 3). This was verified, for instance, by a case study done in Campinas, in which 94.1 percent of the beneficiaries were female (Pires, 2008, p. 347).

Before going into the relevance of women being the recipients of the CCT in this program and the empowerment it provides, it has to be stated that setting up the CadÚnico, one single database for registering all persons receiving some form of assistance through different social programs, is very useful and is considered a huge step forward. The National Secretary of Citizenship Income (*Secretaria Nacional de Renda de Cidadania*, Senarc), which is in charge of the BFP at the MDS, sets up questions for the interviews. The database is made at the municipal level by technicians trained especially to interview the families, then the data is centralized at federal level by the MDS and the *Caixa Econômica Federal* (CEF). The database was set up by the CEF and is managed by it. The CEF also makes all cash transfers. The Senarc defines the criteria for giving benefits and for the amount, as well as those for reducing or stopping them. Having only one database makes it more cost-effective and limits possibilities for cheating (Brière and Lindert, 2005; Bichir, 2010, p. 120). This database has evolved over the years and nowadays contains an impressive quantity of information. Through the information in the CadÚnico, it is determined whether a family fulfils the necessary requirements to receive some CCT from one or more programs. But it also gives insight into the composition of the family: two parents or female-headed household, the age of children, if they are going to school, the level of schooling of the parent(s), etc. Are the parents employed? If so, formally or not? If it is a female-headed household, is there a day care center in the neighborhood? Does the family home have access to running water, electricity and waste disposal? The information gathered by the CadÚnico is so extensive that it can be considered to be a census of the poor of Brazil, and it is updated on a very regular basis. This wealth of information could be used for a better diagnosis of the problems of each family. This could even lead to more focalized action in reducing poverty by addressing specific problems on a family-by-family basis. (Barros, Carvalho and Mendonça, 2009). In 2013 the CadÚnico registered all families with an income of half the minimum salary (339 reais in 2013) or less per capita, or up to three minimum salaries per family. It has registered 25 million families (over 81 million individuals) and is used for over twelve social programs, of which the BFP is the most important.[10] In 2013, 13.8 million families were beneficiaries of the BFP (Paiva, 2013). Under the Dilma administration, the Brazil without Misery Plan (*Plano Brasil sem Miséria*, BSM) was set up. Dilma's main target is the eradication of extreme poverty during her presidency. According to the MDS, this goal should be reached by 2014. It is an extremely ambitious goal and concerns 16 million extremely poor people, who are so isolated that the state has difficulty in locating them, both in rural and in urban areas. However, new strategies have been developed to actively go and find these people and to include them in the BPF and improve their lives through installing electricity and water, providing education, etc. Besides providing an income and services, the state also wants to promote productive inclusion (Dihl, 2012). To this end, in 2011, President Dilma established a program that provides technical courses for those with hardly any previous schooling, and also provides assistance in acquiring a first job. The Ministry of Education is responsible for the courses, for which no fee is charged. Priority is given to the extremely poor or those in vulnerable conditions, like youth living on the streets. In two years' time, about 680,000 young people have taken advantage of this program (Castioni, 2013, pp. 38–42). Special attention is given to children up to 15 years old through the new *Brasil Carinhoso* (Caring Brazil) Program, which gives extra benefits to children – in addition to the BFP benefits – to improve (pre-)schooling, healthy nutrition, etc. (Dihl, 2012).

Other programs falling under the BSM include the Exemption of the Payment of Fees for Public Entry Exams (*Isenção de Taxas de Concursos Públicos*), Social Telephone (*Telefone Popular*), which provides fixed phones at a very cheap rate; Special Pension Benefits for 'Housewives' (*Benefício Previdenciário Especial para 'Donas de Casa'*); and Social Rates for Electricity (*Tarifa Social de Energia Elétrica*). This last program keeps the costs of consumption of electricity low and is a continuation of *Luz Para Todos* (Light for Everybody), a project executed by the Ministry of Energy and Mines to provide electricity to all Brazilians living in isolated rural areas. This provides inclusion through electric energy, as electricity is used for light as well as for refrigeration, television, computers, irrigation systems, etc. These new possibilities seem to help reduce rural migration to urban areas (Camargo, Ribeiro and Guerra, 2008). As more families without electricity were recently discovered, the program was restarted in 2011 and will run until 2014. As at May 2012, 2.9 million families had benefited from this program and this got the highest praise during the Rio+20 event (Informativo Luz para Todos, 2012). Since 2011, the BSM also includes the Water for All program (*Água para Todos*), which provides water tanks and irrigation systems.

Bolsa Família and the empowerment of women

As mentioned above, if possible, the CCT is given to a woman, even if she is married or living with a partner. This gives women the power of decision over how to use this money. The allocation of resources to women is based on the worldwide experience that their spending will be of higher quality than that of men. Women generally spend money on their children and on the household rather than on personal expenditure. Research has shown that this gives women more self-esteem and that they feel more financially secure (Braido, Olinto and Perrone, 2012, pp. 552–555). However, although this seems to hold true for Brazil and for other CCT programs that make women their primary beneficiaries, Maxime Molyneux also sees a number of problems in her analysis of the comparable program *Progresa/Oportunidades* in Mexico. Started in 1997, this program is reportedly responsible for inspiring President Cardoso to set up a CCT program in Brazil in the same year, according to Molyneux.[11] In Brazil, to prevent children from working, they were paid a sort of minimum wage to go to school, as poor families need all the income they can get. In a way, this encourages women stay in the traditional role: taking care of children and families. However, it has the potential to create resentment among the traditional male providers, or make them feel even less obliged to provide for their family, while women have fewer opportunities to search for work as they are kept busy by the program (2007, pp. 69–71). Despite this, women are less subject to domestic violence at home (Soares and Sátyro, 2009, p. 31). More recent studies show that the empowerment of women is happening and that it goes beyond the acquisition of food or clothes for the children. Women buy the medication needed for their children and also contraception, which shows women increasingly taking charge of their own reproductive rights. A new program, launched by the Ministry of Health in 2011, is strengthening the right of women to plan having children or not, by the *Rede Cegonha* (Stork Network). In addition, extra quality care is provided to all those who have children, within the *Sistema Único de Saúde* (Unified Health System, SUS), also a result of the 1988 Constitution.

This is huge, and has effects on the relationships between men and women, on families themselves, and also on the areas in which these women live. Especially in poorer regions, where there has been less monetization than elsewhere, receiving CCTs (money on a regular basis) gives women greater bargaining power (MDS, 2007). In recent years, CCT is seen 'not as financial help, but as a strategy to fight poverty and hunger, to fight the social inequality of gender, low qualification, the lack of professional training and the lack of access to social actions' (Moreira *et al.*, 2010, p. 201). Therefore, the CCT itself is considered to be a form of empowerment. Getting income on a regular basis means that women do not have to work in jobs that are, more often than not, dangerous, not well paid and do not offer much stability. On the contrary, it gives them the opportunity to look for better jobs, as people with a very low income try to find some form of employment, to increase their earnings (Moreira *et al.*, 2010, pp. 200–201). Obtaining money on a regular basis also gives women the possibility of making choices, which is not the case when they receive food baskets (*cestas básicas*).

The *cesta básica* was introduced in 1938, linked to the minimum wage legislation in 1938 and contains a one-month supply of basic foodstuffs such as rice, beans, meat, milk, some cleaning products and products for personal hygiene. The minimum wage is calculated based on the necessities of workers for food, clothing, housing, hygiene and transportation. Over the years, the composition of the food basket has changed, based on an evolving knowledge of nutrition, taste and changing cultural patterns. There are also regional differences, which are related to differences in culture and taste (Barretto, Cyrillo and Cozzolino, 1998, pp. 29–35). The free distribution of food baskets had been part of the Collor and Cardoso administrations, with an extremely wide distribution of 30 million baskets in the election year 1998 (almost twice as many as in 2000), considered to be the high point of the program. At the end of that year, the program that distributed food baskets was cut because, according to the federal government, it did not reduce poverty (Silva, Belik and Takagi 2005, pp. 167–168).

In addition to not offering the possibility of choice, the food basket also 'establishes a relationship of dependency in more competitive areas, while the *Cartão Alimentação* (Food Card) gives spending possibilities to the urban poor and creates opportunities for the local economy and family agriculture' (Silva, 2003, pp. 47–48). This program also pays attention to healthy nutrition. Those who use the *Cartão Alimentação*, which is part of the BFP, have to be registered officially in the *Cadastro Único*, with official documents. The same families may have been literally excluded before, as they did not technically exist in the Brazilian bureaucracy (Ibid., p. 49).

The CCT that can be used to buy food and other items gives women 'more status in their neighborhoods, with shopkeepers treating them with more respect' due to their stable incomes, as Molyneux noted for the Mexican program *Progresa*, which later become *Oportunidades* (2007, p. 71). The same has been seen in Brazil, where the fact that women are the beneficiaries of the CCT has had three main impacts: (1) women become visible consumers; (2) women assume more authority at home; and (3) women feel more self-respect as citizens. This is due to the fact that women participate in meetings concerning the program and have their own documents. However, it is not yet clear if the BFP has changed traditional gender patterns, or if this would have been possible in such a short time. The case study done in the municipality of Vargem Alegre, Minas Gerais, shows that traditional patterns persist, but at the same time changes were noticeable, as husbands started to share in domestic activities, for instance. As their responsibilities increased, women felt more self-esteem as individuals, not only as mothers. (Moreira *et al.*, 2010, pp. 199, 203, 209–210). This has been confirmed by extensive research carried out between 2006 and 2011 in the Northeast by Walquiria Rego and Alessandro Pinzani. The importance of having the ability to choose, and the positive influence of a regular income, cannot be overstressed. It really changed the lives of the women who are beneficiaries of the BFP (Rego, 2010, pp. 141–151). According to Pinzani, the right to choose is also part of a working democracy and also has an impact (outside consumption) on moral aspects (apud Nascimento, 2013). Another positive factor of the program is that it decreases the isolation of women; poverty often leads to social isolation. Now women get out of their houses more because they have to go shopping for food, clothes and other items. Furthermore, they participate in group meetings with other beneficiaries (Soares and Sátyro, 2009, pp. 30–31).

Special attention is given to women working in rural areas as they are confronted with specific problems. To improve gender equality in rural areas, an important program was created in 2004: the National Program of Documentation for the Rural Female Worker (*Programa Nacional de Documentação da Trabalhadora Rural*). This has long been a request of women themselves. This program, under the responsibility of the Ministry of Rural Development, provides for free basic documents, such as a birth certificate, an identity card, registry in the National Institute for Social Security (INSS), the Individual Taxpayer Registry and the Employment Record Card.[12] It is available for women working in rural areas, artisanal fisherwomen, indigenous women and female descendants of runaway slaves who live in isolated places, known as *quilombolas*.[13] A clear majority of the rural population without documents is female. In fact, the majority of the rural population in Brazil is female. In the twenty-first century only 15 percent of the Brazilian population lives in rural areas, as 85 percent has become urbanized. That makes this problem quite acute. Without basic official documents, women cannot receive credit for programs for family agriculture, to give just one example (Heredia and Cintrão, 2006, pp. 18–19). Rural women are pre-registered in the Cadastro Único, which allows them to participate

in the BFP and also have access to the benefits of other social programs provided by the federal government. Once they have their civil
documents, they can open their own bank accounts, etc. The National
Documentation Program reached its first million rural women in June
2013 (Portal Planalto, 2013). Having documents fosters citizenship and
social inclusion. This, together with inclusion through electricity and
water, certainly helps promote empowerment of women in rural areas.

An evaluation of *Bolsa Família*

Amongst the topics of discussion that followed the start of the program
Fome Zero, was whether or not it should be considered universal or focalized. The whole discussion among academics about the program being
universal or focalized has been very heated. Yasbek states that it is universal (2004, p. 109), and the PT wanted it to be universal. (Bichir, 2010,
pp. 119–120). However, when the BFP was introduced, most academics
considered it to be a focalized program, as it is concentrated on people
who have the lowest incomes in the country, and its goal is to reduce
the problem of poverty (Hall, 2008, p. 807; Castro et.al., 2009, p. 336).

In any case, for the first time, the largest CCT program in Latin
America is really reaching poor people, including the more isolated
ones, such as indigenous groups (or *quilombolas*) and persons with no
fixed housing who are living on the street (Hall, 2008, p. 807). The
consequence of this program has been a real reduction in poverty and
inequality. As the majority of the poor are female, the program has a
double positive effect on women. For the first time since the 1970s,
the Gini index – which gives an indication of income distribution in a
country – has been changed in a positive way, although there is still a
long way to go (Hall, 2008, pp. 809, 811–812; see also Neri this volume).

However, the monitoring of the conditions, certainly during Lula's
first term in office, could have been improved in a number of municipalities. It started to get much better in 2006 and progressed considerably during his second term (Vaitsman, Rodrigues and Paes-Sousa,
2006). The most difficult to monitor are those living in extreme poverty,
because often these families live in greater isolation and have more difficult access to schools and health centers than those who are a bit better
off (Soares and Sátyro, 2009, pp. 14–17).

In that same year, the promised target of 11 million families was
reached, which means that over 44 million people were included in the
BFP. As the expansion of the program happened three months before the
election of 2006, this led to criticism or was construed as a way of getting

votes (Hall, 2008, pp. 812–813). But then again, any public policy could be construed as a way to get votes (Castro *et al.*, 2009, pp. 337–338); cases of fraud receive considerable attention in the media. But, with a program of this magnitude, the cases of fraud are found with limited frequency (namely a couple of hundreds), which is negligible in a program with several millions of beneficiaries (Soares and Sátyro, 2009, pp. 23–24). Nevertheless, in a study of the perceptions of the BFP in Brazilian society, fraud was the main criticism, with 82 percent concurring with the idea that the program includes persons who do not fit the criteria because their income is too high. Research on this aspect has not uncovered any basis for this allegation. Besides, those just above the poverty line might still be confronted by many problems associated with poverty. Incomes can also vary, which is often the case with low earnings that are, more often than not, not very reliable (Bichir, 2010, p. 125). The second issue mentioned in the study on perceptions was that beneficiaries of the BFP would not make an effort to get a job. Most poor people want to have a job, and most of them stress the importance of education for getting (better) employment. Having work is seen as something positive and the beneficiaries of the program do participate more in the job market than others in comparable situations (Castro *et al.*, 2009, pp. 348–349). The last preconceived idea is that the people who are on the program will have more children to benefit even more from the program. There is no proof of this allegation and, in fact, the birth rate is decreasing all over Brazil, even in rural or poorer areas (Castro *et al.*, 2009, pp. 345–349). Furthermore, under Lula, the benefits were limited to three children up to 15 years of age per family. Under Dilma, the number increased to five. The number of adolescents is limited to two, aged 16 or 17.

Although there were some negative perceptions, the majority of perceptions regarding the BFP were positive. The great majority of Brazilians, namely 72 percent, consider that the BFP 'brings good things to Brazil'. There are some clear regional differences, with a more positive attitude in the Northeast than in the South and Southeast, but, all in all, the differential is only a couple of percentage points. The fact that the program kept children in school was evaluated as the highest benefit, with 83 percent, while the improvement of the health of pregnant women was the least well-known and got only a 64 percent positive response. The response also became more positive if the interviewee knew some beneficiary of the program (Castro *et al.*, 2009, pp. 338–341). Maybe the perception of the Brazilian population concerning the BFP is also becoming more positive because a number of positive consequences of this program are coming to the forefront.

The positive impact of the BFP on life expectancy was disclosed by the IBGE in 2013. In 30 years, life expectancy in the Northeast of Brazil has improved by nearly 13 years, and even more so in the last ten years. In other regions, there was also a big increase. The 2013 yearly World Health Organization Report established that, thanks to the BFP, the infant and child mortality rate for children up to five years of age has decreased substantially in Brazil. Similar findings were recently reported by Rasella *et al.* (2013, pp. 57–64). According to other studies, school results have started to improve for children in the BFP.

Notwithstanding these positive results, there are a number of problems with the BFP: it is does not have clear exit policies, such as *Chile Solidário*, which gives benefits for three years, after which families should be able to provide for themselves. The BFP does not provide these possibilities, but different complementary programs do, by providing literacy programs, professional education, microcredit, etc. Therefore, the BFP does not invest directly in human capital, as *Oportunidades* in Mexico does, but the various social programs taken together do create the opportunities for this investment. Both programs, the Mexican and the Brazilian, have no time limit. The BFP does not provide a guaranteed income, as conditions are imposed, and it is dependent on the budget allocated to it, which represents less than 0.5 percent of the whole federal budget on a yearly basis. This also means that the BFP is not a right, and does not provide systematic social protection. Soares and Sátyro consider it somehow a hybrid program (2009, pp. 19–20, pp. 31–33; Bichir, 2010, pp. 129). Especially in the first years of the BFP, some families, who fulfilled all the criteria, were not included in the BFP due to lack of funds in that year. Since then, the budget has increased considerably, and many more families are included. The numbers are growing even more with the active search for those living in extreme poverty, under the BSM. Furthermore, within the Program *Brasil Carinhoso*, not only children up to six years old are included but also those from seven to fifteen years old, as of the end of 2012.

The budget for the BFP in 2013 is 23.95 billion reais (Paiva, 2013). It reached nearly 24 billion by the end of 2013. When it started 10 years ago, it was 4.2 billion reais, and 3.6 million families were beneficiaries of the BFP in 2003. In 2013, the number increased to 13.8 million, which represents nearly 50 million people. Through 2014, the government wants to include another 600,000 families that live in extreme poverty and are not yet included in the BFP, 14.8 million children within the program go to school and fulfil the conditions. According to the statistics presented by the MDS, these children are doing better in primary and secondary school than the national average. Another positive result is that 70 percent of those receiving the BFP have a job, again above the national average (MDS, 2013).

Meanwhile, arrangement, over 1.69 million families left the program of their own accord over the ten years that BFP has existed, as they are now earning more than the maximum allowance for participation in this program. Therefore, the BFP has helped people go beyond the program. Eventually, this seems to be the way to go, maybe only for part of this generation, but certainly for their children. In addition to the benefits of the BFP, this generation gets extra schooling, financial help such as microcredit, and the necessary documentation to be able to enter the formal work place. Their children have their health monitored, go to school on a regular basis, get more possibilities to enter a university, or get more professional schooling, which should all lead to a more promising future in which the BFP is no longer needed.

Conclusion

The Constitution of 1988 must be considered extremely important in that, for the first time in Brazil, it was stated clearly that the federal government had to protect those who cannot protect themselves. Therefore, the government must provide an income for those who cannot earn one themselves, because they are old or otherwise incapacitated. It must provide free education of quality, a good health system and social protection for those in need. This new constitution led to a proliferation of CCT programs in the 1990s at three levels, mostly at municipal level, but also at the state and national level. There existed a multitude of programs, which had their own criteria and transfers and worked alongside each other, without knowing what the others were doing. The creation of the BFP meant a huge step forward, as the programs became centralized at the MDS, payments were done by the CEF and the municipalities had their role to play, as municipal civil servants got in touch with the beneficiaries and had to monitor whether or not the conditions were met. The program became much more efficient, coherent, cost-effective and transparent.

The BFP started in October 2003 and has completed its 10th anniversary, with a budget that expands yearly and the number of families covered by the BFP increases continuously (Figure 6.1). In all the studies of the BFP, it is stated clearly that poverty in Brazil has decreased tremendously, that the lower middle class is growing and consumption in

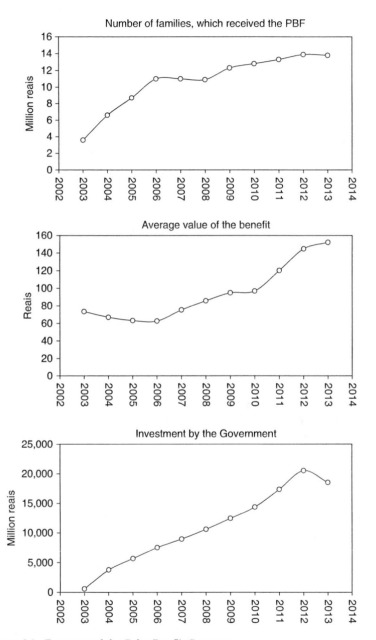

Figure 6.1 Ten years of the *Bolsa Família* Program

the country is increasing (a good indication). The BFP is also helping to improve indicators in the areas of education and health. The program is certainly helping to empower women. This has also been confirmed by an evaluation of the BFP by the United Nations Development Program in 2012. During the evaluation, interviewers were especially surprised by one particular response from existing beneficiaries. Given a scenario in which the budget was to be increased and could be used either to provide higher benefits for existing beneficiaries or to include more families in the program, 80 percent of beneficiaries interviewed answered that they would prefer to have more families participating (UNDP/PNUD, 2012). This report also confirmed the empowerment of women, that they make more decisions about different topics, including reproductive rights. But more could be done for women, especially in view of the specific problems of many female-headed households. Thanks to the CadÚnico, it is clear that women might want to work and cannot do so because they have no place to leave their children, as there is no day care center in their neighborhood.

The BFP is a crucial program within the context of social policies in Brazil and it has certainly been fundamental in reducing poverty in the country. With a relatively small investment of the federal budget, it goes a long way in improving the living conditions of millions of families. It has become the largest CCT program in the world. It could be even more focalized if it used the incredible amount of information accumulated in the CadÚnico. At the same time, it is continuously being adapted and improved. It is possible that too much focalization would make the biggest CCT program of the world unworkable or extremely expensive. Finally, there is certainly continuity between the social programs under Lula and Dilma. Dilma is expanding the budget, reaching more families and incorporating some new and even more focalized programs. She is paying even more attention to improving the situation of women and, already in 2013 (earlier than planned), no beneficiary of the BFP lives in extreme poverty, according to the minister of Social Development, Tereza Campello (Gombata, 2013). The *Bolsa Família* Program is here to stay, no matter who wins the next elections. Eventually, in the long run, the program should no longer be necessary.

Notes

1. The military regime lasted from 1964 until 1985; in 1985 Brazil got a civilian president again. However, he had been elected indirectly by Congress, despite a huge campaign for direct elections. Those were held in 1989, after

a new constitution had been voted in. Known as the 'Citizens' Constitution' because of the protection of civil liberties and the inclusion of social rights in a very large and unprecedented way (Companhole and Companhole, 1992).

2. Lula got nearly two-thirds of the votes, not only from Brazilians interested in his social programs but also from citizens who wanted a president who promised more national policies than those of his predecessor Cardoso, who was responsible for a large privatization program.

3. 'É ter a certeza de que os seus filhos vão estudar numa escola de qualidade e que os filhos das pessoas mais pobres deste País têm que sonhar em ter acesso à mesma universidade do filho do mais rico deste País, porque é assim que a gente vai construir uma democracia forte, uma democracia sólida' (translation by the author).

4. The quota system for higher education was started in 1998 under the Cardoso Government, along color lines. The Brazilian Institute of Geography and Statistics (Instituto Brasileiro de Geografia e Estatística, IBGE) uses five colours in its census: white, yellow, brown, black and indigenous. The latest census was in 2010. The new program will be implemented in stages and has to reach the stated 50 percent in four years' time (Law n. 12.711, 2012).

5. For Lula, this topic is so fundamental that he did not limit his fight against hunger to Brazil. He launched a program against hunger and poverty on an international scale, which he started simultaneously with his Brazilian campaign. Lula presented his vision in different forums and international meetings, such as the Economic World Forum in Davos, the G8 Summit – in which Brazil participates as a member of the group of five, or outreach-group (Brazil, China, India, Mexico and South Africa) – and then in September 2004, at a specific meeting during the annual meeting of the General Assembly of the United Nations. The objective is to decrease the problem of hunger and poverty in the world. Lula presented this plan, together with two other presidents and one head of government – the former from Chile, Ricardo Lagos, the former from France, Jacques Chirac, and the Prime Minister of Spain, José Luis Zapatero – with the support of the former secretary-general of the UN, Kofi Annan. The first four were known as the four musketeers. With Kofi Annan they set up the New York Declaration on action against hunger and poverty, which has been signed by over 110 governments. These five leaders, who form the World Alliance Against Hunger in the eyes of some media, have participated in a summit on the topic, 'A Fair Globalization: Implementing the Millennium Declaration', to transform the fight against hunger into a political and ethical world priority, according to Lula. The big problem is how to finance this project. Until now, no agreement has been reached among the many different suggestions about where to find the necessary funds.

6. The amounts change in accordance with the minimum salary. When it increases, the amounts are also adapted.

7. In addition to the Brazil Literacy Program, there was another program established under the Cardoso administration, *Programa Alfabetização Solidária*, which was done outside the formal structure of education and was conducted by lay teachers and with state and private funds (Barreyro, 2010).

8. The Gas Subsidy was terminated on 31 December 2008 (Decree n. 6392, 2008). For this subsidy there was no conditions attached.

9. In Brazil, the Minimum Wage is the parameter for all kinds of social programs. It is the basis for setting pensions as well as for determining the amount of fines in the case of traffic offenses. When the minimum wage increases, it has an enormous impact on all incomes, pensions, etc. (See Neri, Chapter 5).

10. These programs are: BFP, Eradication of Child Labor (PETI), National Access to Technical Education and Employment (Pronatec), Street Resident, National Urban Housing (PNHU) and Rural Housing (PNHR), Social Rate for Energy, Social Rate for Water, Popular Telephony, Continuous Cash Benefit (BPC), Waste Recyclers and Cards for the Elderly.

11. In Brazil CCT programs started in 1995 and the first national program dates from 1996, PETI. In 1997 the Federal Government funded some municipal CCT programs.

12. The Individual Taxpayer Registry, known as *Cadastro de Pessoas Físicas* (CPF), which might translate as Social Security Number, is an absolutely essential document in Brazil. To give just one example, it is needed for any receipt asked in a shop, restaurant, etc. The Employment Record Card (*Carteira de Trabalho*) is required for any formal job.

13. *Quilombolas* are found mostly in the Northeast and northern regions, where runaway slaves escaped and their descendants now live (see Castro, Chapter 10).

References

Barretto, S.A.J. Cyrillo e, D.C. and Cozzolino, S.M.F. (1998) 'Análise Nutricional e Complementação Alimentar de Cesta Básica Derivada do Consumo', *Revista de Saúde Pública* 32(1): 29–35.

Barreyro, G.B. (2010), 'O "Programa Alfabetização Solidária": Terceirização no Contexto da Reforma do Estado', *Educar em Revista* 38: 175–191.

Barros, R.P. Carvalho, M. and Mendonça, R. (2009) 'As Utilidades do Cadastro Único', *Textos para Discussão* 1414, IPEA.

Bichir, R.M. (2010) 'O Bolsa Família na Berlinda? Os Desafios Atuais dos Programas de Transferência de Renda', *Novos estudos CEBRAP* 87: 115–129.

Braido, L.H.B. Olinto, P. and Perrone, H. (2012) 'Gender Bias in Intrahousehold Allocation: Evidence from an Unintentional Experiment', *Review of Economics and Statistics* 94(2): 552–565.

Brière, B. and Lindert K. (2005) 'Reforming Brazil's Cadastro Único to Improve the Targeting of the Bolsa Família Program, *Social Protection Discussion Paper Series* 0527, Social Safety Net Primer Series, Social Protection Unit, Human Development Network, The World Bank.

Cacciamali, M.C. Tatei, F. and Batista, N.F. (2010) 'Impactos do Programa Bolsa Familia Federal sobre o Trabalho Infantil e a Frequencia Escolar', *Revista de Economia Contemporanea* 14(2): 269–301.

Camargo, E. Ribeiro, F.S. Guerra, S.M.G. (2008) 'O Programa Luz para Todos: Metas e Resultados', *Espaço Energia* 9: 21–24.

Castioni, R. (2013) 'Planos, Projetos e Programas de Educação Professional: Agora é a Vez do PRONATEC', *Revista Sociais e Humanas* 26(1): 25–42.

Castro, H.C.O. Walter, M.I.M.T. de Santana, C.M.B. and Stephanou, M.C. (2009) 'Percepções sobre o Programa Bolsa Família na Sociedade Brasileira', *Opinião Publica* 15(2): 333–355.

Companhole, A. and Companhole, H.L. (1992) *Constituições do Brasil* (São Paulo: Atlas).

Dihl, K. (2012) 'A Política de Ccombate à Pobreza do Plano Brasil sem Miséria (Governo Dilma Rousseff): Erradicação da Pobreza ou Controle sobre os Pobres?' *XX Seminario Latinoamericano de Escuela de Trabajo Social.* http://www.ets.unc.edu.ar/xxseminario/datos/1/1br_Kelly_dihl_stamp.pdf

Heredia, B.M.A. and Cintrão, R.P. (2006) 'Gênero e Acesso a Políticas Públicas no Meio Rural Brasileiro, *Revista Nera* 9(8): 1–28.

Morais, E.V. Morais, A.V. Brandini, A.C. and Paula, E.M. (2007) 'Democratização Digital, Uso do Computador às Crianças do Projeto PETI de Cassilândia – MS', *Anais do XXVII Congresso da SBC.* http://www.br-ie.org/pub/index.php/wie/article/viewFile/957/943.

Gombata, M. (2013) 'Não se Discute mais Quem é Contra ou a Favor do Bolsa Família, Diz Ministra', *Carta Capital* published on 24 August 2013. http://www.cartacapital.com.br/sociedade/nao-se-discute-mais-quem-e-contra-ou-a-favor-do-bolsa-familia-diz-ministra-946.html

Hall, A. (2008) 'Brazil's Bolsa Familia: A Double-Edged Sword?', *Development and Change* 39(5): 799–822.

Holmes, R. Jones, N. Vargas, R. and Veras, F. (2010) 'Cash Transfers and Gendered Risks and Vulnerabilities: Lessons from Latin America' *ODI Background Note* 1–6.

Informativo Luz para Todos. (2012) *Luz para Todos é Elogiado no Rio+20* n. 39 (Brasilia: Ministerio de Minas e Energia – MME). http://luzparatodos.mme.gov.br/luzparatodos/downloads/Informativo%20nr.39.pdf

Keck, M. (1992) *The Workers' Party and Democratization in Brazil* (New Haven: Yale University Press).

Ministério do Desenvolvimento Social e Combate à Fome. (MDS) (2007) 'Avaliação de Impacto do Programa Bolsa Família'. http://189.28.128.100/dab/docs/portaldab/documentos/avaliacao_impacto_programa_bolsa_familia.pdf.

Ministério do Desenvolvimento Social e Combate à Fome. (MDS) (2013) 'Bolsa Família 10 anos', http://bolsafamilia10anos.mds.gov.br/

Moehlecke, S. (2009) 'As Políticas de Diversidade na Educação no Governo Lula', *Cadernos de Pesquisa* 39(137): 461–487.

Molyneux, M. (2007) 'Two Cheers for CCTs', *IDS Bulletin* 38(3): 69–74.

Moreira, N.C. de Almeira, A.L.T. Ferreira, M.A.M. and de Matta, I.B. (2010) 'Programa de Transferência de Renda Mínima e Atividade Complementar de Renda: Uma Análise sobre o Empoderamento das Mulheres', *Revista de Ciências Humanas* 10(1): 198–212.

Nascimento, P.C. (2013) 'Livro Revela como o Programa Bolsa Família Transformou a Vida de Beneficiárias', *EcoDebate, Cidadania & Meio Ambiente*. http://www.ecodebate.com.br/2013/05/02/livro-revela-como-o-programa-bolsa-familia – transformou-a-vida-de-beneficiarias/ date accessed on 2 May 2013

Paiva, L.H. (2013) 'Inovações Recentes no Programa Bolsa Família e Impactos na Superação da Extrema Pobreza', *Painel Técnico Internacional sobre Programas de Transferência de Renda Condicionada na América Latina*. http://www.mds.gov.br/

148   *Marianne Wiesebron*

bolsafamilia/painel-tecnico-internacional-sobre-programas-de-transferencia-de-renda-condicionada-na-america-latina/apresentacoes date accessed on 17 June 2013.

Pires, A. (2008) 'Bolsa Família e Políticas Públicas Universalizantes: O Caso de um Município Paulista', *Cadernos de Pesquisa* 38(134): 341–366.

Portal Planalto. (2013) 'Programa de Documentação da Trabalhadora Rural Já Beneficiou um Milhão de Mulheres no País', 18 June 2013. http://www2.planalto.gov.br/imprensa/noticias-de-governo/programa-de-documentacao-da-trabalhadora-rural-ja-beneficiou-um-milhao-de-mulheres-no-pais

Projeto Fome Zero. (2001) *Uma Proposta de Política de Segurança Alimentar para o Brasil* (São Paulo Place OK : Instituto da Cidadania/Fundação Djalma Guimarães).

Rasella, D. Aquino, R. Santos, C.A.T. Paes-Sousa, R. and Barreto, M.L. (2013) 'Effects of a Conditional Cash Transfer Program on Childhood Mortality: A Nationwide Analysis of Brazilian Municipalities', *The Lancet* 382(9886): 57–64.

Rego, W.D.L. (2010) 'Política de Cidadania no Governo Lula: Ações de Transferência Estatal de Renda: O Caso do Programa Bolsa Família', *Temas y Debates* 20: 141–154.

Sicsú, J. (2013) 'O (des)emprego Dez Anos Depois' *Carta Capital*, published on 19 February 2013. http://www.cartacapital.com.br/economia/o-desemprego-dez-anos-depois.

Silva, J.G. (2003) 'Segurança Alimentar: Uma Agenda Republicana', *Estudos Avançados* 17(48): 45–51.

Silva, J.G., Belik, W. and Takagi, M. (2005) 'The Challenges of a Policy of Food Security in Brazil', in A. Cimadamore, H. Dean and J. Siqueira (eds), *The Poverty of the State: Reconsidering the Role of the State in the Struggle Against Global Poverty* (Buenos Aires: CLACSO).

Silva, L.I.L. da (2003) 'Pronunciamento do Presidente da República, Luiz Inácio Lula da Silva, na sessão solene de posse no Congresso Nacional Brasília – DF, Secretaria de Imprensa e Divulgação Discurso do Presidente da República'. http://www.biblioteca.presidencia.gov.br/ex-presidentes/luiz-inacio-lula-da-silva/discursos-de-posse/discurso-de-posse-1o-mandato/view

Silva, L.I.L. da (2007) 'Pronunciamento à nação do Presidente da República, Luiz Inácio Lula da Silva, na cerimônia de posse. Palácio do Planalto'. http://www.biblioteca.presidencia.gov.br/ex-presidentes/luiz-inacio-lula-da-silva/discursos-de-posse/discurso-de-posse-2o-mandato.

Singer, P. (2009) 'Políticas Públicas da Secretaria Nacional de Economia Solidária do Ministério do Trabalho e Emprego', *Mercado de Trabalho* 39: 43–48.

Siqueira, A.C. de (2006) 'O Plano Nacional de Pós-Graduação 2005–2010 e a reforma da Educação Superior do Governo Lula', *Educação Superior: Uma Reforma em Processo* (São Paulo: Xamã).

Soares, S. and Sátyro, N. (2009) 'O Programa Bolsa Família: Desenho Institucional, Impactos e Possibilidades Futuras', *IPEA Texto para Discussão* 1424 https://www.ipea.gov.br/agencia/images/stories/PDFs/TDs/td_1424.pdf

UNDP/PNUD. (2012) 'Pesquisa Avalia Impactos do Programa Bolsa Familia', 20 July 2012. http://www.pnud.org.br/Noticia.aspx?id=3632

Vaitsman, J. Rodrigues, R.W.S. and Paes-Sousa, R. (2006) 'O Sistema de Avaliação e Monitoramento das Políticas e Programas Sociais: A Experiência do Ministério do Desenvolvimento Social e Combate à Fome do Brasil, *Management of Social Transformations*, UNESCO Policy Papers 17.

Yasbek, M.C. (2004) 'Programa Fome Zero no Contexto das Políticas Sociais Brasileiras', *São Paulo em Perspectiva* 18(2): 104–112.

7
Violence, Crime, and Insecurity since 2000: Local Dynamics and the Limitations of Federal Response

Kees Koonings

Violence, crime, and insecurity cast a shadow over the acclaimed success of Brazil as a consolidated democracy that champions human rights, promotes social reform, and claims greater international prominence as an emerging power. Violence and crime, especially in cities, reflect the deep rooted structures of inequality and exclusion. Public security policies, especially law enforcement, are often ineffective, repressive and harmful to human and citizenship rights. Violence and insecurity in Brazil are embedded in a perverse dynamic of legal and extralegal networks and interactions that undermine the quality of democracy and reproduce social, spatial and cultural segregation in its cities.

This chapter explores these complex issues by, first, examining recent trends in violence and insecurity, initially offering a national-level perspective but then focusing on the urban context. Secondly, the emblematic case of Rio de Janeiro is used to arrive at a more thorough understanding of these local and state-level dilemmas. In particular the prospects and impact of the recent public security strategy of 'favela pacification' will be assessed. During the 2010 electoral campaign, the then Workers' Party candidate for the presidency, Dilma Rousseff, presented the national implementation of the UPP[1] (Unidade de Polícia Pacificadora) model as the cornerstone of her public security strategy. In the final section, I review recent federal-level policy efforts aimed at public security and law enforcement – in particular the PRONASCI (Programa Nacional de Segurança Pública com Cidadania (National Programme for Public Security with Citizenship)) launched in Lula's second term and inherited by Dilma's government – to show the limits faced by such policies.

Trends and patterns of Brazil's 'new' violence

In this section I will examine the basic trends of violence and insecurity in the country as a whole during the past two decades. I will argue that trends in lethal violence show variation in time and place, despite the overall pattern of high violence levels since 1990. Then I will discuss the social and political implications of sustained levels of violence in a country that is not at war and is considered to be a consolidated democracy.

If we look at the levels of lethal violence expressed by its most conventional indicator (the homicide rate, i.e. death by acts of violence per 100,000 inhabitants per year) it is immediately clear that this level has been steadily on the rise between 1980 and 2002, after which the indicator showed annual variation without any visible downward trend (Figure 7.1).

The initial rise in homicide rates during the 1980s is often associated with rising poverty and inequality during the 'lost decade', the transition to democracy and concomitant 'loosening' of policing, and, above all, the rise of cocaine trafficking, especially in the peripheral zones of the major cities (Leeds, 1996; Peralva, 2000). This developed into a self-sustained cycle during the 1990s as homicide rates grew by more than

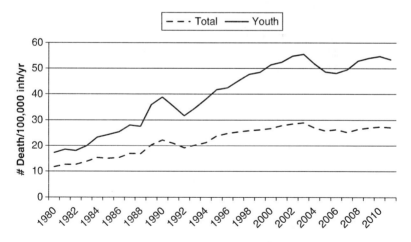

Figure 7.1 Homicide rates in Brazil (total population and youths aged 15–24), 1980–2011
Source: Waiselfisz (various years; compiled by the author).

50 percent. After the turn of the millennium, the rate has been hovering somewhat below 30 per 100,000 with no visible downward trend. This is a clear indication of the overall tenacity of the phenomenon. What can be said about the phenomenology of contemporary violence and insecurity in Brazil reflected in these statistics? A first characteristic is the steady rise of lethal violence from the mid-1980s until the early 2000s in the country as a whole. This reflects the rise of so-called 'new violence' and the debates concerning this phenomenon. New violence is defined as having primarily social and (criminal) economic motives, while not directed at state power per se (Koonings and Kruijt, 2004; 2007). It involves the proliferation of armed actors that perpetrate citizen-on-citizen violence (Pereira and Davis, 2000; Rotker, 2002), having multiplier effect of insecurity, fear, and distrust through what Caldeira (2000) calls 'talk of crime'. Although not directly motivated politically (in the sense of securing state power), new violence in Brazil (and other Latin American countries, notably Mexico, the countries of Central-America, Colombia, and Venezuela) has a clear political impact (Koonings, 2012). This includes persistent popular demand for repressive security policies, that, in turn, not only have a negative impact on human rights standards in general but also are largely ineffective, contributing to the further spread of insecurity (Caldeira and Holston, 1999; Caldeira, 2000). Often, violent actors seek to coerce the citizenry and the state in direct ways to achieve specific objectives, as in the case of the uprising in São Paulo in May 2006, orchestrated from prison by the *Primeiro Comando da Capital* (PCC) faction (Carosamigos, 2006; Pereira, 2008).

A second notable feature is that Brazil has been consistently classified among the (moderately) high homicide rate countries of Latin America (see for instance PNUD 2013, pp. 46–47). While, between 1995 and 2010, (see Figure 7.2), levels and hence country rankings on the homicide rate list of the region varied considerably, by 2010 Brazil's rates were close to Colombia's and higher than Mexico's, two countries suffering, respectively, from a protracted (drug-fueled) armed conflict and warfare among powerful drug trafficking organizations and the state. As we will see in the next section, this raises particular questions, in the case of Brazil, regarding the apparent compatibility of high levels of violence and public insecurity and democratic consolidation.

Third, specific categories within Brazil's population are particularly vulnerable. The homicide rate for youths (age 15–24) has been growing much faster than the average rate, as can be observed in Figure 7.1 above. Since 1980 homicide rates for youths have grown by more

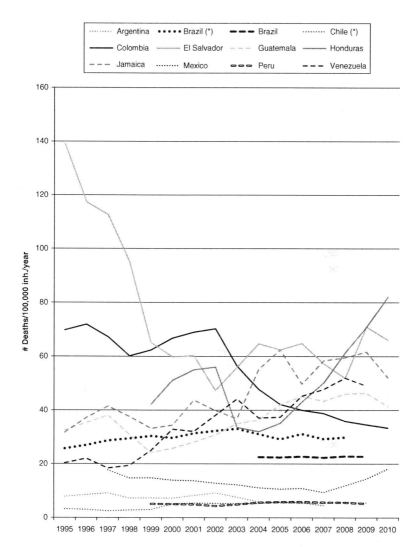

Figure 7.2 Evolution of homicide rates of selected Latin American and Caribbean countries, 1995–2010

All data are official national police data, except for (*) which are PAHO (Pan American Health Organization) data.

Source: UNODC, 2011 (Table 9.1; elaboration by the author).

than 200 percent, against 100 percent for the non-youth population (Waiselfisz, 2011, p. 77). We see at least three spikes of lethal violence against youths: in the late 1980s, the mid-1990s, and again the mid-2000s. Youth homicide rates are consistently close to twice the homicide rate for the entire population since the late 1990s. This reflects a particular characteristic of lethal violence: the proliferation of drug trafficking, the rise of gangs, and the concomitant involvement of male youths in the violence of the urban peripheries. This pattern also explains other characteristics of violence in Brazil apart from the high vulnerability of youths: the disproportionally higher victimization rates of non-whites and the high proportion of homicides caused by small firearms (Fernandes, 2005; Waiselfisz, 2013).

A final feature is the substantial subnational variation of homicide rates underneath the relatively constant national average over the past decade. This is illustrated here by homicide patterns in selected major cities but is a general feature that also reflects variation within states, smaller towns, and across rural areas (Waiselfisz, 2007; 2011). Especially after 2000 we observe a marked decline of homicide rates in São Paulo and, to a lesser extent, Rio de Janeiro, but a simultaneous increase in other cities, especially Salvador, the third largest metropolitan area in the country (see Figure 7.3). According to Waiselfisz (2011, pp. 41ff.) violence has been spreading from the large urban agglomerations to many other parts of the country, a trend he calls 'interiorization'. In addition, some areas (cities and federal states) that had high and

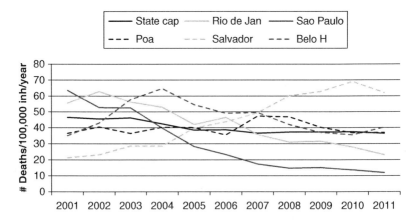

Figure 7.3 Homicide rates in Brazil (state capitals and selected cities), 2001–11
Source: Waiselfisz (2011, p. 29; graph compiled by the author).

rising rates during the 1990s saw this trend reversed, while areas with relatively low levels in 2000 experienced rapid increase. This can be explained, according to Waiselfisz (2011, pp. 57–58) by three factors: the economic and demographic expansion of so-called non-central regions, the increased effectiveness of security policies in São Paulo and Rio de Janeiro, and the improvement of homicide data gathering in smaller towns and rural areas. The second factor is in part debatable; I return to that later. In any case, it is clear that there is a concentration of lethal violence in specific urban areas of high insecurity (more or less independent from the average homicide rates of cities as a whole).

In sum, the ensuing profile of violence and insecurity in Brazil is suggestive: lethal violence is to a significant degree urban; it affects young men, more often colored and black men than not; most victims die through the use of firearms. This dominant pattern is, of course, related to other dimensions of the problem. Other forms of victimization, such as non-lethal violence against persons (assaults, kidnapping, domestic violence), and crimes against property have also become a permanent concern (Caldeira, 2000), not to mention the psycho-cultural and structural aspects of violence in everyday life (Linger, 1992; Scheper-Hughes, 1992; Lowell Lewis, 2000). This has led to the erosion of the sense of security and to the spread of fear, particularly visible in cities and urban life where the most prominent forms of violence can be found and its social, political, and cultural consequences are most clearly felt.

Explaining Brazil's shadows of violence

The rise of violence and insecurity over the past two decades can be related to a number of causal and background factors. Many authors point at globalization, in particular the convergence of growing inequality and informalization in the urban peripheries with the inclusion of Brazil in the global and local commodity chains of the drugs and small arms economies. This has contributed to the consolidation of small-scale local gangs as well as broader networks of drug trafficking (called *comandos*) that, in the case of Brazil, mainly operate at the city level (Leeds, 1996; Peralva, 2000; Amorim, 2007). As we will see later, this has had a profound impact on the social construction of insecurity in urban areas. A second factor is the failure, by and large, of public security and law enforcement, especially in the field of policing, criminal justice, and the prison system (Nunes, 2005; Sapori, 2007). Finally, a generalized sense of insecurity among the citizenry merges with fear of victimization and with distrust in the capacity and willingness of public authorities to deal with crime and violence (Caldeira, 2000). This, in turn, spawns the peculiar combination of popular clamor for repressive law enforcement and the systematic use of private security and extralegal measures of 'popular injustice' (Huggins, 2000).

This complex of features has been casting a permanent shadow over Brazil as a consolidated democracy (Koonings, 1999), inspiring the application of a series of adjectives: ugly, illiberal, disjunctive, uncivil, violent (Caldeira and Holston, 1999; Diamond, 1999; Pereira, 2000; Arias and Goldstein, 2010). From this perspective, it is possible to review the way violence in Brazil has been approached: between, on the one hand, governance failure, through 'unrule' of law, to urban warfare and 'violent democracies'. These perspectives are not necessarily contradictory or mutually exclusive; rather they reflect different frames and point at the complementarity of the different dimensions of the problem.

The governance failure approach sees the problem of violence and insecurity as a lack of resources, institutional aptitude, administrative focus or political will. In particular, this entails in the first place a lack of political synergy: the dispersion of authority and jurisdiction over public security matters among the federal, state and municipal levels of governance; second, institutional fragmentation, not only in policing where, at the frontline of public law enforcement, tasks are divided between the two police forces of each of the 26 federal states (*Polícia Militar* and *Polícia Civil*); third, cultural-organizational deficiencies of police and policing in the sense that these forces are either militarized of unruly, ineffective, and violent, lacking resources, skills and public ethos (Pereira, 2000; Kahn, 2002; Zaverucha, 2005). Often, this interpretation sees such governance failure as a handover from the period of military authoritarianism; consequently, the solution is sought in the domain of 'security sector reform' (especially the police and the judiciary). However, Pereira (2008) has convincingly argued that security sector reform in Brazil is hampered by what he calls fragmentation, politicization, and privatization (see also Soares, 2000 and Husain, 2007 for the limitations of police reform in Rio de Janeiro). The problem of privatization refers to the proliferation of private security arrangements, ranging from private security companies and the 'organic security' of gated communities, shopping malls, and businesses to more or less legal neighborhood watches and often quite illegal informal vigilantes (*justiceiros*) operating in popular neighborhoods. Off – (or on-) duty police officers are regularly involved in these activities, blurring the divide between public policing and private disciplining (Huggins, 2000).

As we will see later, the governance failure approach lies behind grand strategies to improve public security policy since the 1990s (during the Cardoso and Lula administrations). More sophisticated strategies were designed to take into account the context and complexity of violence and insecurity in alignment with citizenship rights and social justice, in other words, 'citizen security'. Such an approach has inspired the workings of the *Secretaria Nacional de Segurança Pública* (SENASP) and, especially, the ambitious PRONASCI program put in place in 2007 at the beginning of Lula's second term. As we will see, PRONASCI has not been successful despite high expectations (see Pereira, 2008, p. 205) and the relatively large budget available. The concept of citizen security as the foundation for 'correcting' previous misdirection in public security governance also underlies local strategies for public security such as the pacification strategy in Rio de Janeiro. As we will see later, this approach also reflects some of the other frames to be discussed in this section, especially the view that (gang) violence in peripheral urban areas has warlike characteristics.

The unrule of law approach also takes the dysfunctions of law enforcement as its starting point but moves beyond the idea of institutional and policy failure in search of more deeply engrained fault lines that run through democracy and citizenship in Brazil. The key notion in this approach is that of 'disjunction', developed by Caldeira and Holston (Caldeira and Holston, 1999; Caldeira, 2000; Holston, 2008). They speak of disjunctive democracy and disjunctive citizenship to explain the discrepancy between, on the one hand, the consolidation of political rights and the stability of electoral democracy, and, on the other hand, the systematic disrespect for civil rights and protective responsibilities of the Brazilian state vis-à-vis specific populations that are seen as incomplete or second-class citizens. Echoing O'Donnell's (1993) seminal distinction between 'blue' (full rule of law) and 'brown' (unrule of law) social domains in Latin America's transitional democracies, this view no longer sees the failure of public security as a governance problem or as a leftover from military authoritarianism. Rather, it is seen as a systemic aspect of a formally democratic system that generates dualities in terms of citizenship rights, differentiating between deserving and undeserving subjects (Murilo de Carvalho, 2002). Waqcuant (2003) connects this idea to his notion of 'penalization' of poverty, and to the collapse of the classical welfare functions of postwar developed capitalism and to the rise of advanced marginality under neoliberalism in the Global North (Waqcuant, 2008), but he sees Brazil as a particularly straightforward example of the penalization of poverty by the state and by public opinion. This involves not only repressive law enforcement against the urban underclass and the overcrowding of prisons by predominantly young, poor and colored males, but also by framing *favelas* as spaces of urban exclusion, contained, under a regime of marginal surveillance, in which there is no room nor need for citizen security. In fact, it is commonplace among Brazilian elites and middle classes to reject the notion of human rights and citizenship for the poor in general and alleged criminals (*marginais, elementos, bandidos*) in particular (Caldeira, 2000).

The widely discussed issue of lethal police violence (Caldeira, 2000; 2002; Ahnen, 2007) is a central aspect of the 'unrule of law' frame. It is often stated that, in democratic Brazil, the police killed far more civilians than the number of lethal victims (killed and disappeared) of the 1964–85 military dictatorship. Police in 19 of the 26 Brazilian federal states killed a total of over 7,800 persons between 1994 and 2001 (Ahnen, 2007, p. 153). Police killings in Brazil are, generally, not registered as homicides, but as casualties of armed confrontations or resistance against arrest (regardless of the autopsy evidence that usually contradicts such claims). Recent statistical evidence is not easily available but there is no reason at all to assume that police killings have been dropping after 2000. In 2009 alone, for instance, police in 14 states killed a total of 2,227 persons (according to official SENASP data – see Figures 7.4 and 7.5 for breakdown and source citation). In line with this appalling absolute magnitude, their rates (annual deaths caused by police per 100,000) in 2009 were disturbing (equaling total homicide rates in average Western European or East Asian countries), and alarmingly in the state of Rio de Janeiro the rate of police killings in 2009 (6.5) accounted for more than 20 percent of the total homicide rate (31.6) in Rio the Janeiro city (see Figure 7.4). Furthermore, it has been well established that the number of people killed by police far exceeds the number of wounded, as well as exceeding the number of police killed in action. This runs counter to claims that police kill out of necessity in the line of duty; rather, police kill because they apply a de facto death penalty on the streets (Caldeira and Holston, 1999, pp. 703–704).

It is a small step from the notion of unrule of law for non-citizens framed as 'undesirable others' to applying repressive, even unbounded violence to what are considered to be social enemies. In this view, especially in the urban peripheries, violence and insecurity appears as an endemic condition that can best be regarded as warfare. Violence and insecurity are the permanent features of warlike confrontations between and among public security forces, mandated to apply counterinsurgency

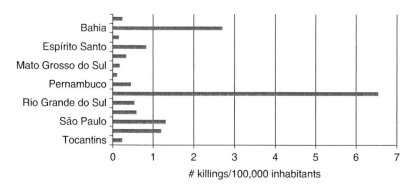

Figure 7.4 Rates of police killings in selected states, 2009 (per 100,000 inhabitants)

Source: Ministério da Justiça/Secretaria Nacional de Segurança Pública – SENASP; Secretarias Estaduais de Segurança Pública. Compiled by Forum Brasileira de Segurança Pública (http://www2.forumseguranca.org.br/lista/estatisticas/2898).

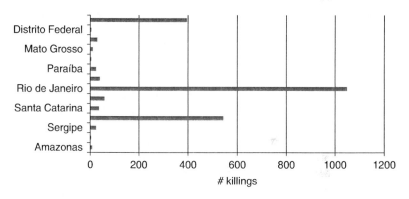

Figure 7.5 Numbers of police killings in selected states, 2009

Source: Ministério da Justiça/Secretaria Nacional de Segurança Pública – SENASP; Secretarias Estaduais de Segurança Pública. Compiled by Forum Brasileira de Segurança Pública (http://www2.forumseguranca.org.br/lista/estatisticas/2898).

style violence, and heavily and ostentatiously armed criminal gangs that seek to control urban spaces for the pursuit of illicit business. This view has been popularized by journalistic and testimonial work (such as Barcellos, 2003; Soares, Batista and Pimentel, 2006; Soares *et al.*, 2010), literary fiction (Lins, 1997) and motion pictures such as *Cidade de Deus* and *Tropa de Elite*. This urban warfare is depicted as dirty but maybe also as unavoidable. Warfare, in turn, corrupts and, in combination with systematic impunity, creates the conditions for police immersion in criminal activities beyond brutality: extortion, extrajudicial executions, drug trafficking and small-arms trade.

The urban warfare paradigm brings in another type of social agent, namely organized crime, especially neighborhood gangs and cartel-type factions known in Rio de Janeiro and São Paulo as *comandos*. During the 1990s, these criminal armed actors appeared not only as visible agents of illicit economic activities but also as more or less organized forces of domination and order in the urban peripheries 'abandoned' by the state. Leeds' (1996) seminal piece ignited the debate on this issue by framing it as the rise of a 'parallel power' in which the drug gangs (of Rio de Janeiro) not only carved out separate spaces of control in the city but also sought to dominate the existing structures of grassroots democracy and community governance, such as the neighborhood associations (*Associações de Moradores*, AM).

Subsequent and equally pioneering work by Arias (2006) dismissed the notion of parallel (in the sense of separate, mutually exclusive) powers and revealed the (clandestine) connections between politicians, police, drug traffickers and slum residents in Rio de Janeiro. In general terms, this means, according to Arias and Goldstein (2010; for the case of Rio see also Gay, 2009; 2010) that the coercive operations of criminal and other extralegal armed actors are integral to what they have been dubbed 'violent democracies'. This notion refers to the use of violence by a variety of social and political agents as an established option within the broader reach of electoral politics and democratic governance. This includes the use of violence and coercion by legitimate politicians and public agencies (such as the police) but also the targeting of the state and public resources by extralegal violent actors, to the extent that the distinction between legal politics and extralegal violence is blurred. From this perspective, Brazil, given its positive track record in terms of transformative democratic consolidation (especially under the rule of the Workers' Party; see Power in this volume), appears as a particularly emblematic and problematic case of 'violent democracy'.

The urban pattern of violence and insecurity: The case of Rio de Janeiro

Briceño-León and Zubillaga (2002) argue that one of the defining elements of new violence in Latin America is its urban setting. Hence, it is relevant to focus on the urban dimension of violence and insecurity in Brazil because it frames much of the country's experiences and discourses. This is not meant to disregard the relevance of violence in other social domains, that often have acquired high profile and visibility, such as violent conflicts over land and social rights in the countryside (Hammond, 1999; Branford and Rocha, 2002) or in the notoriously lethal prison system (Nunes, 2005). Still, as I have already suggested above, Brazilian cities have turned into prime sites of violence, insecurity, and fear. As a first example we can consider the notorious wave of violence that paralyzed the São Paulo conurbation in May 2006. A wave of attacks by criminal gangs on police posts, buses, shops and restaurants was orchestrated from prisons by the leadership of the PCC as a strategy to avoid the announced transfer of PCC kingpins to maximum security facilities in the interior of São Paulo state. In retaliatory response, the São Paulo police set out on a killing spree, victimizing almost 500 people (Feltran, 2011, p. 181), alleged gangsters according to the authorities. In practice, most victims turned out to be innocent young men who happened to fit the profile of the 'undesirable other' or simply were in the wrong place at the wrong time. The event shook São Paulo and the country, also because violence rates in the city had been dropping significantly during the preceding couple of years. This drop, although in part attributable to more effective policing, has also been related to the consolidation of law and order under the quasi-sovereign reign of the PCC in the urban periphery of greater São Paulo, operative in allegedly tacit understanding with state authorities (Willis, 2009; Feltran, 2010; Feltran, 2011, pp. 185–188).

Rio de Janeiro is very different. None of the drug factions (among which the three most prominent are the *Comando Vermelho* [Grassroots Democracy, CV], the *Terceiro Comando* [Third Command, TC] and the *Amigos dos Amigos* [Friends of Friends, AdA] ever established firm and durable control over the city's thousand-plus *favelas*. Gangs related to these factions regularly engaged in violent disputes among themselves or with the Rio military police. In addition, after the year 2000 the spectrum of violent actors was broadened by the rise of so-called *milícias* that came to dominate a growing number of *favela* communities. Looking at the case of Rio de Janeiro is therefore instructive not only because since the 1980s the city has been regarded as the textbook example of warlike urban violence in Brazil, but also because in recent years the city has been applauded as a success story in reversing the trend of violence through the so-called strategy of 'pacification', applied since late 2008.

Gay (1994) observed the arrival of drugs and gang violence in Rio de Janeiro in his research on the workings of Grassroots Democracy during the democratic transition of the 1980s. It is interesting to quote his early observations of this, then, new, and increasingly disturbing phenomenon:

> The majority of favelas are also unpoliced, and it is largely because they have been abandoned by the state that they have increasingly fallen prey to elements involved in the drug trade. All but a few favelas in the city of Rio provide cover for armed gangs that peddle cocaine and marijuana to local elites, to tourists, and, increasingly, to the inhabitants of the favelas themselves. These gangs are often the perpetrators of extreme violence in their dealings with local police, who are themselves often involved in the buying and selling of drugs, and in their dealings with rival gangs. They are also, however, a source of welfare in their own favelas, playing the occasional role of Robin Hood in return for public support and the protection of anonymity.
>
> (Gay, 1994, p. 12)

Gay's pioneering research focused on the dynamics of *favela* politics, traditionally dominated by clientelism and brokerage. Especially in the case of the *favela* known as Vidigal, he observed the growing role of *traficantes* that up till the late 1980s used to maintain a low profile by not interfering in community politics. He states:

> During the past four or five years, however, the drug gang has become increasingly violent in its dealings with other traficantes, with the local police, and with residents of the favela itself. A the same time, however, the drug gang has been cultivating its own basis of support in the favela by financing small public works projects at the top of the slum and by making the occasional donation of a truckload of food and provisions to the more needy families of the community.
>
> (Gay, 1994, p. 97).

He goes on to describe the operation of the *bocas de fumo* (local sale outlets for marihuana and cocaine) and the gang's physical surveillance of the neighborhood, the corruptive interaction with the police, the precariousness of gang life coupled to the attractiveness of gang membership for the *favela* youngsters (Gay, 1994, pp. 97–98). From the perspective of the community association's leadership, the gang is a competitor in efforts to muster up loyalty and support from the population but not seen as an actor that seeks active control of community affairs (Gay, 1994, p. 98).

This would soon change. Violence in Rio de Janeiro since these early years has followed a bizarre logic of territorial fragmentation, economic interests and socio-political control.[2] I already referred to Leeds' (1996) analysis of parallel power, meaning that drug gangs constituted separate micro-monopolies of violence in the communities and were seeking to control the AM's and even to impose forms of informal justice known as the *Lei da Favela* (law of the *favela*). Contrary to São Paulo during the past decade, this never evolved into a stable system of hybrid order and legitimacy (Arias and Rodrigues, 2006).

In the course of the 1990s, almost every *favela* came to be the domain of drug gangs (*quadrilhas*) led by a local *dono* (drug lord). The size and scope of these gangs varied (Leeds, 1996, p. 59) but the pattern along which they operate is fairly constant. Drug lords seek to maintain exclusive control of one or more *favelas*. The key objective is to control the local system of drug trade focusing on one or more selling points in the *favela* (Zaluar, 2000). In the course of time, these gangs consolidated at the level of the city into the three major syndicates (or factions) already mentioned: the CV, the TC, and the AdA. The largest and most powerful was the Red Command, locked in constant confrontation with the Third Command (Lima, 1991; Amorim, 1993). The Friends of Friends developed as a small split-off group of the Red Command. Not only the name of the Grassroots Democracy echoes its early inspiration from leftist revolutionaries.[3] Also the groups linked to the syndicate still refer to themselves as *o movimento* (the movement) and combine the practice of crime and violence with a discourse (and sometimes a practice as well) of taking care of the poor and fighting the injustices of Brazil's economic and political system.

The confrontations of the gangs and the criminal factions have been mainly about territorial control. This leads to violence when one gang or faction tries to invade and take over the area of another gang or faction. This violence often takes the form of street fighting in which small arms but very often also heavier weaponry such as mortars and RPG launchers are used. The enlisting of child soldiers was common practice (Dowdney, 2003). At the same time, the state military police (PM) of Rio de Janeiro acquired notoriety for its violence interference in the drug-gang controlled parts of the city (Husain, 2007; Gay, 2009). In general, the way the police dealt with the drug gangs and the violence derived from the militarized, repressive and exclusionary approach to public security and law enforcement within the 'unrule of law' frame discussed above. Second, it implied becoming stakeholders themselves in the various rackets of drug trafficking, arm sales and extortion.

The paradox implied in these two combined logics of policing in Rio de Janeiro is that they serve various objectives and this makes them in a certain sense compatible. The tough approach to crime fighting as 'undeclared warfare' responds to societal fears and appeals for 'zero tolerance' from politicians, the media and middle class constituencies; in addition, it contributes to the militaristic esprit de corps held in high esteem by the security forces, especially among the notorious *Batalhão de Operações Policiais Especiais* (Battalion for Special Police Operations, BOPE) created in the early 1990s and featured in the two *Tropa de Elite* motion pictures (see Soares, Batista and Pimentel, 2006; Soares *et al.*, 2010). At the same time, the arbitrary violence so to speak 'allows' certain elements within the police force to engage the gangs on their own terms and to become actors in criminal racketeering. The generalized and apparently disorderly violence turns into an effective smokescreen for this degradation of law enforcement. It contributes to the notion of *favela* violence being an intractable problem, best left to the experts in official violence without undue scrutiny from the public.

In addition to the violence of gangs and police, other armed actors have appeared as part of the spectrum of the privatization and informalization of security and law enforcement. Historically this appeared in the form of *justiceiros* or *polícia mineira* consisting of off-duty or retired armed police – and firemen – claiming to deal with petty crime and local gangs in 'their' communities. After 2000, in a growing number of *favelas* 'paramilitary' groups appeared as a response to the increasing power of the drug gangs. These groups, the so-called *milícias*, succeeded in taking over communities from gang control. The use of excessive force by *milícias* has been commonplace since many of them consider themselves as part of law enforcement or 'above the law'. This allowed them to set up their own range of illegal activities. These activities are typical 'rackets' of extortion or monopolized sale of goods and services. They include, besides offering protection, the sale of gas bottles, the distribution of (illegally tapped) cable television and internet connections and the control of local means of transportation such as vans and *mototaxis*. The militias profess to fight the criminal violence of the drug gangs, but they employ the same violence to force their way into communities and to keep control over their 'economic interests'. Those suspected of ties with the drug trade are dealt with in a swift and ruthless way (Cano and Iooty, 2008; Machado da Silva, 2008). Hence, *milícias* have added a new dimension, that of security provision-as-criminal racketeering, to the continuum suggested by Huggins (2000, pp. 119–120) between on the one hand legal on-duty policing, through corporate private security provision to clients, off-duty moonlighting by policemen, and organized vigilantism, to the individual *justiceiro* on the other hand. Until recently, the militias enjoyed a certain amount of institutional and political support. Police units cooperated with militias in certain areas, important local politicians praised the 'patriotic' efforts of restoring security, and a few deputies in Rio de Janeiro's state legislature had ties with militia organizations. However, after the use of violence by militia members in the Batam *favela* against undercover reporters from the local newspaper *O Dia* in May 2008, the state legislature started an official inquiry to unveil the nature and scope of the militia phenomenon. Following the publication of the final report of the Rio de Janeiro State Assembly Inquiry Commission (*Comissão Parlamentar de Inquerito*, CPI), authorities denounced the militias while public opinion started to turn against them.[4]

Pacification in the 'wonderful city': panacea or placebo?

The persistence of gang power, police violence and corruption, and the increasingly bold and politically backed operations of the *milícias* in the closing years of the 2000s finally incited new political and policy responses. The selection of Brazil as host for the 2014 FIFA World Cup (Rio being the most important 'match venue') and Rio de Janeiro as the seat of the 2016 Summer Olympics (to be held during Rio's mild winter) heightened the sense of urgency that something had to be done. This resulted in the much applauded and debated strategy of 'pacification' initiated as a pilot in the Santa Marta *favela* in late 2008.[5] This strategy entails a particular combination of initial bellicose operations and discourse (using overwhelming force by the BOPE or military units for occupying the *favelas*, ousting the drug gang or *milícia*, and establishing 'peace') and community policing (or *polícia de proximidade*, policing in close contact with the citizenry, as it is called in Rio) to be carried out by newly trained and established permanent police units in the *favelas*: the *Unidades de Polícia Pacificadora* (UPP, Pacification Police Units).

In the course of 2009 this approach was transformed into a general strategy for 'pacification' in the city and indeed in the state. The official goal, adopted by Rio de Janeiro major Sérgio Cabral and the State Secretary for Public Security Mariano Beltrane, was to make pacification and the UPP the new model for public security. The strategy was supposed to lead to the recovery by the state of permanent control of urban territories and communities dominated by the drug trade and *milícias*, to end violent confrontations between drug factions, to promote the interaction of *favela* residents and police, and to bring in social policies. In sum, pacification sought to re-instate the state in territories that had been 'occupied for decades by traffickers and, more recently, by milicianos' (Willandino *et al.*, 2011, p. 153). The State Secretariat for Public Security (SSP) saw an explicit link between social inclusion of stigmatized communities and the poorest and most vulnerable segments of the urban population. SSP conducted a feasibility study to identify priority communities for the implantation of UPPs: criminal territorial control, the 'ideological presence' of criminal factions, and the open use of heavy firearms. Forty-seven communities were identified for pacification (Willandino *et al.*, 2011, pp. 154–155).

The official strategy of pacification contains four steps. First, the recovery of urban territory, for which terms such as invasion and occupation are used, involving the, often violent, entry of the security forces into the community and the expulsion of the drug gangs. Second, stabilization of the presence of the police (or other security forces, such as the army, as has been the case in Complexo do Alemão) by setting up key facilities (such as stations). Third, the permanent occupation of the communities, by installing a high profile UPP facility and making UPP policing a part of everyday routines of the community. Finally, 'post-occupation' meaning consolidation of police presence and the entry of other social services. It is noteworthy that combatting drug trafficking per se is not the main objective. Rather, changing its modalities is sought to end the explicitly territorial operations of the criminal factions and their use of heavy arms, violent confrontations and intimidation of the local population. It was supposed to make drug trafficking a 'normal crime' rather than a dominant feature of insecurity in the city and the state (Willandino *et al.*, 2011, p. 155).

The base line to date in terms of the results of pacification and the implantation of UPP as a permanent police presence in the communities is that open violence, meaning public display of weapons by gang members, armed confrontations between gangs of different factions, and massive and arbitrary police incursions in the form of *blitz* (raids), have largely ended. The pacified communities have been opened up as urban spaces, so that people (residents and outsiders) can more easily transit to and from the communities. The direct threat to personal security seems to have diminished (Machado da Silva, 2010). Permanent police presence changed the parameters of law enforcement while residents saw the immediate impact (sharply reduced violent confrontations, improved personal physical security, increased mobility) as a step forward. But this is not the same as reorganizing policing and law enforcement along the lines of democracy, citizenship, inclusion and participation. A thorough assessment is beyond the scope of this chapter, but the key complications for this to be achieved are the following (see Koenders and Koonings, 2012; Rodrigues, Siqueira and Lissovsky, 2012 for a detailed analysis):

First, the nature of UPP presence prioritizes spatial and physical control of the communities. The UPP appears as a mini-state in its own right, behaving arbitrarily, affecting patterns of everyday life in the sense of imposing more control and restrictions, and affecting the relationships with grass root organizations such as the *associações de moradores*, bypassing them or reducing their influence. These factors contribute to continuing low levels of trust between residents and the agents of the law. Is the UPP captain the new *dono* of the hill? Will the UPP become the next *milícia*?

Second, the presence of criminal actors (especially drug traffickers) and their use of force, coercion and intimidation vis-à-vis residents, and recently also UPP units in some *favelas*, has not ended. Although criminal activities have become more low profile, drug traffickers continue to be active in the communities and deploy tactics of control. This is done through intimidation that can be backed up by real violence. If and how the UPP is able or even willing to counter this, given the continuation of the climate of distrust and fear, is unclear. A related issue that is far from resolved is whether the UPP is immune from the criminal interaction with the drug trade that was widespread under the conventional regime of policing.

Third, questions can be raised with regard to the scope and long-term effectiveness and relevance of pacification. By 2014, pacification has reached less than 30 of more than 1,000 *favelas* in Rio de Janeiro, at already considerable expense. Questions are raised as to the financial feasibility of expanding the strategy to other areas. Other obstacles include the gentrification effect of pacification (the expulsion of poorer residents due to real estate value and rent hikes, especially in the *favelas* of Rio's wealthy Zona Sul), expulsion as a result of urban improvements related to the sporting mega-events, the problems to be expected in really engaging *favelas* dominated by *milícias*, the limitations of controlling the drug factions and gangs solely on the basis of a micro-local approach, given the trans-communal networks sustained by the traffickers, and the future political sustainability of the pacification strategy, especially after the 2016 Olympic Games.

The limitations of federal response: PRONASCI

Pacification in Rio de Janeiro was engendered by local and regional governments, notably the state governor and the mayor of the city of Rio de Janeiro, who both belonged to a political party (PMDB) that had allied itself at the federal level to the ruling Workers' Party but at the local level often behaves as a rival. In fact, there are hardly any examples of direct effective Workers' Party management of public security in major states or cities, during the past two decades. Even in the often positively appraised examples of Workers' Party-led municipal participatory budgeting (Koonings, 2004; Wampler, 2007), public security did not acquire much prominence given the formal jurisdiction over policing and the judiciary being in the hands of the state governors and not the city mayors.

In fact, after initial efforts through the establishment of SENASP by the Cardoso administration in 1998, Lula's first term did not generate a specific, let alone new, approach to public security apart from creating a *Sistema Único de Segurança Pública* (SUSP, Unitary System for Public Security) as an effort to enhance institutional streamlining at the different administrative levels. The obstacles analyzed by Pereira (2008): fragmentation, politicization, and privatization, combined with the complexity of the security issue at the local level and the prime policy prerogative at the state level, seemed to deter the Workers' Party from embarking upon a transformative strategy at the federal level. Nevertheless, Lula's second term saw the advent of such an effort, based on the concepts of citizen security, social inclusion and prevention. This was the *Programa Nacional de Segurança com Cidadania* (PRONASCI, National Program for Security with Citizenship). In this final section I will briefly discuss the nature and limitations of the program (see also Koonings, 2013).

This program, that started in 2007, aimed at enhancing public security efforts at all administrative levels with a multipronged strategy, a wide variety of partnerships, and a considerable amount of funding. PRONASCI contained the following components: strengthening of policing capacity through training of personnel and coordination; covenants with decentralized authorities to strengthen public security policy-making and implementation; the introduction of the notion of 'peace territories' in which specific interventions could be financed on the basis of citizen participation; prevention programs aimed at at-risk social categories; and finally, improvement of the penitentiary system. The objective was to allocate BRL 6.7 billion to a wide variety of programs and projects during the 2007–11 period (basically coinciding with Lula's second term). This should happen through numerous agreements with state and municipal authorities. An estimated target population of 3.5 million direct beneficiaries should have been reached, including police officers, youngsters in at-risk situations (like living in shantytowns or being black), prison guards, inmates, and so on. The master aim was to lower the homicide rate by more than half from 29 per 100,000 in 2007 to 12 in 2011 (FGV, 2009).

If this had been the decisive criterion for assessing the relevance and effectiveness of PRONASCI, the program obviously failed. As Figure 7.1 shows, homicide rates in 2011 and 2012 continued more than twice the level of the PRONASCI target. Since, simultaneously, homicide rates in São Paulo and Rio de Janeiro dropped significantly (mainly as a result of specific local dynamics, as we have seen), the program must have had very little impact in the country as a whole. So what happened with PRONASCI?

The few available assessments, that by no means amount to a rigorous public policy evaluation, speak favorably about the contributions of the program in terms of its adoption of a multi-causal approach to violence, the citizenship rights priority designed into the program (including participatory interventions), capacity-building and training, and the decentralized prevention projects (Carvalho and Fatima e Silva, 2011). Mention is made of the proliferation of new policing practices, among which the UPP in Rio de Janeiro (PRONASCI was a source of institutional support and seed money funding for Rio's pacification approach). Overall, PRONASCI spent on average more than BRL 1 billion each year and a large number of covenants were signed. During its first year, 2008, the budget was mostly spent on capacitation scholarships *à distância* (meaning 'at a distance', not involving class meetings with instructors) for officers of the security forces, strengthening of police forces, including acquisition of new equipment, and preventive social programs (FGV, 2009). On the other hand, observers point at the enormous diversity of activities leading to fragmentation and thin spread of the program. In addition, PRONASCI had to face the perennial problem of bureaucratism, low implementation capacity of many municipal administrations and the long time horizon implied in many of the program's activities.

This very much reads like a recipe for ineffectiveness. A budget assessment carried out in late 2010 by INESC (Pereira *et al.*, 2010) showed that by October of that year less than half of the approved annual budget had been spent, of which 70 percent went on training of police officers through a *bolsa formação* (training stipend) without '...altering the institutional environment in which these police officers operate' (ibid., 11). In a more detailed version of the assessment (INESC, 2010), blame for PRONASCI's ineffectiveness is put on the shift in focus of the program, away from its original innovative aspirations. It is instructive to quote from the executive summary of the assessment:

> The analysis found that, despite its innovative conception, PRONASCI proved insufficient to confront the complex spectrum of violence in the country. The reason for this was that PRONASCI's original conception, designed within a human rights framework, was abandoned at the moment of planning the activities and projects that should have put these ideas into practice. (...) These data prove that the Program, until this moment [2010 – kk], is reduced to a policy of salary increase for security agents.
>
> (INESC, 2010, p. 3)

As a result, federal-level ambitions with respect to public security slowly evaporated during Rousseff's term. Although her 2010 presidential campaign rested, as far as public security was concerned, on maintaining the program and on nation-wide deployment of close to 3,000 Rio-style UPP units, both were ditched in 2012 and 2013. Since then, the federal government focused on specific security issues related to the 2014 FIFA World Cup and the 2016 Olympic Games, emphasizing technical solutions, such as mobile command and control centers to be deployed in the sportive venues (Agência Brasil, 2013).

Conclusion

This chapter showed that, since the 1980s, Brazil experienced the emergence and consolidation of a complex spectrum of violence and insecurity. Taking homicide rates as a proxy for this complicated problem, after 2000 no reversal of this state of affairs happened, despite declining rates in the two largest urban agglomerations, São Paulo and Rio de Janeiro. Homicide rates, however, are just the tip of the massive iceberg of the exclusion of a substantial part of the Brazilian citizenry from public and legal protective capabilities. This means that violence and insecurity in Brazil reflect much more than the mere failure of public security governance. It is a structural condition that testifies to the 'disjunctive' nature of democracy and citizenship in the country (Caldeira and Holston, 1999) as far as civil rights and citizen security is concerned. Especially in urban areas (discussed for the case of Rio de Janeiro), this leaves the ground open to perverse and criminal interaction of a variety of violent actors (Arias, 2006): drug gangs and factions, 'unchecked', corrupt and criminalized police, *vigilantes*, and extortion rackets of violent *milícias*.

The decline in average lethal violence in the two megacities São Paulo and Rio de Janeiro cannot hide the increase of violence elsewhere. Insecurity as a key concern, not only in specific areas and for specific populations but in urban Brazil in general, continues as one of the most tenacious problems the country is facing. In São Paulo, Rio de Janeiro, and other major cities, many areas are still marked by high rates of lethal violence and other forms of crime, coercion and insecurity, despite the advance, to a certain degree, of 'pacification' in the case of Rio de Janeiro.

The overall pattern emerging from my discussion is that Brazil failed, after 2000, to make a significant break away from the vertiginous rise of violence and spread of insecurity during the preceding 15 years. The problem of violence, crime, and insecurity has proved notably immune to federal public policy intervention during Lula's second term and into Dilma's 2011–14 term, despite the good intentions, high ambitions, and ample funding set out for the federal citizen security program PRONASCI during 2007–11. In other words, the reign of the Workers' Party has not provided the silver key to unlock the conundrum of violence and fear as an expression of inequality and exclusion in Brazil.

Notes

1. Pacification Police Unit, a public security strategy in the city of Rio de Janeiro aimed at the expulsion of drug gangs from *favelas* and the establishment of permanente police posts in these neighborhoods.
2. Parts of this section are based on Koenders and Koonings (2012).
3. In the 1970s, groups of imprisoned urban guerrillas who as a rule had a middle class or student background came into contact with detained criminals and drug dealers. The former passed their organizational expertise (vertical command lines and the cell structure) on to the crime leaders who used it first to secure their power within the penitentiaries and then to consolidate drug gangs and syndicates outside (Leeds, 1996, pp. 52–58; Peralva, 2000, pp. 73ff.).
4. See Assembléia Legislativa do Estado do Rio de Janeiro, *Relatório final da Commisão Parlamentar de Inquérito destinada a investigar a ação de milícias no âmbito do Estado do Rio de Janeiro* (Rio de Janeiro, 2008). See for the subsequent introduction of permanent 'pacification' policing in Batam (and a few other *favelas*), 'Polícia para mil e uma utilidades. ' In *O Globo*, 15 August 2009, p. 12.
5. This section draws on Koenders and Koonings (2012).

References

Agência Brasil. (2013) 'Dilma Diz que Reforço da Segurança Pública Ficará como Legado dos Grandes Eventos'. http://memoria.ebc.com.br/agenciabrasil date accessed on 13 June 2013

Ahnen, R.E. (2007) 'The Politics of Police Violence in Democratic Brazil', *Latin American Politics and Society* 49(1): 141–167.

Amorim, C. (1993) *Comando Vermelho: A História Secreta do Crime Organizado* (Rio de Janeiro: Record).

Amorim, C. (2007) *CV-PCC: A Irmandade do Crime* (Rio de Janeiro: Record).

Arias, E.D. (2006) *Drugs and Democracy in Rio de Janeiro. Trafficking, Social Networks and Public Security* (Chapel Hill: University of North Carolina Press).

Arias, E.D. and Goldstein, D.M. (eds) (2010) *Violent Democracies in Latin America* (Durham: Duke University Press).

Arias, E.D. and Rodrigues, C.D. (2006) 'The Myth of Personal Security: Criminal Gangs, Dispute Resolution, and Identity in Rio de Janeiro's Favelas', *Latin American Politics and Society* 48(4): 53–81.

Barcellos, C. (2003) *Abusado. O Dono do Morro Dona Marta* (Rio de Janeiro: Record).

Branford, S. and Rocha, J. (2002) *Cutting the Wire: The Story of the Landless Movement in Brazil* (London: Latin American Bureau).

Briceño-León, R. and Zubillaga, V. (2002) 'Violence and Globalization in Latin America', *Current Sociology* 50(1): 19–37.

Caldeira, T. (2000) *City of Walls. Crime, Segregation, and Citizenship in São Paulo* (Berkeley: University of California Press).

Caldeira, T. and Holston, J. (1999) 'Democracy and Violence in Brazil', *Comparative Studies in Society and History* 41(4): 691–729.

Cano, I. and Iooty, C. (2008) *Seis por Meia Dúzia: um Estudo Exploratório do Fenômeno das Chamadas Milícias no Rio de Janeiro* (Rio de Janeiro: Fundação Heinrich Boll).

Carosamigos. (2006) *PCC* (Edição Extra, 10[28]) (São Paulo: Casa Amarela).

Carvalho, V.A. and de Fatima e Silva, M. do R. (2011) 'Política de Segurança Pública no Brasil: Avanços, Limites e Desafios', *Revista Katál* 14(1): 59–67.

Diamond, L. (1999) *Developing Democracy: Towards Consolidation* (Baltimore: Johns Hopkins University Press).

Dowdney, L. (2003) *Children of the Drug Trade: A Case Study of Children in Organized Armed Violence in Rio de Janeiro* (Rio de Janeiro: ISER/Viva Rio).

Feltran, G.S. (2010) 'Crime e Castigo na Cidade: Os Repertórios da Justiça e a Questão do Homicídio nas Periferias de São Paulo', *Caderno CRH* 23(58): 59–73.

Feltran, G. de S. (2011) *Fronteira de Tensão. Política e Violência nas Periferias de São Paulo* (São Paulo: Editora UNESP).

Fernandes, R.C. (ed.) (2005) *Brasil: As Armas e as Vítimas* (Rio de Janeiro: Letras).

FGV. (Fundação Getúlio Vargas) (2009) *PRONASCI em Números* (Rio de Janeiro: FGV).

Gay, R. (1994) *Popular Organization and Democracy in Rio de Janeiro. A Tale of Two Favelas* (Philadelphia: Temple University Press).

Gay, R. (2009) 'From Popular Movements to Drug Gangs to Milicias: An Anatomy of Violence in Rio de Janeiro', in K. Koonings and D. Kruijt (eds), *Megacities: The Politics of Urban Exclusion and Violence in the Global South* (London: Zed Books).

Gay, R. (2010) 'Toward Uncivil Society: Causes and Consequences of Violence in Rio de Janeiro', in E.D. Arias and D.M. Goldstein (eds), *Violent Democracies in Latin America* (Durham: Duke University Press).

Hammond, J. (1999) 'Law and Disorder: the Brazilian Landless Farm Workers' Movement', *Bulletin of Latin American Research* 18: 469–89.

Holston, J. (2008) *Insurgent Citizenship: Disjunctions of Democracy and Modernity in Brazil* (Princeton: Princeton University Press).

Huggins, M.K. (2000) 'Urban Violence and Police Privatization in Brazil: Blended Invisibility', *Social Justice* 27(2): 113–134.

Husain, S. (2007) *In War Those Who Die Are Not Innocent: Human Rights Implementation, Policing, and Public Security Reform in Rio de Janeiro, Brazil* (Amsterdam: Rozenberg).

INESC. (2010) *Segurança Pública e Cidadania. Uma Análise Orçamentária do Pronasci* (Brasília: Instituto de Estudos Socioeconômicos).

Kahn, T. (2002) *Velha e Nova Polícia. Polícia e Políticas de Segurança Pública no Brasil Atual* (São Paulo: Sicurezza).

Koenders, S. and Koonings, K. (2012) *Winning the Urban war in Rio de Janeiro? Citizen Security and the Favela Pacification Strategy* (San Francisco: paper presented at LASA Conference).

Koonings, K. (1999) 'Shadows of Violence and Political Transition in Brazil. From Military Rule to Democratic Governance', in K. Koonings and D. Kruijt (eds), *Societies of Fear. The Legacy of Civil War, Violence and Terror in Latin America* (London: Zed Books).

Koonings, K. (2004) 'Strengthening Citizenship in Brazil's Democracy: Local Participatory Governance in Porto Alegre', *Bulletin of Latin American Research* 23(1): 79–99.

Koonings, K. (2012) 'New Violence, Insecurity, and the State. Comparative Reflections on Latin America and Mexico', in Wil Pansters (ed.), *Violence, Coercion, and State-Making in Twenthieth-Century Mexico. The Other Half of the Centaur* (Stanford: Stanford University Press).

Koonings, K. (2013) 'Democracia y Gobernabilidad en Brasil: Los Desafíos de la Pobreza, la Corrupción y la Inseguridad', in F. Rojas and P. Silva (eds), *Gobernabilidad y convivencia democrática en América Latina* (San José: FLACSO).

Koonings, K. and Kruijt, D. (eds) (2004) *Armed Actors: Organised Violence and State Failure in Latin America* (London: Zed Books).

Koonings, K. and Kruijt, D. (eds) (2007) *Fractured Cities. Social Exclusion, Urban Violence and Contested Spaces in Latin America* (London: Zed Books).

Leeds, E. (1996) 'Cocaine and Parallel Politics in the Brazilian Urban Periphery: Constraints on Local-Level Democratization', *Latin American Research Review* 31(3): 47–84.

Lima, W. (1991) *Quatrocentos Contra Um: Uma História do Comando Vermelho* (Rio de Janeiro: ISER/Vozes).

Linger, D.T. (1992) *Dangerous Encounters: Meanings of Violence in a Brazilian City* (Stanford: Stanford University Press).

Lins, P. (1997) *Cidade de Deus* (São Paulo: Companhia das Letras).

Lowell Lewis, J. (2000) 'Sex and Violence in Brazil: Carnaval, Capoeira, and the Problem of Everyday Life', *American Ethnologist* 26(3): 539–557.

Machado da Silva, L.A. (ed.) (2008) *Vida sob Cerco: Violência e Rotina nas Favelas do Rio de Janeiro* (Rio de Janeiro: Nova Fronteira).

Machado da Silva, L.A. (2010) *Afinal, Qual é a das UPPs?* (Rio de Janeiro: UFRJ [www.observatoriadasmetropoles.ufrj.br].

Murilo de Carvalho, J. (2002) *Cidadania no Brasil: O Longo Caminho* (Rio de Janeiro: Civilização Brasileira).

Nunes, A. (2005) *A Realidade das Prisões Brasileiras* (Recife: Nossa Livraria).

O'Donnell, G. (1993) 'On the State, Democratization, and Some Conceptual Problems: A Latin American View with Glances at Some Postcommunist Countries', *World Development* 21(8): 1355–1369.

Peralva, A. (2000) *Violência e Democracia. O Paradoxo Brasileiro* (São Paulo: Paz e Terra).

Pereira, A.W. (2000) 'An Ugly Democracy? State Violence and the Rule of Law in Postauthoritarian Brazil', in P.R. Kingstone and T.J. Power (eds), *Democratic Brazil: Actors, Institutions, and Processes* (Pittsburgh: University of Pittsburgh Press).

Pereira, A.W. (2008) 'Public Security, Private Interests, and Police Reform in Brazil', in P.R. Kingstone and T.J. Power (eds), *Democratic Brazil Revisited* (Pittsburgh: University of Pittsburgh Press).

Pereira, A.W. and Davis, D. (2000) 'Introduction: New Patterns of Militarized Violence and Coercion in the Americas', *Latin American Perspectives* 27(2): 3–17.

Pereira, A.C.J. Graça, E.M. Barbosa, L.B. and de F. Reis, S. (2010) *Segurança Pública com Cidadania: Uma análise orçamentária do Pronasci (atualização)* (Brasília: INESC and CFemea, Nota técnica 172)

PNUD. (2013) *Seguridad Ciudadana con Rostro Humano: Diagnostico y Propuestas para América Latina* (New York: United Nations Development Program/ Programa de las Naciones Unidas para el Desarrollo; Informe Regional de Desarrollo Humano 2013–2014).

Rodrigues, A. Siqueira, R. and Lissovsky, M. (eds) (2012) *Unidades de Polícia Pacificadora: Debates e Reflexões* (Rio de Janeiro: ISER).

Rotker, S. (ed.) (2002) *Citizens of Fear: Urban Violence in Latin America* (New Brunswick: Rutgers University Press).

Sapori, L.F. (2007) *Segurança Pública no Brasil: Desafios e Perspectivas* (Rio de Janeiro: FGV Editora).

Scheper-Hughes, N. (1992) *Death without Weeping. The Violence of Everyday Life in Brazil* (Berkeley: University of California Press).

Soares, L.E. (2000) *Meu Casaco de General. Quinhentos Dias no Front da Segurança Pública do Rio de Janeiro* (São Paulo: Companhia das Letras).

Soares, L.E. Batista, A. and Pimentel, R. (2006) *Elite da Tropa* (Rio de Janeiro: Objetiva).

Soares, L.E. Ferraz, C. Batista, A. and Pimentel, R. (2010) *Elite da Tropa 2* (Rio de Janeiro: Nova Fronteira).

UNODC. (2011) *Global Study on Homicide 2011: Trends, Contexts, Data* (New York: United Nations Office on Drugs and Crime).

Waiselfisz, J.J. (2007) *Mapa da Violência dos Municípios Brasileiros* (São Paulo: Instituto Sangari).

Waiselfisz, J.J. (2010) *Mapa da Violência 2010: Anatomia dos homicídios no Brasil* (São Paulo: Instituto Sangari).

Waiselfisz, J.J. (2011) *Mapa da Violência 2012: Os Novos Padrões da Violência Homicidano Brasil* (São Paulo: Instituto Sangari).

Wampler, B. (2007) *Participatory Budgeting in Brazil: Contestation, Cooperation, and Accountability* (University Park: Pennsylvania State University Press).

Waqcuant, L. (2003) 'Towards a Dictatorship over the Poor?: Notes on the Penalization of Poverty in Brazil', *Punishment and Society* 5(2): 197–205.

Waqcuant, L. (2008) *Urban Outcasts: A Comparative Sociology of Advanced Marginality* (Cambridge: Polity Press).

Willandino, R., Sento-Sé, J.T., Dias, C.G. and Gomes, F. (eds) (2011) *Prevenção à Violência e Redução de Homicídios de Adolescentes e Jovens no Brasil* (Rio de Janeiro: Observatório de Favelas).

Willis, G.D. (2009) 'Deadly Symbiosis? The PCC, the State, and the Institutionalization of Violence in São Paulo, Brazil', in G. A. Jones and D. Rodgers (eds), *Youth Violence in Latin America. Gangs and Juvenile Justice in Perspective* (New York: Palgrave MacMillan).

Zaluar, A. (2000) 'Perverse Integration. Drug Trafficking and Youth in the Favelas of Rio de Janeiro', *Journal of International Affairs* 53(2): 654–671.

Zaverucha, J. (2005) *FHC, Forças Armadas e Polícia. Entre o Autoritarismo e a Democrcacia 1999–2002* (Rio de Janeiro: Record).

8
Urban and Housing Policy from Lula to Dilma: Social Inclusion with Territorial Segregation

Nabil Bonduki

Between the severe economic crisis of the early 1980s, which resulted in dismantling the Housing Finance System (*Sistema Financeiro de Habitação*), and the creation of the Ministry of Cities (*Ministério das Cidades*) in 2003, which initiated a new phase of housing policy under the Lula administration, Brazil underwent one of the most interesting processes of transition from dictatorship to democracy (Stepan, 1989; Kingstone and Power, 2000; 2008). Thanks to this process, not only was the election of a leftist president with a popular background possible in 2002, but also Lula's government was successful in its commitment to structural transformations that would confront the country's severe social inequalities and guarantee social rights to the excluded population. This transition can only be fully understood in light of a series of phenomena: a wide range of popular and social mobilizations, the construction of civil organizations, and the formulation of public policies with the participation of society at large, all of which characterized the country during this period.

One facet of this process was the struggle for the construction of new paradigms in urban and housing policies, based on principles such as the social function of property, the right to proper housing, the universalization of access to basic sanitation and to quality public transportation, and the democratic administration of the city. These principles were articulated in a widespread movement, one that was both complex and multifaceted, known as the Movement for Urban Reform (*Movimento pela Reforma Urbana*). By aggregating numerous organizations and mobilizations, the movement surged forward throughout this period, garnering victories and concrete experiences in the name of ensuring urban rights. The proposals crafted during this period, later incorporated into the municipal administrations that were dominated by the Workers' Party, served as examples of public policies formed 'bottom up,' with significant popular participation.

This long series of events, in which society took the leading role, began with a popular initiative to include urban reform in the 1987–88 debates during the elaboration of the new Constitution. For the first time, the initiative enabled the establishment of a specific department for urban development in the Brazilian Constitution, thereby introducing the principles of the social function of property and the right to housing. This development unfolded along with the concrete experiences of municipal administrations that, throughout the 1990s, introduced participative forms of management: the mobilization in support of the City Statute, approved by National Congress (2001); the approval of the Constitutional Amendment Bill that introduced housing as a constitutional social right (2000); and the formulation of the Housing Project (1999–2000), structuring a strategy for resolving the country's housing deficit.

This process culminated in the creation of the Ministry of Cities by the Lula administration in 2003, enlisted with the responsibility of coordinating a new urban policy at national level and thereby involving sectorial policies such as housing, environmental sanitation and urban transport, which opened new horizons for ensuring the right to housing.

This chapter seeks to assess the housing and urban politics of both the Lula administration and the (early) Dilma administration, with the aim of identifying advances and obstacles with regard to ensuring the right to housing and to the city itself.

Background: the crisis of the military regime, democratization and the dismantling of the housing policy

The failure of the economic model implemented by the military regime in the early 1980s generated a recession, a higher rate of unemployment and a drop in wage levels; it marked the beginning of a new era. This process had enormous repercussions in the Financial Housing System (*Sistema Financeiro da Habitacão*, SFH), generating a strong credit default among borrowers and consequently reduced investment capacity of the SFH. In a climate of substantial popular mobilization alongside the democratization process, the critics of the National Housing Bank (*Banco Nacional de Habitação*, BNH) were incensed and joined the fight against the authoritarian regime with which the institution was closely associated (Maricato, 1997).

With the end of the military regime, it was hoped that the 'New Republic' would renovate housing policy. However, for political expediency, President José Sarney (PMDB, 1985–89) resolved that the BNH would be abolished rather than housing policy be reformulated, thus transferring management of the Financial Housing System to the Federal Savings Bank (*Caixa Econômica Federal*). The decision had nothing to do with housing policy: its aim was to empower the president, who formerly had neither control of the BNH nor the political force to change its direction, as indicated by the state governors of the PMDB (Aragão, 1999).

The decision to abolish the BNH, without replacing it with another institution, was executed without the resistance of society and public opinion, as the bank had become one of the most hated institutions in the country. With inflation reaching frightening levels, the BNH was characterized by the image that 'the more you pay, the more you owe.' Outstanding balances and installments of borrowers, by virtue of the monetary adjustment mechanism, were growing at a faster pace than salaries, which were subjected to a sharp crunch in the beginning of the 1980s, while scandals involving the misuse of SFH funds were reported with high frequency.

With the end of the BNH, what was lost was a nationwide structure that, for better or worse, had accumulated enormous experience, trained professionals and financed the greatest housing project in the history of the country that, albeit with misconceptions, was at least established. As a result, there emerged a void and an effective national housing policy ceased to exist. Shortly thereafter, the Ministry of Urban Development (*Ministério do Desenvolvimento Urbano*) was also abolished, further dismantling the nascent institutional structure focused on the urban and housing sector, which had barely begun to be organized.

From this moment onwards, the lack of priority for urban issues became obvious. Between the abolishment of the BNH in 1986 and the creation of the Ministry of Cities in 2003, the sector of the federal government responsible for the administration of housing policy was subordinated to seven different administrative structures, evidence of discontinuity and a lack of strategy to tackle the problem (Bonduki, 1998a).

The Federal Savings Bank became the financial agent of the SFH, precariously absorbing the expertise, personnel and archives of the former BNH. The regulation of housing credit and of the SFH as a whole passed to the National Monetary Council (*Conselho Monetário Nacional*), becoming an instrument of monetary policy that led to tighter control over the granting of mortgage loans. Misguided policy decisions marred by allegations of corruption, along with a release of contracts beyond the control of the Fundo de Garantia do Tempo de Serviço (FGTS) during the Collor administration in 1990, resulted in a total shutdown of financing through FGTS resources between 1991 and 1995 (Carvalho and Sobrinho, 1992).

The financial deficit generated by the default crisis of the early 1980s led to a reduction in housing investment in order to recover the funds of the SFH. In this regard, financing and housing production was further limited, while housing problems for the poor became more severe with unemployment and loss of income among the urban population, which characterized the last two decades of the twentieth century. The favelas (shantytowns) began to grow at much higher rates than the urban population as a whole.

To cope with this situation, several municipalities and states launched housing programs that were financed through alternative sources, particularly budgetary resources, thereby adopting principles and assumptions different from those that had been adopted by the BNH. However, given the State's fiscal crisis, these investments fell short of necessity and, moreover, the absence of a financial design prevented their use as subsidies for the loans granted by the SFH (Bonduki, 1998b).

During this period, a national strategy to address the issue of housing ceased to exist, leaving a void that was filled in a fragmentary, yet creative, way by municipalities and states. This led to a gradual transfer of responsibilities to the states and municipalities, keeping the Constitution of 1988 as a framework, which made housing a competitive assignment for the three branches of government. With democratization and the growth in mobilization of housing movements, the pressure heightened for the greater participation of local authorities in the housing issue. As we shall see later, local administrations became the principle interlocutors of popular organizations and assumed responsibility for addressing social demands, as they were in direct contact with the problems of the poor population.

The legacy of the FHC government: economic stability, low investment and recovery of the SFH

During the administration of Fernando Henrique Cardoso (PSDB, 1995–2002) and with the introduction of the real (BRL), economic stability and a gradual resumption of financing for housing and sanitation were achieved at a national level through the resources of the FGTS, after several years of paralysis. A consistent housing policy was not structured at this time, but the assumptions that guided the action were fundamentally different from those that predominated during the period of the BNH, thereby directing the formulation of new programs (*Ministério do Planejamento e Orçamento*, 1996a; 1996b). Macroeconomic policy, marked by a restriction of credit and public spending, prevented any forceful or massive action to addressing housing problems. The restrictive character adopted by the government created a culture of fiscal responsibility that, although exaggerated, had the merit of generating conditions for a recuperation of the financial health of the FGTS and the investment capacity of the SFH. This opportunity was little exploited in the Fernando Henrique Cardoso (FHC) administration and the first two years of the Lula administration, but permitted the great leap that was initiated in the year 2005 (Instituto Via Pública, 2004).

Although, at first glance, the changes introduced could indicate a renovation in the way that the housing issue was treated by the federal government, breaking the rigid perspective inherited from the times of the BNH, they did not in fact succeed in leveraging a new housing policy and ultimately generated a set of adverse effects in social, economic and urban terms. Between 1995 and 2003 (including the first year of the Lula administration), around 1.7 million loans were contracted, totaling a little more than BRL 22 billion. Out of these funds, only 22 percent of the contracts and 36 percent of the funds were allocated to produce 364,000 new units in nine years. To understand this in comparative terms, the FGTS had financed the same number of units in only one year (1980) (Instituto Via Pública, 2004).

These programs hardly had a noticeable impact in the fight against the housing shortage, particularly in low-income segments. A traditional characteristic of housing policy in Brazil was maintained or even accentuated: privileged treatment of the middle class. Between 1995 and 2003, 78.8 percent of the total funds were allocated to households with an income higher than five times the minimum wage, with only 8.5 percent destined for low-income households (up to three times the minimum wage), which constitutes 83.2 percent of the quantitative deficit (Instituto Via Pública, 2004).

The Residential Leasing Program (*Programa de Arrendamento Residencial*, PAR) was created in 1999 and was dedicated to the production of new rental units, together with the Housing Subsidies Program (Programa de Subsídio Habitacional). The two programs brought with them an important novelty at the federal level: subsidies with funds from the National Treasury to support the construction of housing for the low-income population.

The PAR brought an innovation, incorporated as a cornerstone in the housing policy proposals formulated by the Housing Project and implemented by the Lula administration: a mix of resources comprised of a returnable source (FGTS) and a non-returnable source, so as to enable assistance to the population that did not have income compatible with the cost of financing a housing unit. It can be said that these two programs, by way of introducing a non-returnable fund (the Federal Budget or other sources), were unchartered territory for federal government actions under the new National Housing Policy (*Política Nacional de Habitação*) implemented by the Lula administration.

The roots of Lula's national housing policy: municipal experiences and the Workers' Party approach to government

Given the absence of a national policy, the trend of decentralized housing policies grew (as we saw previously, facilitated by the Constitution of 1988) and a broad set of pioneering experiences emerged with social housing by municipal administrations, based on assumptions alternative to those employed by the centralized and homogeneous model of the BNH. These proposals were marked by diversity and by innovative assumptions about tackling the housing problem that would become one of the formative elements of the policy implemented by the Lula administration 20 years later (Maricato, 2001). This new housing policy formulated by the Lula administration, therefore, inherited the long development process that originated in the first directly elected state and municipal governments (Bonduki, 1997).

Although these initiatives were not implemented on the scale required, they were important seeds because they had been dialogued with the actual city and were realized with budgetary funds that had been provided to promote popular participation. Out of all the municipal experiences, the social housing program of the municipality of São Paulo (1989–92) that was implemented by the Luiza Erundina administration, elected by the Workers' Party, stands out as a true laboratory experiment for alternatives addressing the issue in an innovative way; within this process were born several proposals that were later developed by the Lula administration. The intervention was remarkable, pointing to the inclusion of housing as a fundamental element for the creation of the city, and for the implementation of new forms of management, with a great diversity of programs and quality of projects (Bonduki, 2014).

The housing intervention in Sao Paulo during this period occurred at an unprecedented scale for municipal programs: in four years, almost

250 projects were developed and nearly 70,000 families were involved. It was not a pilot, but rather a program with the objective of generating a demonstrative effect that another kind of housing policy was possible. With high-quality architecture and appropriate urban integration, innovative project references were developed and associated with new forms of administration, such as self-governed *mutirão* (collective work effort). A relationship between housing production and urban policy was pursued despite institutional and political constraints.

An aggressive policy of expropriation of vacant urban spaces with existing infrastructure introduced a new logic of urban integration, which broke with the traditional peripheral locations of large housing complexes. The projects were aligned with the urban policy that proposed to combat empty properties and unused plots of land. In the favelas, the policy attempted to facilitate urbanization, except if the favela was very dense and was very well located, in which case it would opt for a full reconstruction of the settlement to keep the population in the same area. Along the same lines, another program was implemented in Rio de Janeiro with a different urban design. Led by mayor César Maia, the conservative administration introduced *Favela-Bairro* (favela-neighborhood), the biggest program of favela upgrading until that time, reinforcing the proposition that urbanization is the best option for dealing with the problem of precarious urban settlements.

Enabling social housing projects in city centers was another innovation of this period. Pilot projects developed in São Paulo between 1989 and 1992 showed that this was possible at costs consistent with the income from traditional projects and that it even had advantages for the city, with a reduction in transport needs, mixture of social classes, diversified use of urban space, and the effective utilization of infrastructure and equipment. In this seemingly utopian era, at the turn of the century, it began to be advocated more broadly that it was possible to break the historic urban segregation that cast the poor out to the periphery.

These pioneering experiments served as effective demonstrations for the housing movement, which continued to advance its cause, not only for the right to housing but also the right to the city. Beginning in 1996, the occupation of vacant buildings in historic city centers was becoming common, initially in São Paulo and then in other major Brazilian cities such as Rio de Janeiro, Porto Alegre, Salvador and Recife.

The creation of the federal government's Residential Leasing Program (PAR) in 1999 gave some encouragement to this approach and opened up the possibility of financing interventions in city centers. However, this type of venture was unimpressive from a quantitative point of view; less than 1 percent of units financed by the PAR were of this type (Maleronka, 2004).

Municipal and state experiments, funded by resources from their respective levels of government, showed to the housing movements that it was fundamental to fight so that the State would make available budgetary resources to finance the production of low-income housing.

In 1996, several programs of this new phase were selected as successful examples to be included in the Brazilian Report for the United Nations Conference on Human Settlements – Habitat II, which helped to bolster support for a new way to address the housing problem (Bonduki, 1997). This group of experiments was fundamental for the creation of a large program for the urbanization of favelas under the Lula administration.

The national housing policy of the first Lula administration: The construction of a bottom-up public policy

From the outset of the twenty-first century began a new period in the history of public housing policy in Brazil (Bonduki, 2014). By any interpretation, it is undisputable that the inclusion of the right to housing in the Constitution (2000), the Statute of the City (2001), the creation of the Ministry of Cities (2003) and the formulation of a new national housing policy (2004) are important milestones. Beyond that, the economic situation of the country changed significantly throughout the first decade of the century, thus allowing for a significant increase in investment, in both social and commercial housing.

The point of departure of the new National Housing Policy occurred in 1999 and 2000, when the Citizens' Institute (*Instituto Cidadania*), coordinated by Luiz Inácio Lula da Silva, launched an enticing proposal: to develop a plan that would permit stabilization, in terms to be defined, of the housing problem in the country. The proposal was part of a set of projects from the institute aimed at the construction of development projects that would associate the resolution of social issues with economic growth and job creation, having in mind the electoral campaign of 2002 (Instituto Cidadania, 2000).

Launched in 2000, the housing project presented proposals in three dimensions – social management and control, financial design, and urban-land elements – and faced the issue not only in the context of the federal government, but also in consideration of the various agents who bear some responsibility for the housing problem, in both the public and private domains. The establishment of the National Housing

System (*Sistema Nacional de Habitação*) was proposed, formed by the three branches of the federal government, it would act as a formal structure under the coordination of a new ministry known as the Ministry of Cities (Instituto Cidadania, 2000; Maricato, 2001).

Social control would be exercised by the Council of Cities (*Conselho das Cidades*) and similar agencies in states and municipalities, which would be fit to manage housing funds that concentrate budgetary resources to subsidize the poor. In this regard, the priority would be the approval of the bill by popular initiative for the establishment of the National Housing Fund (*Fundo Nacional de Habitação*), a flagship of the housing movement that had been bogged down in Congress since 1991.

In summary, taking into account all three dimensions of the housing project, the proposals would be: to approve the Statute of the City to facilitate access to land and make this cheaper, combat idle property speculation, and implement real estate development in the municipalities according to master plans; to create a new institutional structure, with social participation and control, as well as intergovernmental and inter-sectorial coordination; and to create a new financing and subsidy model. With this base established, there should be a wide enough range of programs to ensure handling of the various types of urban and housing problems, with a level of diversity that would encompass the different regions and categories of cities.

In the initial phase of the first term of the Lula presidency (from 2003 to July 2005), the proposals related to institutional and urban issues advanced more rapidly than the financing model. The Ministry of Cities was created on the first day of the government, seeking to establish sectorial policies and to address the urban issue with four national secretariats (Housing, Sanitation, Urban Mobility and Urban Programs). A team committed to the urban reform agenda, the struggle for the right to housing and the proposals of the housing policy, assumed the key posts of the ministry. In October of 2003, the First National Conference of Cities (*1ª Conferência Nacional das Cidades*) was held, with 2,500 delegates elected in an extensive process of social mobilization in more than 3,000 municipalities, consolidating the foundations of government action. As a result, the creation and composition of the National Housing Council (*Conselho Nacional de Habitação*) was proposed, and consequently installed in 2004 (Ministério das Cidades, 2004).

The Statute of the City began to be implemented through a national campaign for the Participative Master Plan (*Plano Diretor Participativo*), developed by the Department of Urban Programs. It sought to qualify professionals and community leaders who, among other things, would introduce urban instruments capable of combatting real estate speculation and ensuring urbanized land for housing production. Between 2001 and 2006, about 2,000 municipalities developed their own master plans with very different results. Regardless, the federal government had achieved for the first time, through a democratic and participative process, broad action throughout the entire territory to implementing a planning instrument, which was furthermore associated with the housing issue. This milestone ushered in a debate and the possibility of putting into place instruments of urban reform.

In spite of this considerable progress, the staff of the Ministry of Cities, under the coordination of Minister Olívio Dutra, encountered enormous difficulties in implementing proposals in the area of financing, given a rigid monetary policy still under the relatively orthodox control of the Ministry of Finance (*Ministério da Fazenda*) and Central Bank (*Banco Central*). In 2003 and 2004, budgetary resources became scarce, while the FGTS programs created in the previous administration continued to prevail, despite the efforts of the Ministry of Cities to prioritize the low-income population. Even a more flexible use of the FGTS was met with resistance, and therefore was adopted only gradually.

During this period the new National Housing Policy (*Política Nacional de Habitação*, PNH) was formalized. Without significant subsidies, though, the fiscal vision of the federal savings bank prevailed and alterations in the granting of credit were minimal. The creation of the National Social Housing Fund (*Fundo Nacional de Habitação de Interesse Social*, FNHIS), proposed by a popular legislative initiative, reiterated a commitment made by the president at the first National Conference of Cities that public resources would be directed toward enabling housing subsidies. FNHIS, however, encountered opposition from the government's economic policy team, delaying the Fund's approval until 2005 and, after strong pressure from the housing movement, its installation in 2006. Instead of being institutionalized like a financial fund, which was the original proposal, it was introduced as a budget fund with a more limited role. The government, meanwhile, pledged to contribute BRL 1 billion per year to subsidize housing programs, a value that had never before been reached. Additionally, a resolution of the FGTS trustee council extended the possibility of the fund being utilized for housing subsidies.

The same legislation that created the FNHIS also established the National System of Social Housing (*Sistema Nacional de Habitação de Interesse Social*, SNHIS), as a basis for enabling the coordination of the three federal entities. It also required that states and municipalities create an institutional structure with municipal or state funds, council and plans, as a condition to having access to federal resources and thus contributing to a new, decentralized institutional design.

Little by little, key elements for the implementation of a new housing policy were being incorporated, with the support and mobilization of the social sectors represented in the Council of Cities. In 2005, housing subsidies were amplified with funds from the FGTS, enabling greater service to the low-income population. Despite these advances, the established regulations failed to provide appropriate solutions for the poor population in metropolitan areas. Services provided to those individuals and families earning up to three times the minimum wage constituted 26 percent of the total in 2003, reached 46 percent in 2005 and jumped to 65 percent in 2007. These official numbers released by the Federal Savings Bank, however, should be relativized because the minimum wage increased significantly during this period.

The Lula administration's reconciliation with the construction industry

The strategy formed by the National Housing Policy was based on strengthening the ability of the market to use the resources of the SFH to respond to the needs of the middle and lower middle classes in a way that would ensure that government subsidies could be directed toward the low-income population. In this sense, the government substantially altered its previous position and began to support the strengthening of the private sector and to stimulate investment in the construction industry.

Therefore, the Lula administration undertook fundamental measures to increase market-driven production of housing. A new Resolution of the Central Bank began requiring banks to use the resources of savings accounts to finance housing, as stipulated by the law that regulated the SFH. In 2004, Congress approved Public Law 10-931 with strong support from the government and the private sector, providing for legal security in the market through mortgaging housing loans and by obligating the payment of undisputed debt in the case of a legal conflict between the borrower and financial agent and/or promoter.

In a favorable environment of high economic growth, these measures generated an enormous increase in the production and sales of housing units to the middle class. The investment in housing in the private sector, with resources from the Brazilian Savings and Loan System (*Sistema*

Brasileiro de Poupança e Empréstimo, SBPE) jumped from BRL 2.2 billion in 2002 to BRL 50 billion in 2010. While focusing on the middle class, the significant supply of housing units contributed to tackling the housing shortage because the formal and informal housing markets were interconnected. The lack of available housing options in the medium segments tended to elevate the cost of popular housing, even if informal, and those social housing units that were produced with subsidies were 'milked' by those who didn't have the appropriate necessities, as has happened in the entire history of public production.

This new situation led to the initial public offerings of twenty-four real estate companies, a significant investment of foreign capital and an overwhelming demand for land. The speculative process that took place between 2007 and 2008 came to be known as the real estate 'boom'. This demand created land disputes with devastating effects on the production of social housing.

Faced with the need to expand their market, many companies that were traditionally focused on the upper and upper-middle classes created subsidiaries specialized in cheaper products and targeted the lower-middle class, a segment that had grown significantly with the economic and wage policies of the Lula administration but still had insufficient income to obtain housing built for the private market. The feasibility of private mortgages for this segment has been crucial for tackling the housing issue.

The national housing plan and the My House, My Life Program (*Programa Minha Casa Minha Vida*)

A new housing policy was heading toward implementation, linked with other sectorial policies, and influenced by the ideals of the urban reform movement. The macroeconomic conditions of the country had been improving significantly, suggesting that the proposed financial model could be viable and thus implying that a significant extension of mortgage credit and non-onerous resources would be directed toward housing subsidies, elements that were indispensable for definitively coping with the problem. This framework was validated by the creation of the Acceleration of Growth Program (*Programa de Aceleração do Crescimento*, PAC) in 2007 and the My House, My Life Program (*Programa Minha Casa Minha Vida*, PMCMV) in 2009. PAC was concentrated on implanting large infrastructure projects, and included among its components a social program known as the Urbanization of Precarious Settlements

(*Urbanização de Assentamentos Precários*). The program allocated unused budgetary resources to the housing sector, thereby enabling the implementation of the largest territorial inclusion program that had ever been conducted in the country.

As a result, between 2002 and 2008, the total resources dedicated to housing increased from about BRL 8 billion to more than BRL 42 billion, as illustrated in Figure 8.1. For the first time since the days of the BNH, which saw the allocation of sufficient resources to develop massive housing programs, there arose the tangible prospect of a significant contribution of resources to the subsidy. As a result, a much stronger impact on the housing shortage of low-income sectors was made possible.

In this context, from 2007 to 2008, the National Housing Plan (*Plano Nacional de Habitação*, or PlanHab) was formulated as one of the proposed components of the new PNH (Ministério das Cidades, 2009a). Its objective was to satisfy the housing needs of the country within 15 years. Developed by a participative methodology along with the consultation of the Housing and Human Settling Laboratory (*Laboratório de Habitação e Assentamentos Humanos*) of the College of Architecture and Urbanism at the University of Sao Paulo (FAU-USP) and the Via Pública Institute, PlanHab was conceived as a strategic long-term plan with a

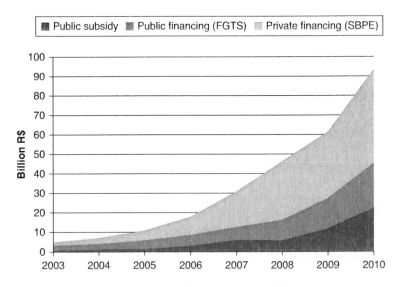

Figure 8.1   Evolution of investments in housing in Brazil, 2003–10

temporal horizon of 2023, but was structured with operational mile-stones to be implemented in the short and medium term.

To overcome the traditional homogeneity with which the housing issue was treated in the past, PlanHab developed proposals, action strat-egies and goals that took into account the diversity of the housing issue, the different categories of municipalities, regional specifications and the different perspectives of each social segment. The strategy proposed simultaneous actions in four areas considered to be indispensable: (1) financing and subsidies; (2) institutional arrangements; (3) production chain in the construction industry; and (4) urban, land and environ-mental strategies.

A progressive extension of budgetary resources was proposed to achieve a stable allocation of 2 percent of the federal budget (*Orçamento Geral da União*) and 1 percent of the state and municipal budgets – a percentage three times greater than that which was being applied until the intro-duction of the PAC – the level of support required to achieve a massive alleviation of the housing shortage through the creation of a new sub-sidy policy. This was based on the segmentation of demand by levels of service, grouped according to the borrower's capacity to repay the loan.

According to the proposed financial design, the poorest group with-out the capacity to repay a loan would benefit from a complete subsidy, while families who had taken financing as part of the total cost of a housing unit, but were considered risky by financial agents, would have access to partial subsidies. At the same time, the Guarantee Fund (*Fundo Garantidor*), upon its creation, would have the role of extending the capacity of this group of families to obtain financing.

The vision that guided PlanHab, however, considered the Brazilian housing problem to be not only a financial issue, but also one that required the development of other fundamental elements. It observed, among other things, the lack of capacity of the municipalities, state and even the financial agent (Caixa, the Federal Savings Bank) to operate on a large scale; the constraints of the production chain, whose output is generally low in productivity and lacks the architectural and urban planning quality to meet the most urgent demand; the difficulty of access and the cost of urbanized and regularized land for the production of social housing, in adequate urban and environmental conditions.

All of these aspects were considered obstacles to massive production, even though there was a significant investment of resources. Because of this, strategies and actions were proposed to simultaneously involve the four elements mentioned above (financial resources, operating capacity of the banks, the construction sector, and land) as a prerequisite to be able to achieve good results. In this sense, PlanHab was a fundamental instrument for directing housing policy in the long term, finding itself in a more favorable situation than ever to face and resolve the housing shortage in a new way.

In the second half of 2008, however, when PlanHab was just being completed, the international economic crisis hit Brazil and generated uncertainty and paralysis of the real estate sector, caught in the counter flow as it was in the process of accelerating production. The situation seemed out of control, with sharp drops in share prices of these companies on the stock exchange and obvious impacts on the activities of the sector, which suffered a substantial decline for the last months of the year. This situation was crucial to the government's decision to invest vigorously in the housing sector to prevent the crisis from worsening. As a result, formulation of what would become the My House, My Life (*Minha Casa, Minha Vida*) Program was initiated. The proposal, developed initially within the Ministry of Finance, originated as an anti-cyclical emergency action to support the private sector and avoid an increase in unemployment and the risk of a severe recession, a credible threat at the turn of 2008–2009.

The intervention of the National Housing Secretary of the Ministry of Cities, launched during the development of the National Housing Plan (PlanHab), made it possible for the anti-cyclical action to gain popular support, incorporating part of the strategy that was still being formulated. Born of this process, with the goal of enabling the construction of 1 million houses by the end of 2010, was the My House, My Life Program (PMCMV). The government's willingness to apply abundant resources to boosting construction, an attitude generated by the crisis, accelerated its decision to implement the financial aspect of PlanHab, which under normal conditions would have been met with strong resistance from the Ministry of Finance and would have undergone a lengthy implementation process. Under these circumstances, the government decided to allocate BRL 26 billion in subsidies to the production of new units, adding value to what was already planned by the PAC for the urbanization of precarious housing. The proposal was eventually adopted, which in practice was the most optimistic scenario proposed by PlanHab, attaining an investment of 2 percent of the federal budget for housing subsidies, a level that, according to the original proposed strategy, should take a few years to reach (Ministério das Cidades, 2009b).

In addition to this sudden increase in resources, other measures for financing PlanHab were proposed and adopted to reduce the cost of housing, such as tax relief for Social Housing (*Habitação de Interesse Social*, HIS), a decrease in the price of homeowners insurance and the creation of the Guarantee Fund (which resumed the idea of the guarantee fund proposed in the Housing Project), all of which had a positive impact on access to both social and commercial housing.

The PMCMV eventually incorporated the logic that provided for the allocation of subsidies and funding proposed by PlanHab, related to the creditworthiness of beneficiaries. With the contribution of this program, plus the significant increase of investments based on resources from the Brazilian Savings and Loan System, the growth of investment of resources in housing was extraordinary from 2006 onwards, reaching more than BRL 90 billion in 2010, as shown in Figure 8.1.

The new program, however, left out numerous guidelines proposed by PlanHab to ensure better housing assistance and better urban integration. Just as BNH did during the military regime, it was focused exclusively on the production of finished units, an approach that attended to the demands of the construction industry but brushed aside other options for dealing with the housing shortage. In addition to funding and grants for finished units, PlanHab had designed a range of housing programs to lower unit costs and to be better attuned to the popular process of housing production (such as urbanized lots complemented by the financing of construction materials and technical assistance). The program had the potential to assist a greater number of families at a lower unit cost, a prospect that was very suitable for medium and small municipalities.

For this reason, the quantitative goal of the My House, My Life Program 1 (from 2009 to 2010) directed toward the low-income population, which amounted to 400,000 units, was timid compared to the need, despite the enormous resources available for subsidy. As a result, the distribution of units by income level adopted by the PMCMV was far from being proportional to the profile of the housing shortage. In 2009, 91 percent of the accumulated housing shortage (i.e. almost 6.5 million households according to the traditional method of calculation, or 5.9 million if adjusted to the new method of calculation) was borne by those individuals and families earning up to three times minimum wage and who received full subsidies. This income group was considered a priority in the guidelines of the National Housing Policy, yet they were allocated only 400,000 units (40 percent of the overall goal of the program), a number that met only 6 percent of the accumulated deficit. (Bonduki, 2009) (Tables 8.1and 8.2).

Table 8.1   Resources allocated to the My House, My Life Program 1

Type of service	Resources (in billions BRL)
Housing subsidies – up to 1,375	16
Financing subsidies – up to 2,700	10
Infrastructural financing	5
Guarantee Fund for Housing	2
Production Chain Financing	1
TOTAL	34

Source: Brasil – Ministério das Cidades (2009).

Table 8.2   Goals of the My House, My Life Program 1, and the accumulated housing shortage by income level

Income Level (relative to minimum wage)	Accumulated shortage (%)	Goals of PMCMV (%)	Accumulated shortage (thousands)	Goals of PMCMV (thousands)	Accumulated shortage satisfied (%)
up to 3MW	91	40	6,550	400	6
from 3 to 6MW	6	40	430	400	93
from 6 to 10MW	3	20	210	200	95
TOTAL	100	100	7,200	1,000	14

Source: Bonduki (2009), with figures from the FundaçãoJoãoPinheiro (2007).

By not adopting the totality of strategies that PlanHab deemed essential, the PMCMV only managed to address the housing issue in an incomplete manner. Without prioritizing a land strategy, at the same time as the demand for land viable for housing production increased, the program generated an appreciation of land and plot prices and real estate speculation that prejudiced social development projects. This problem tended to generate the transfer of subsidy to the owners of the land, partially undermining the precepts of the program.

PlanHab had proposed a localization subsidy, adding value to its reputation for stimulation projects in dense, central areas; the PMCMV, by establishing a single ceiling of unit value for each region, wound up driving the projects to peripheral locations, in areas poor in employment, infrastructure and equipment, which created a demand for transportation, and hence a financial and human cost. Although it is clear that the proper location of projects depends heavily on the municipalities (on their master plans, their housing plans and the urban instruments that they regulate), it is the role of the federal government to stimulate the deployment of new projects in locations that are better equipped and that generate less urban, social and environmental costs – even more so when it yields a powerful steering tool: abundant resources for subsidy. The PlanHab proposed to incentivize municipalities by granting priority access to resources to those that were structured institutionally and would adopt correct land and urban policies. These policies included the institution of progressive taxes to combat underutilized real estate. That, however, has not been taken forward.

The only breakthrough in the urban land department of the PMCMV, a program that became a priority in the last two years of the Lula administration, was the inclusion of a specific section that facilitated the land regulation of favelas, in the Law Project (*Projeto de Lei*) that governed the program. This enabled the adoption of legal provisions proposed in the revision of Public Law 6.766/79 and which had been stuck in Congress until this point. The initiative shows that the government could have taken advantage of the opportunity of creating this program to incorporate other strategies that fell under the institutional and urban-land departments of the PlanHab.

The results of the PMCMV 1

As predicted, the My House, My Life Program was an important resumption of massive housing production, but from the qualitative point of view it left much to be desired.

As shown in Table 8.3, between 2009 and 2010, the program contracted a total of 1,005,128 housing units in different forms. Of these, only 237,824 units had been delivered by 31 December 2010, and the remaining was still in the production phase. Altogether, these contracts totaled BRL 53.16 billion , including resources from the federal budget and from the FGTS (onerous and non-onerous). By the end of 2011, a total of 719,000 units had been delivered.

According to official data, which can be distorted by the omission of income declarations, the total number of contracted units which were destined to households earning up to three times the minimum wage (BRL 1,395) far exceeded the initial proposal of 400,000 and reached 571,321 units, or 42.8 percent more than the target that was originally provisioned for this income level, which is extremely positive.

Despite the positive performance in quantitative terms, the regional distribution was unbalanced since the number of units contracted in the Northeast in Level 1 (up to 3MW) represented 10.3 percent of the

Table 8.3   Contracted units of the My House My Life Program 1 by income level

Income level (minimum wage – MW)	Original goal (housing units)	Contracted housing units	Contracted relative to goal (%)
Up to 3MW	400,000	571,321	143
From 3 to 6MW	400,000	284,772	71
From 6 to 10MW	200,000	149,035	75
TOTAL	1,000,000	1,005,128	101

Source: Caixa Econômica Federal.

housing shortage in this bracket, and in the Southeast it only accounted for 6.1 percent. This discrepancy and the weak performance in the Southeast region, the most urbanized region of the country, and where the largest cities are concentrated, is evidence of the difficulty of viable housing solutions in metropolitan areas, where the cost of land bears greater weight and where it is necessary to design housing production with a more sophisticated funding and urban policy. This problem is a consequence of the lack of land and urban strategy in the program.

Although there are exceptions – high-quality housing projects embedded within the urban fabric – the vast majority of the projects of the PMCMV are located at the outskirts of cities, far from jobs and disconnected from the existing urban fabric or from urban expansion projects, with housing projects that lack architectural quality and identity within the local communities. Therefore, it can be said that the program, despite its success in regard to resuming housing production, suffers from the absence of a more consistent approach to addressing the urban issue.

It is no coincidence that an administration so esteemed as Lula'a, which on its first day created the Ministry of Cities with the vision of articulating urban policies, ended with a one billion reais building program. The administration succeeded in contributing an impressive subsidy, as had never happened before, to serve the low-income population. It did not, however, pay attention to important urban and land issues, and instead tackled the housing problem predominantly by constructing tiny houses and small apartment buildings on the urban periphery with projects of low architectural quality and poor planning.

This result is one of the consequences of the weakening of the Ministry of Cities which arose from the moment that it was sacrificed for a 'policy of governability', implying that it came to be directed by a political group that did not have a coherent program to address the complexity of the urban issue in Brazil but rather sought only to generate more of the same.

In July of 2005, Olívio Dutra was substituted by Márcio Fortes, who was appointed in the middle of the most severe political crisis of the Lula administration by the Popular Party (*Partido Popular*, PP) of which the president of the House at the time, Severino Cavalcanti, was a member. The change represented the beginning of the process of dismantling a department that sought to structure itself to exercise its role of formulator of a nationwide urban policy. In 2007, with the substitution of all national secretaries of the ministry appointed by Dutra, with the exception of the National Housing Secretary, this process unfortunately advanced even further. At the same time, it is important to note that the heart of the federal government, including the chief of staff's office, the Ministry of Finance, the Federal Savings Bank and the president himself, was all much more concerned to render quantitative results (direct impacts on the economy and generation of jobs and immediate political gains offered by the program) than the city project itself was, with its implicit focus on qualitative solutions.

In summary, it can be concluded, albeit contradictory, that the conditions for solving the housing problem in Brazil – especially from a financial perspective – became much more favorable from the moment Lula took office. However, the administration's success in effectively coping with the housing deficit is questionable. Despite the fact that the shortage may have formally been reduced, the urban and environmental effects may still exacerbate other urban problems such as transport mobility and pollution, contributing to the severe crisis that is faced by Brazilian cities.

From Lula to Dilma: PMCMV 2 and the great urban and housing challenges in Brazil

It is undisputable that Brazil has undergone a very interesting process of constructing a public policy in the area of urban and housing development. It is a true bottom-up policy that began in the 1980s. Social participation in this debate was intense and social actors, especially social movements and progressive technocrats, had a decisive role in the formulation of proposals and alternatives that contradicted the traditional logic of the sector.

Just as the housing policy was structured during the first Lula administration and went on to receive greater resources (that coincided with the change of management executives of the Ministry of Cities, with the departure of some of the key activists committed to this process), there was greater influence from the private sector and therein emerged the adoption of proposals that would distance the agenda from urban reform. This process culminated with the launch of the My House, My Life Program in 2009, where corporate interests weighed much more heavily than the historic allies of the Lula administration. This moment could be considered to be an inflection point, with the project changing from a bottom-up to a top-down public policy.

With its peculiar background in the construction of an urban and housing policy, and conducting itself in a participatory manner, Brazil could advance considerably beyond what was achieved in the first stage of the My House, My Life Program. The launch of a second stage of the program in 2011, during the Dilma administration, presented the opportunity to take one step beyond that which was realized by Lula. The quantitative goal established by the new government was even more ambitious: 2.4 million units, 1.4 million of which being dedicated to households with incomes up to three times the minimum wage, which meant a greater focus on that segment of social interest. During the first year of the new government, 457,000 units were contracted, a considerable result given that the regulation of the PMCMV 2 was only approved in the middle of 2011.

The great challenge that the Dilma administration faced was overcoming a restricted and disjointed vision of urban policy, where sectoral insulation predominates within the Ministry of Cities itself and where physical goals and quantitative results were objectives to be reached without observing qualitative aspects. The federal government, including the Ministry of Cities, did not yet possess the clarity of vision to realize that it was necessary to change the development model of Brazilian cities, which is based on social segregation, real estate speculation and prioritizing of economic interests linked to the supply of urban goods and services, such as the automobile industry, real estate developers, contractors of public works, urban transportation companies, etc.

For these reasons, there seemed to be no real commitment to forcing municipalities to break with this pattern, a shift that could be induced through the creation of stimuli and restrictions on the transfer of resources from the federal to the municipal level, for programs like My House, My Life. Without the interjection of the federal government, only the municipalities that have administrations which are conscientious about the need to create new development patterns, and which are capable of formulating a more consistent urban housing policy, will effectively benefit from the exceptional advantage (from a financial point of view) offered by the new housing policy introduced by Lula and continued by Dilma, in particular by subsidy and financing conditions.

In conclusion, it can be said that there is much to be done to advance the structure of a new urban housing policy that is consistent across the country. The necessary advances require a new management approach, with profound changes in the way that the Ministry of Cities is operated. It is this great challenge that the Dilma administration has not yet dared to face, while the situation of Brazilian cities continues to deteriorate.

It is worth quoting a phrase used frequently by Fernando Haddad in his victorious 2012 campaign for mayor of São Paulo: 'since Lula, life has improved a lot from the doorway into the house, but outside, the situation remains very difficult' (my translation) (Rede Brasil Atual, 2011). Though used in another context, the statement is succinct in describing the results of the new Brazilian housing policy: the housing conditions improved significantly for those who obtained housing and continue to be bad for those who didn't; for both, in the meantime, the urban conditions have become much worse. This is the great challenge that lays ahead for the coming years.

References

Aragão, J.M. (1999) *Sistema Financeiro da Habitação – Uma Análise Sócio-Jurídica da Gênese, Desenvolvimento e Crise do Sistema* (Curitiba: Juruá Editora).

Bonduki, N. (org.) (1997) *Habitat – Práticas Bem Sucedidas em Meio Ambiente, Habitação e Gestão Urbana nas Cidades Brasileiras* (São Paulo: Studio Nobel).

Bonduki, N. (1998a) *Origens da Habitação Social no Brasil* (São Paulo: Estação Liberdade).

Bonduki, N. (1998b) 'O Novo Papel do Município na Questão da Habitação', *Proposta 77* (Rio de Janeiro: FASE).

Bonduki, N. (2009) 'Do Projeto Moradia ao Programa Minha Casa, Minha Vida', *Teoria e Debate*. http://www.teoriaedebate.org.br/materias/ nacional/do-projeto-moradia-ao-programa-minha-casa-minha-vida

Bonduki, N. (2014) 'Os Pioneiros da Habitação Social no Brasil (São Paulo: Editora da UNESP/Editora SESC).

Carvalho, S. and Sobrinho, A. (1992) 'Notas sobre as Tendências Recentes da Política Nacional de Habitação Popular', *IX Congresso Nacional dos Sociólogos* (São Paulo.)

Instituto Cidadania. (2000) *Projeto Moradia* (São Paulo: Instituto Cidadania).

Instituto Via Pública. (2004) 'Diagnóstico de Políticas e Programas Habitacionais'. *Produto 01 de Prestação de consultoria à Secretaria Nacional de Habitação/Mcidades* (São Paulo).

Kingstone, P.R. and Power, T.J. (eds) (2000) *Democratic Brazil. Actors, Institutions, and Processes* (Pittsburgh: University of Pittsburgh Press).

Kingstone, P.R. and Power, T.J. (eds) (2008) *Democratic Brazil Revisited* (Pittsburgh: University of Pittsburgh Press).

Maleronka, C. (2004) *O Programa de Arrendamento Residencial e a habitação na área central*. São Paulo, Master Thesis (São Paulo: Instituto de Pesquisa Tecnologica).

Maricato, E. (1997) *Política Habitacional do Regime Militar* (Petrópolis: Vozes).

Maricato, E. (2001) *Brasil, Cidades: Alternativas para a Crise Urbana* (Petrópolis: Vozes).

Ministério das Cidades (2004) Política Nacional de Habitação, *Cadernos M.Cidades 4*.(Brasilia: Ministério das Cidades)

Ministério das Cidades. (2009a) *Plano Nacional de Habitação* (Brasília: Ministério das Cidades).

Ministério das Cidades. (2009b) *Programa Minha Casa, Minha Vida* (Brasília: Ministério das Cidades).

Ministério do Planejamento e Orçamento – Sepurb (1996a). *Principais Ações em Habitação 1995–9* (Brasília: MPO).

Ministério do Planejamento e Orçamento – Sepurb (1996b). *Política Nacional de Habitação* (Brasília: MPO).

Rede Brasil Atual. (2011) *Para Haddad Vida do Paulistano só Melhorou da Porta de Casa para Dentro*. http://brasilatual.jusbrasil.com.br/politica/8234984 date accessed in 2 February 2014

Stepan, A. (ed.) (1989) *Democratizing Brazil: Problems of Transition and Consolidation* (New York: Oxford University Press).

9
Social Inclusion in Rural Brazil under Lula

Antônio Marcio Buainain, Henrique Dantas Neder, and Junior Ruiz Garcia

Introduction

Historically, the rural population, rural areas and agriculture in general have been neglected economically, socially and politically in Brazil. As a consequence, the development gap between rural and urban territories widened throughout most of the twentieth century. Until quite recently, the massive concentration of poverty and extreme poverty in rural areas has been a key feature of Brazilian 'urban industrial' society. The Brazilian countryside is still stigmatized by certain features, such as highly skewed income and land tenure distribution; massive exploitation of an unprotected workforce, including children and 'modern' forms of slave labor; and landless workers struggling to survive amid the wide expansion of idle land held by private ownership. However, this picture is rapidly changing.

Brazilian agriculture and agribusiness are at the forefront of the recent and unprecedented surge of economic growth and income distribution; rural poverty as measured by income has fallen sharply since the mid-1990s, and in particular during Lula's administration. Conditions of living and welfare indicators have also improved in rural areas. It might not be an exaggeration to think that the neglected rural areas are taking the classic and positive role played by frontiers in today's developed countries. The development lag between urban and rural areas is still abysmal, but rural development policies adopted over the last 15 years might have triggered structural changes that will eventually breach the historical trend of social exclusion in rural areas. An examination of the rich set of databases of social and economic indicators in Brazil will reveal the unequivocal and unprecedented progress registered during Lula's two successive presidential terms.

This paper will provide an overall assessment of social and rural development policies under Lula, with a twofold approach: (1) tracing the roots, evolution and innovation of key rural policies implemented during Lula's administration, and asking to what extent those policies were a virtuous evolution of existing policies and institutions and to what extent they actually represent a break with past policies is still open to future discussion. (2) using official IBGE (Instituto Brasileiro de Geografia e Estatística) data, accredited statistical information, and recognized academic sources, this paper will also attempt to provide a more balanced account of achievements during the Lula administration regarding social inclusion in rural areas.

The paper will look critically at the official versions and eventually provide alternative interpretations and figures regarding the results, virtues and scope of selected social and rural development policies implemented between 2003 and 2010. Particular attention will be paid to the agrarian reform program, the family farm program (PRONAF) and the promotion of sustainable development of rural territories, which form the cornerstones of the rural development strategy adopted by the Lula administration. While it is important to recognize all of the merits of Lula's administration, academics – engaged or not with government and political parties – have the obligation to look critically at social processes and to separate what may be political propaganda from actual ongoing developments. That is the underlying philosophy of this chapter.

From poverty to social inclusion in rural areas

Brazil can be characterized as a changing country. In 1970 its population totaled 93 million (56 percent in urban areas and 44 percent in rural areas) and it had 17.6 million households (58 percent urban and 42 percent rural). Forty years later, in 2010, the number of households had jumped to 67.6 million and the total population was 190.8 million, with the vast majority (84 percent, or 161 million) living in urban areas (IBGE, 2012). Notwithstanding this high urbanization rate, almost 30 million people still live in rural areas, and the rural population is larger than the total populations of most Latin American countries. The countryside still plays an important role in the Brazilian economy: agriculture accounts on average for 6 percent of gross domestic product (CEPEA/USP/CNA, 2012) and directly employs about 28 million people (IBGE, 2006). A steadily growing proportion of the agricultural workforce lives in small urban centers that can be considered 'country townships'. If these townships (with less than 50,000 inhabitants) and their inhabitants were counted as 'rural', the rural population would rise to 34 percent of the total.[1]

To some extent, average per capita household income illustrates the structural changes undergone by the Brazilian population since the 1980s and the impact of public policy during the intervening period. A glance at Figure 9.1 suffices to highlight two patterns: first, the wide and abrupt variation in the level of average per capita income; and second, a moderate uptrend since 2003. However, it is striking that average per capita income in 2009 was still below the 1986 level.

Income inequality fell during this period, but not enough to remove Brazil from the list of the world's most unequal countries.[2] The number of people living in extreme poverty[3] in the countryside fell from 20.2 million in 1992 to 9.9 million in 2009 (Table 9.1). Although this decline intensified after the economy was stabilized, roughly half of it occurred under the Lula administration. Income concentration remains very high in rural areas, as do the numbers of people considered to be poor and extremely poor.

In 1992 the numbers of poor and extremely poor people in rural areas accounted for 84 percent and 67 percent of the total rural population respectively, compared with 55 percent and 33 percent respectively in 2009. The decline intensified from 2004 to 2009, a period that corresponds to part of President Lula's two terms in office.

The improvement in literacy rates can also be considered symptomatic of a change in individuals' basic capacity to exercise full citizenship, in this case through access to information, in particular regarding

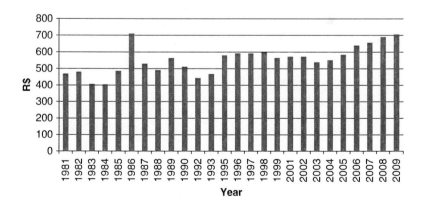

Figure 9.1 Evolution of household income per capita average BRL in Brazil, 1981–2009
Source: Prepared by the authors based on Ipeadata (2012).

Table 9.1   Number of people in extreme poverty, poverty, and Gini coefficient in rural areas in Brazil

Year	Extreme Poverty	Poverty	Extreme Poverty (%)	Poverty (%)	Gini coefficient
1992	20,179,998	25,188,482	67.2	83.9	0.5422
1998	17,758,772	23,607,573	56.7	75.3	0.5483
2004	14,997,433	21,460,595	49.3	70.6	0.5178
2009	9,926,354	16,527,467	33.0	54.9	0.4902

Source: Prepared by the authors based on PNADs microdata (National Survey by Household Sample) – IBGE.

legal rights. In 1991 the rate of illiteracy in rural areas was 39 percent, compared with 14 percent for the urban population. For the Northeast alone, however, it was 56 percent (IBGE, 2012). Rural illiteracy had fallen to 23 percent by 2010, although this remained much higher than the illiteracy rate for urban areas, which was then 7.1 percent. Despite this improvement, the situation is still far from satisfactory, as illustrated in the findings of IBGE's National Household Sample Survey (PNAD), according to which 41 percent of the rural population was functionally illiterate in 2009, compared to 17 percent of the urban population (Figure 9.2). Therefore, illiteracy in the countryside is not restricted to the poor but extends to a far larger proportion of the rural population, underscoring the anti-rural bias of Brazilian development.[4] It should be noted that on average 30 percent of the rural population works in precarious conditions, and this indicator has not improved significantly in recent years. Precarious work is defined here as poorly paid work (earning less than the minimum wage) or work performed without a formal employment relationship.

The pattern is similar for access to drinking water and electricity in rural areas: the proportions without both have fallen considerably but the deficit in each case remains very large. The proportion of the rural population living in extreme poverty without access to drinking water fell from 74 percent in 1992 to 50 percent in 2009. The proportion of households in rural areas without electricity also fell significantly, for all three income groups as well as for the total population. The improvement was the result of a major government initiative for rural areas, culminating in the Light for All Program (*Luz para Todos*).

In sum, improvements can be observed in practically all social indicators (see Figure 9.2 and Figure 9.3), which show that social development

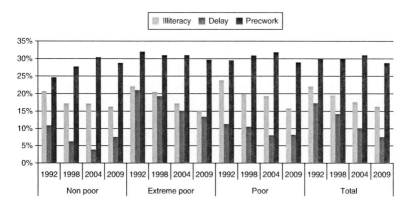

Figure 9.2 Evolution of illiteracy, students with schooling delay, and people in precarious works proportion in Brazilian rural areas, 1992–2009
Source: Prepared by the authors based on PNADs microdata (National Survey by Household Sample) – IBGE.
Note: illiteracy = proportion of illiterate people (above 14 years old); delay = proportion of students with schooling delay; precwork = proportion of precarious work (unregistered for less than minimum wage or unpaid).

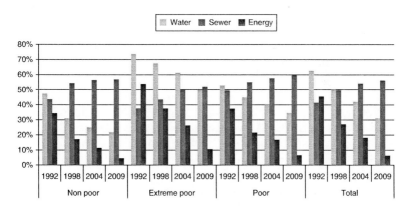

Figure 9.3 Evolution of the percentage of Brazilian rural households without access to water, sewage, and energy services, 1992–2009
Source: Prepared by the authors based on PNADs microdata (National Survey by Household Sample) – IBGE.
Note: water – proportions of households without water supply; sewer = proportion of households without appropriate sewage conditions; energy – proportion of households without energy.

in Brazil in the recent past has roots and trends that extend beyond any one particular federal administration and are explained by a development trajectory grounded in institutional changes dating from the late 1980s and early 1990s. From a multidimensional standpoint, the reduction in overall poverty, both rural and urban, has been uniform in the past few decades and is a process that began before the Lula era – influenced by the social advances enshrined in the 1988 Constitution – by the defeat of galloping inflation and by the economic and institutional reforms implemented in the last 20 years.

Social policy innovations and legacies

The public policy legacy and the political and institutional construction of public policies are more important than the numbers achieved. Therefore, no matter how the reforms and social policies introduced or expanded during the 1990s are appraised, no academic study can legitimately deny the importance of the innovations introduced and the institutional legacy bequeathed by the administration of President Fernando Henrique Cardoso (FHC) and those of his predecessors.

Notwithstanding the strength of the common view that Lula inherited a 'cursed legacy' and was therefore the godfather of the social progress registered during his terms in office, the bare data reviewed in the previous section suffices to at least raise doubts about whether or not the Lula administration signifies a turning point as far as the positive evolution of social progress is concerned. In our view Lula has received a 'blessed heritage' from the previous administrations – not only from Cardoso's – which, amid tremendous institutional, economic and political constraints, managed to set in motion a virtuous process of social progress and laid down the basic institutional and operational framework for the massification of social policies during the Lula administration. The recognition of a heritage of social problems but also of significant social and institutional progress does not reduce Lula's merits nor does it diminish the progress achieved during his two terms in office.

The 'blessed heritage' can be symbolized by a tripod, each leg built by a set of institutional reforms and economic and social policies and programs that were introduced in the late eighties and have since been revised, improved, reoriented and expanded by the successive governments that ruled the country in the last 30 years, including state and municipal administrations. The three legs are: (1) democratization and the 1988 Constitution, (2) macroeconomic and institutional reforms during the 1990s, and (3) social and sectorial policies introduced during the Cardoso Administration.

Re-democratization and the 1988 Constitution

The return to democracy after 1985 was undoubtedly the main positive institutional reform, which affected all others in the following decades. Approved in October 1988 as the 'Citizenship Constitution', the 1988 Constitution created and/or extended social and civil rights to the Brazilian population without identifying sustainable funding to ensure its proper enforcement. It soon became the 'Villain Constitution', blamed for the stagnation and successive inflationary crises experienced by the country until 1994, when the Plano Real was successfully enforced.[5]

Nevertheless, in the context of the ongoing re-democratization process, the legal definition of social rights created social and political dynamics that, irrespective of fiscal distortions and budget problems, established the pillars of the Brazilian social protection system that has since been built and that experienced significant expansion during the Lula years.

One of the most important constitutional legacies is the universalization of social security regardless of prior contribution.[6] The progressive enforcement of this right, irrespective of each government's will, was responsible for the inclusion of millions of families in both rural and urban areas, hitherto totally helpless, as beneficiaries of the social security system. It is largely a consensus amongst specialists that social security benefits are probably the most relevant factor behind the reduction of poverty and inequality, particularly in rural areas.

The inclusion of all rural workers in the social security system (Law No. 8.213/1991) foreseen in the Constitution, regardless of previous payment of contribution, was greatly important for the reduction of rural poverty and also helped to boost the local economy in many stagnant rural communities: local trade and agricultural production flourished with the injection of resources paid as pensions and retirement benefits to the elderly in rural areas. For example, in the state of Alagoas, cash transfers that included the social security benefits accounted for 40 to 99 percent of the GDP of the municipality in 1998 (Buainain *et al.*, 2009). The Constitution also laid down the foundation, defined policy instruments, assigned responsibilities amongst the federal and state governments, and set the limits for agricultural policy and land reform that would be implemented from the 1990s onwards, and which reached maturity during the Lula administration.

However, the Federal Constitution has by no means been implemented in its entirety. Far from it, in fact. Genuine recognition and enforcement of constitutional rights depend on the passage of legislation by Congress as well as action by the executive, and often by the judicial, branches. Social progress typically responds to political pressure from organized groups to defend vested interests and specific rights, alongside the political interests of Congress and the executive, rather than by virtue of the importance of such constitutional issues to society as a whole. Thus, governments were also responsible for building the social safety net and for the massification of social policies seen mainly during FHC's second term and both of Lula's terms.

Macroeconomic and institutional reforms in the 1990s

The second leg that supported the social progress during the Lula administration is the set of macroeconomic and institutional reforms implemented during the Cardoso administration. The most important was undoubtedly the Plano Real, which succeeded in stabilizing the national currency after 20 years of high inflation, two hyperinflationary crises and recurrent institutional breakdowns in the economy, which led to the moratorium of foreign debts in 1986 and the freezing of financial assets in 1990, including assets of small savers and retirees invested in the popular saving account *Caderneta de Poupança.*

The importance of stability is obvious: none of the social policies adopted would be effective without monetary stability. The recovery of the real minimum wage and the real income of workers, which began during the Cardoso administration and became one of the pillars of the new Brazilian middle class that emerged most clearly during the Lula administration, would have been thwarted by inflation, as had already happened in the past when several governments and trade unions attempted to raise wages above the current inflation rate. It is well known that high and accelerating inflation overrides the redistributive effects of public policies and produces the opposite effect of concentrating income.

The reforms allowed for the recovery of the Brazilian public sector from financial bankruptcy and from a pattern of erratic and ineffective intervention. In fact, following years of severe fiscal and institutional restructuring during the Cardoso administration, the State gradually regained the ability to spend, formulate and implement sustainable public policies, which were refined and expanded after 2003. It is also worthwhile highlighting the strengthening of the domestic financial sector, which gradually regained the ability to finance the expansion of domestic consumption, thereby supporting the welfare aspirations of families as they emerged from poverty.

Social and sectoral policies introduced during the FHC administration

Finally, the FHC administration introduced a set of social and sectoral public policies that, at the very least, facilitated the work of its successor. It is a well-known fact that the FHC administration established, in a disorganized manner, several income transfer and social protection programs for the poorest groups of the Brazilian population (for a balance of FHC Administration, see Giambiagi, Reis and Urani, 2004). FHC linked all programs under the umbrella of the Community of Solidarity (*Comunidade Solidária*) and then the Active Community (*Comunidade Ativa*), a component of the Alvorada Project (*Projeto Alvorada*) and the Brazilian Social Protection Network (*Rede Brasileira de Proteção Social*). These programs were important innovations that marked a divergence from the conditional cash transfer instruments articulated by *Comunidade Solidária*. The Brazilian Social Protection Network was based on a central registry, whose implementation began in 2001 under the operational responsibility of the Federal Savings Bank (*Caixa Econômica Federal*). Its aim was to coordinate the benefits hitherto granted haphazardly by a range of ministries and other government agencies, which had made the efforts to combat poverty less effective and failed to make a significant difference to the well-being of the families concerned. FHC's 2002 budget allocated 3 percent of GDP to spending on social protection in this broad sense and 6 million families are estimated to have benefited from these programs in the same year (Barros and Carvalho, 2004).

The main initiatives for the countryside were the Family Farming Support Program (PRONAF), launched in 1996, and the resumption of land reform.[7] In 2002, PRONAF distributed almost BRL 2.4 billion at current prices (Figure 9.4), benefitting 830,000 families (MDA, 2012). The two land reform programs are estimated to have settled 600,000 families during the FHC administration (INCRA, 2012). It is also important to mention the initiatives to assist debt restructuring by farmers in general and the reactivation of the public-sector farm loan program. Both were key drivers of the robust growth seen in the Brazilian agricultural sector during the first decade of the twenty-first century.

These experiences and innovations paved the way for the expansion of social policies that took place in the early years of Lula's first term.

Rural development and social policies under Lula: beyond the legacy

The Lula administration took office amid intense social conflicts in the countryside, particularly with regard to the prospects of land reform, which the social movements were criticizing strongly for their pace and scope. Theoretically, the rural development and anti-poverty policy adopted by the Lula administration rested upon four pillars: (1) land reform, (2) support for family farming, (3) social protection, and (4) investment to improve the quality of life for the rural poor.

In 2003 the Lula government launched the Second National Land Reform Plan (PNRA II), which defined land reform as urgently needed to transform society, create jobs, generate income and guarantee food security. The program's targets were ambitious and called for the settlement of at least 400,000 families by 2006, when Lula's first term was due to end (PNRA II, 2004). As noted below, this pillar received less attention and the achievements in land reform fell far short of the targets (see Figure 9.5).

The second pillar, support for family farming, occupied a central place in the Lula administration's rural development policy. PRONAF was financially reinforced, operationally enhanced and extended in terms of territory, situations and targeted beneficiaries. In addition, in its first year the administration launched new initiatives in this area, particularly the National Program for the Sustainable Development of Rural Territories (PRONAT), which resembled *Projeto Alvorada* in its main thrust – of linking up the federal government's interventions in poor territories and organizing marginalized social groups in those territories – to pursue an inclusive and sustainable local development agenda.

The third pillar consisted mainly of conditional cash transfer programs to combat rural poverty, spearheaded by *Bolsa Família* (a build-up of the National Social Assistance Program) and a widening of the scope of education and healthcare policies for rural areas.

The fourth pillar comprised a large number of interventions designed to reduce the deficits in access to public policy for the rural population in general, and its poorest members in particular, and to improve their living conditions by supplying water, electricity and housing. This always involved participation by state governments, using their own funds or via loans from multilateral lenders such as the World Bank, the Inter American Development Bank and IFAD (International Fund for Agricultural Development).

Initially, the Lula administration repackaged all its actions to combat rural poverty as part of Zero Hunger, which in practice was more of a movement to mobilize society behind a cause with strong emotional appeal (the fight against hunger) than a proper public policy with objectives, strategies, instruments and clearly-allocated resources. All government actions in the social area and those dedicated to promoting development were given the Zero Hunger hallmark and motivation, so much so that the program eventually became watered down by so many initiatives that it ceased to be effective. Toward the end of Lula's first year in office, it was replaced as the backbone of the administration's social policy by a return to conditional cash transfer programs.

Social protection and conditional cash transfer

It is impossible to discuss the reduction in rural poverty, or indeed the Lula administration's rural development policy as a whole, without highlighting the importance of the *Bolsa Família* Program (BFP) (see Wiesebron this volume).[8] During the Lula administration the number of families in the BPF jumped from 6.6 million enrolled in the previous programs to 12.8 million at the end of 2010. Moreover, while in the previous schemes the benefits were not regularly distributed, the BFP introduced monthly payments and all families received the full amount. In 2011, the program was attending to approximately 13.3 million families, which received a total contribution (transfer value) of BRL 17.4 billion (USD 8.58 billion) (MDS, 2012).[9] This may well be considered a case of dialectical qualitative leap whose positive impacts would not qualify without the extraordinary quantitative jump. In the rural areas, what made the difference was the fact that millions of families (entire poor rural communities) became beneficiaries of the BFP and now received cash transfers on a regular basis. This is a major breakthrough achieved by the Lula administration, the importance of which cannot be minimized by the previous existence of conditional income transfer programs. In fact, it is worthwhile emphasizing that building up the *Bolsa Família* represented a major political, operational, institutional and fiscal challenge that would only succeeded with the personal involvement and will of the President himself.

The BFP was particularly successful in targeting the extremely poor and poor rural families. It may be argued that this was not a planned policy result but rather a consequence of the need to expand the program within a stringent fiscal policy regime adopted during Lula's first term, which has shaped social policies. The motivation does not matter so much if the outcome is positive, as in this case.

Although the amount of cash paid to BFP beneficiaries each month is not enough to eradicate food insecurity for families living in extreme poverty (Ferreira de Souza, 2012),[10] the program's significance to rural families is qualitatively different from what it means to urban families. In the countryside, the program signifies a guaranteed monthly income for families without regular earnings, families who would otherwise have to migrate to find income between harvests or at times of adverse weather. In the past this migration emptied entire towns and villages. Moreover, the cash transfer is worth more in the countryside than in the town.

The BFP focuses undoubtedly on the poorest and most vulnerable families. Still, women constitute the majority among the beneficiaries of the BFP. This represents a major impact on community and family life in rural areas, where the role and status of women are historically underestimated and denied. This is a direct result of the targeting policy, which has set women as primary cardholders instead of the traditional head of household criteria. According to research carried out by IBASE (2008), 94 percent of the beneficiaries are women, with 85 percent of those being women between 15 and 49 years old and 27 percent being single mothers. Still, 78 percent of beneficiaries' households are located in urban areas and the Northeast region alone accounts for 50 percent of total rural households.

Support for family farming (PRONAF)

In 2006 Brazil had 4.27 million family farms according to that year's agricultural census (compared with 4.14 million in 1996). They represented 85 percent of all farms, occupied 24 percent of the area surveyed by the census, and provided livelihood for 12.3 million people. Most family farms in Brazil (2.28 million) are very small, with areas of less than ten hectares, while 52 percent are too small to keep the family above the poverty line (IBGE, 2006).

One of the key instruments deployed by the Lula administration to combat rural poverty and strengthen the income-generating capacity of the rural poor was the National Family Farming Support Program (PRONAF). The seed was sown in 1995 with the implementation of a program to provide cheap loans to small farmers. PRONAF was launched a year later by Decree 1946, issued on 28 June 1996. In 2003–04 PRONAF's budget exceeded BRL 4.5 billion (now about USD 2.2 billion); by 2009–10 it had risen to more than BRL 13 billion, and it is set to reach BRL 22.3 billion (USD11 billion) in 2012–13, from which some 2 million family farmers will benefit (MDA, 2012) (Figure 9.4).

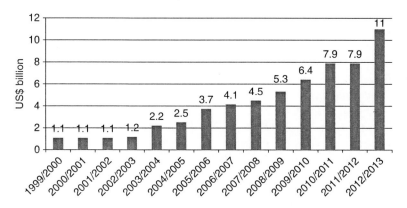

Figure 9.4 Amount of financial resources released by PRONAF, 1999/2000–2012/2013
Source: Prepared by the authors based on MDA, 2012.
Note: Exchange rate is the average of July 2012: BRL 2.028/USD1

PRONAF's objective is to enhance the production capacity of family farms, to foster employment and income in rural areas, and to reduce rural poverty and improve overall quality of life in rural areas. Its specific objectives are: the adjustment of public policies to the needs of family farms; the provision and improvement of rural infrastructure required for sustainable development of family farms; the strengthening of support services to family farms; the strengthening of family farmers' managerial and technological capacity; and the facilitation of family farmers' access to financing and support services. During Lula's terms the beneficiary group was extended to include rural households involved in non-agricultural activities; new and innovative funding mechanisms were also added to cope with different regional contexts and beneficiaries' socioeconomic profiles. Irrespective of its ambitions, PRONAF has remained, in essence, a rural credit program focused on family farming.

PRONAF expanded considerably in scale and scope during the Lula administration. Several other grants, allowances, and lines of credit were introduced for specific purposes and groups such as youth, women, fishermen, *quilombolas* (former runaway slaves), cottage industries and so on. In practice these facilities differed little from the program in general terms and conditions, but they played an important role in raising awareness and supporting a range of marginalized groups. They also served as a link for the leaders of the various groups, who were able to present themselves to their communities as empowered by the possibilities opened up by PRONAF and to the government as representatives of social movements that were dedicated to demanding that promises be kept and policies carried out fully, including disbursement of the promised funds. This practice, which permeated social policy management under Lula, may be one of the most innovative and democratizing aspects of the social policies implemented during the period.

Bridge loans[11] accounted for over 80 percent of the credit extended by PRONAF, while financing for investment – the real source of structural improvement and income growth for small farmers – played a secondary role. Therefore, despite all the support for and commitment to family farming, the Lula administration also failed to surmount the difficulty of financing investment for poor farmers who could not provide loan security because of the small scale on which they operated.[12] Nevertheless, the importance of bridge loans is far from negligible, as they helped farmers to keep producing and stay on the land, averting migration to the towns. PRONAF was indeed a significant step forward in agricultural policy and enabled the inclusion of millions of previously marginalized small farmers.

A survey conducted by Neder and Buainain (2012) to assess the impact of PRONAF on a range of economic and social indicators produced several important findings.[13] They showed, first of all, that in the Northeast the program had a positive impact on both the numbers employed by family farms and the value added by family farms. The survey also found that PRONAF reduced rural poverty, confirming that access to credit in poor areas reinforced the effects of policies such as cash transfer programs and the increase of the minimum wage, which are frequently seen as responsible for reducing poverty. For Brazil as a whole, the positive impact on employment growth and poverty reduction was weaker. This finding may appear paradoxical, since farmers in the North and Northeast are less organized and capitalized than elsewhere and do not receive the lion's share of PRONAF loans. The explanation may lie in the socio-economic profile of farmers in the South, who are more financially sound and operate more stable production systems, so that they mostly require PRONAF to finance investment rather than running costs. Although the tests did not show that PRONAF had a positive impact on employment growth or poverty reduction in the South, it cannot be inferred that access to credit is irrelevant without considering the counterfactual, that is to say what would have happened to employment and poverty if farmers had not had support from PRONAF. Based on historical experience, it can be argued that migration would have been significant and family farming would have shrunk, neither of which was the case. No significant impact on land concentration indicators was observed for the period from 1996 to 2006.

One of the consequences of the massification of PRONAF is that it raised the default level among family farmers, which incidentally is a general and traditional problem among Brazilian farmers. The payment delays result from poor harvests and falling prices due to the opportunistic attitude of farmer pressure groups that have enough political power to impose the renegotiation of rural debt payment terms and conditions and to gain advantages from the federal government during situations of crisis.

The findings confirmed the conclusions of previous surveys (Guanziroli, 2007; Guanziroli, Buainain and Sabbato, 2012), that production-financing policies alone lack sufficient force to drive significant change in the structure of land ownership. One of the reasons given is that poor farmers, even with access to credit, remain subject to a range of insufficiencies and risks that reduce their production capacity, income and accumulation. Moreover, they are frequently forced to take losses due to adverse weather, natural disasters or market factors, all of which tend to offset the accumulation achieved during good years, have severe adverse effects on family wealth and capital, and erode their capacity to generate income.

In fact, one of the most serious problems faced by small producers is the high risk associated with climate, market conditions and family health. Small producers are generally unprotected by traditional risk management strategies. A bad harvest may be enough to undo years of effort, a disease may consume all family assets accumulated over years of hard work and sacrifice, or a slight drop in prices may force small farmers to face the dilemma of defaulting or cutting down household consumption, which may already be too low. The family and community safety nets are important, but not sufficient to significantly avoid and reduce the negative effects of these events.

Rural insurance, assistance and extension programs

Here it is relevant to mention two of the main innovations introduced by PRONAF during the Lula administration: first, reactivation of PROAGRO, an insurance program focusing on family farmers that had been practically left dormant; and second, a crop insurance program (*Seguro Safra*) designed specifically for family farmers in the semi-arid areas of the Northeast, who suffer most from the effects of the region's frequent droughts. Its aim is to mitigate the effects of crop losses due to drought or excessive rain. It benefits only the poorest regions (the Northeast, northern Minas Gerais and northern Espírito Santo). Municipal governments and small farmers are eligible if they contribute matching funds equivalent to 1 percent of the forecast annual benefit as estimated by a steering committee (MDA, 2012).

The program expanded rapidly during the decade in terms of both the number of municipalities and the number of farmers benefited. In 2002, 333 municipalities and 200,000 farmers participated, rising to 859 municipalities and 662,000 farmers by 2009–10. It continued to expand after the end of Lula's second term, covering more than 771,000 farmers in the 2010–11 crop year (MDA, 2012). The number of family farmers who participated throughout the period from 2003 to 2010 totaled about 3.1 million, with 2 million reporting proven crop losses and receiving support from the crop insurance program (Presidência da República, 2012). The program pays out up to six times the minimum wage in monthly installments as compensation for crop losses due to drought. It temporarily reduced migration in periods of drought and enabled farmers to survive until the time came to sow the next crop.

The PROAGRO Family Farm Insurance (SEAF) was created in 2004 and since then it has benefited more than 600,000 family farmers and paid over BRL 200 million per year as compensation (USD 68.4 million). The amounts insured by SEAF rose from BRL 2.5 billion to BRL 4.8 billion (USD 1.4 billion to USD 2.7 billion). From the 2010–11 harvest, the farmers had a secure climate for investment (MDA, 2012).

There were also initiatives to bolster agricultural extension, but these gained scope only at the end of Lula's second term with the discussion (and approval in 2010) of the National Policy of Technical Assistance and Agricultural Extension for Family Farming and Land Reform (Pnater).[14] Nevertheless, the frequency with which farmers across Brazil resort to technical assistance is extremely low. According to the 2006 Agricultural Census, only 22 percent (1.1 million) had received some form of technical assistance at the time; of these, 337,000 had farms of less than ten hectares (IBGE, 2012). Moreover, the poor quality of technical assistance is widely recognized. Typically it is limited to one or two short visits by technicians during an entire year, rather than continuing supervision and guidance to foster the adoption of innovations.

Food purchasing and the *Mais Alimento* (More Food) programs

Another very important strategy adopted by the government was the creation of secure markets for family farm production. This followed previous initiatives of state and local governments that occasionally purchased food from local smallholders, either for distribution or for use in schools, hospitals, prisons and so on. The Food Purchasing Program (PAA), launched in 2003 under the Zero Hunger umbrella, institutionalized this support for family farming and has since been one of the strongest drivers for new investments by organized groups of family farmers. Although research has not yet been done to prove this, a guaranteed market for family farm products can be said to have had a significant impact in all regions of Brazil, enabling many areas that had fallen into decline because of the family farming crisis to recover and gain strength. The outstanding example is the dairy industry. Family producers who had been forced out of business by the big dairy combines and by imports at prices distorted by developed-country policies were back in business and were responsible for almost 58 percent of total milk production in 2006 (IBGE, 2006).

Federal Law number 10,696 (July 2nd, 2003) established the PAA, whose main objectives are: (1) to ensure access to food in quantity and regularity for the populations vulnerable to food insecurity; (2) to contribute to the formation of strategic stocks; (3) to enable farmers to store their products; and (4) to promote social inclusion. The main actions of PAA are formation of stocks and direct purchase from family farming (MDA, 2012). From 2003 to 2010 the government allocated around BRL 3.4 billion (USD 1.7 billion) to PAA, benefiting on average 118,154 families per year in 25 Brazilian states and attending to an average of 10.4 million people per year facing food insecurity (MDA, 2012). In 2011, the Brazilian government purchased, under the PAA, around 492,000 tons of food from 162,283 family farmers (MDS, 2012).

In the same context another interesting initiative is the More Food Program (*Mais Alimentos*). Launched in 2008, the program aims to stimulate the supply of agricultural products by family farmers in general, and targets precisely those groups that are struggling to respond to the incentives offered by the program mentioned above. More Food finances investment in infrastructure and equipment, which is expected to have a direct impact on production capacity and productivity. In the 2008–09 and 2009–10 crop years the program disbursed BRL 3.58 billion to more than 85,000 farmers (Presidência da República, 2012).

In particular, significant progress has been achieved in the promotion of access of small farmers to governmental food purchases. The purchase of food produced by smallholding/family farmers by public institutions and programs (food distribution programs, hospitals, schools, military forces and so on) had, in many areas, a positive impact on smallholding farmers. It triggered institutional mobilization of small producers for additional resources and support to respond to this market opportunity. In many rural territories small producers have regained market share in value chains in which they have traditionally participated, and in some cases they have even increased their role in relevant local markets.

The access to public food purchases (institutional markets) has played a catalytic role in combining several so-far isolated initiatives, such as the operating credit, focalized investments in plots and in strategic associations'/cooperatives' assets (such as refrigerated milk reception posts to collect scattered production), and guaranteed price. The main problem is the very low ceiling on the amount that each producer can sell under the program scheme. It is indeed too low and does not even ensure an income level above the poverty line for the very poor, and it restricts growth of the more dynamic ones who could lead a local accumulation process amongst smallholders.

Agrarian policy: the land reform program on hold

In spite of radical promises before being elected, the agricultural and rural development policies introduced before and during the Lula administration have not significantly changed the structure of land ownership, which remains highly concentrated. As a result, income inequality in the agricultural sector is also very severe. In the period from 1995 to 2008, about 80 million hectares were compulsorily purchased for land reform and almost 1 million families were settled during this relatively short time. Today, according to INCRA's (Instituto Nacional de Colonização e Reforma Agrária) official statistics, there are an estimated 8,360 land reform settlements with a population of 1,119,000 families (INCRA, 2012). Despite these impressive figures, the traditionally skewed pattern of land tenure remains unaffected, as shown by the Gini coefficient, which was 0.857 in 1985 and 0.854 in 2006 (Hoffmann and Ney, 2010). This finding can be interpreted in two ways: it is evidence either of the government's reluctance to tackle structural imbalances in the countryside or of the ineffectiveness of compulsory land redistribution to promote structural change in land ownership patterns.

In 1993 the Brazilian government resumed the agrarian reform initiative[15] (Emergency Settlement Program) and has since settled over 1 million of the families in agrarian reform projects[16] (Figure 9.5). In Brazil, the basic objective of agrarian reform is to reduce the concentration of land ownership and to promote access to land for landless workers and small producers or for those with insufficient land. The direct beneficiaries of agrarian land are the landless, small farmers, traditional rural communities, riverside populations (affected by dams and other major

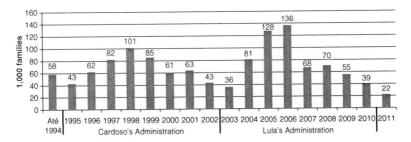

Figure 9.5 Families settled between 1994 and 2011
Source: Prepared by the authors based on INCRA (2012).

infrastructure works), non-Indian occupants of the indigenous areas, rural women, young workers and other groups.

The Brazilian government has four basic instruments of intervention: (1) the expropriation of unproductive estates for agrarian reform (traditional agrarian reform program) carried out by INCRA; (2) financing acquisition of land by organized farmers (Market-assisted land reform (MALR)); (3) direct acquisition of land for distribution, carried out by INCRA and state institutions in special cases (Decree 433, 1992); and (4) settlement on public land owned by the Brazilian government.

In the period from 2003 to 2010 the federal government settled approximately 614,000 families in 3,551 land reform projects with a total area of 48.3 million hectares (Figure 9.5). These results were achieved at a cost of BRL 7.45 billion in that period (INCRA, 2012). The land reform program has come under heavy fire both from traditional critics and from allies, especially from the social movements that have close links with the ruling Workers' Party (PT) and which have always supported Lula and other PT leaders.

The critics point out that most of the families to which land has been given under the land reform program are in the North (305,000 families) and Northeast (186,000) (INCRA, 2012), in territories considered fragile from an environmental standpoint and, at least in the North, lacking in infrastructure. Practically all land reform settlements in the Northeast are located in chronically drought-stricken areas subject to accelerating desertification and likely to be severely affected by climate change (PAN-Brasil, 2004). Moreover, compulsory purchases and settlements were driven by a dynamics determined by land disputes instead of ushering in an era of properly planned settlement, as promised by the second National Land Reform Plan (PNRA II). One of the results is the predominance of very small holdings so as to make room for large numbers of families on these settlements. Technically speaking, these very small holdings cannot support family reproduction and indeed are smaller than the legal minimum established by INCRA itself for the purposes of registering rural properties. In the opposite camp, the allies, who have put down their weapons and ceased holding noisy demonstrations as they did during the FHC administration, complain mainly of the slow pace of land reform, as well as a lack of attention and even abandonment, especially after Lula's re-election. The evidence suggests that the Lula administration decided to put the land reform program on hold to take stock, taking much longer to approve new projects and leveraging the decompression created by the upswing in the business cycle and massification of social protection policies.

National Land Credit Program (PNCF)

The National Land Credit Program (PNCF) was created in 2002 as a continuation of the *Cédula da Terra* Pilot Program and the Land Bank, launched in 1997 and 1998 respectively. All of these programs followed the so-called market-assisted land reform approach introduced by the World Bank in the 1990s and aimed at improving access of poor and small farmers to land through land purchase rather than land redistribution. In Brazil they should complement – not replace – the so-called traditional 'expropriation-redistribution' program implemented by INCRA. *Cédula da Terra* and then *Crédito Fundiário* supported poor landless families' claims to land through the provision of subsidized loans to enable the purchase of land by poor families and of non-refundable funds to invest in productive infrastructure on the acquired lands.

The coexistence of both 'traditional' and 'market assisted' programs has never been peaceful and the implementation of the PNCF, under clear political influence of the Rural Workers' National Confederation (CONTAG), has always been questioned by the Landless Workers' Movement (MST). The eligibility criteria for the PNCF and INCRA are pretty much the same, and in 2006 the PNCP defined as eligible all rural families with proven agricultural experience, earning less than BRL 9,000 per year and with total assets below BRL 15,000. As a compromise between CONTAG and MST, unproductive land that may be subject to compulsory purchase by INCRA under the agrarian reform rules is excluded from *Crédito Fundiário* operations.

Crédito Fundiario operates two lines of action: the first is the Rural Poverty (CPR) component, which provides credit to land purchase and a basket of credit and non-refundable funds for investments in productive assets (infrastructure and equipment) for the use of the entire group of beneficiaries; the second line is the Family Agriculture Strengthening Credit (CAF), which replaced the Land Bank Program and provides credit for land purchase without additional resources for investments. While the CPR line is focused on the poorest families, and operates almost exclusively in the Northeast and Northern regions, the CAF line is also open to the participation of small family farmers with insufficient land. Another difference is that the CPR allocates funds to associations of beneficiaries whereas the CAF provides loans to families within the target group.

The quantitative achievements of PNCF are far from 'inexpressive', as claimed by MST. From 2003 to 2010 a total of 83,000 families purchased a plot of land through the program. Almost 1.4 million hectares were transferred and redistributed through land market operations funded by PNCF, as shown in Table 9.2. And the impact is rather positive, as there is evidence that beneficiaries have increased their income after joining the program. Ferreira, Sielawa and Helfand (2013) carried out an evaluation of PNCF and concluded that 'the program achieved the first part of its primary objective – to create productive activities – through the evidence of increased total agricultural production for program beneficiaries, which is in fact causing an increase at least within the first six years of land ownership'. The authors concluded that during the last

Table 9.2 National Land Credit Program *(Programa Nacional de Crédito Fundiário –* PNCF), 2003–10

Year	CPR		CAF	
	Families	Area (ha)	Families	Area (ha)
2003	4,310	98,996	4,597	69,255
2004	6,006	125,735	97	1,452
2005	7,309	144,199	2,141	23,644
2006	8,842	173,619	7,611	77,202
2007	7,463	152,590	10,589	121,330
2008	4,301	85,728	7,786	101,341
2009	405	8,555	5,790	87,487
2010	2,265	43,722	4,277	59,463
Total	40,901	833,144	42,888	541,174

Source: Prepared by the authors based on MDA (2012).

year, 'total agricultural production – not including any of the costs – increased to an average of BRL 539.74 per person in the household after four years of land ownership'.

National Program for the Sustainable Development of Rural Territories (PRONAT)

Another innovation introduced by the Lula administration was the National Program for the Sustainable Development of Rural Territories (PRONAT). The Territorial Development Department created in 2003 by the Ministry of Agrarian Development (SDT/MDA) identified 116 poor rural territories with a high concentration of family farmers, and embarked upon a campaign of mobilization and social organization that gave rise to PRONAT. The program's aim was to promote planning, implementation and self-management for sustainable development in rural territories. It does so mainly by fostering social management of the territories concerned, bolstering their social capital, reactivating their economies, and building bridges between institutions. PRONAT is present in 164 rural territories throughout Brazil (MDA, 2012), covering 2,500 municipalities with an aggregate population of 52.2 million people. These territories account for 61 percent of the direct beneficiaries of the government's actions via MDA. In 2010 the amount disbursed under this program is estimated to have reached BRL 323 million (Presidência da República, 2012). One of PRONAT's subprograms, called Identity Territories, aims to identify the defining characteristics of rural territories as a basis for strategy and action.

Despite few instruments for action and scant public policy coordinating capacity, PRONAT played an important role in disseminating the territorial approach and creating conditions for the development of the Territories of Citizenship Program, launched in 2008 under the direct responsibility of the Office of the Presidential Chief of Staff, which has ministerial status and is the most powerful portfolio in a Brazilian president's cabinet.

Territories of Citizenship seeks to promote economic development and universal access to basic citizenship programs in poor rural territories. The underlying concept is that territorial development is essential to any effort to combat rural poverty. Execution of the program depends on social participation and integrated action by the federal, state and municipal governments. A rural territory is defined as a group of municipalities that share a sociocultural identity as well as having the same economic and environmental profile. The program covers 120 territories, 57 of which are in the Northeast (Portal da Cidadania, 2011).

The Food Purchasing Program (PAA), which supports family farming, is part of a subdivision of Territories of Citizenship called Sustainable Organization of Production.

A balance sheet of achievements and gaps

Table 9.3 summarizes in simplified form the trajectory of the main rural-related social policy instruments and the progress achieved by different governments since the democratization process started in Brazil. It shows that the programs were enhanced and extended by each administration, alongside the implementation of new programs, either in response to new social pressures or owing to operational problems, ineffectiveness or lack of sustainability in the case of some initiatives. The Lula administration was no exception. In several cases it introduced important reforms. In education, for example, it replaced the Primary Education Development Fund (FUNDEF) with the Basic Education Development Fund (FUNDEB), thereby extending the scope of funding for education, a necessary step to respond to the very success of FUNDEF. The latter had achieved universal access to primary education and this in turn required the strengthening of both preschool and secondary education. Another striking example was reform of the income transfer programs in place, engineered by merging them all into one program to do away with the fragmentation of actions and benefits that reduced their positive effects and made the transfer of income less effective.

In other areas the Lula administration combined extension of scope with important innovations. An example is PRONAF, described above. Perhaps the most significant contribution of the Lula administration was to give social policy a special place on the public policy agenda, so that it ceased to be treated as an appendix of other policies. Social protection policies, with the conditional cash transfer programs at their heart – and promoting inclusion for the rural poor centering on PRONAF – were prioritized at the expense of other social policies.

Despite all these efforts the rural poor have not yet reaped the full benefits of social protection, as illustrated by the survey of 'invisibles' conducted by Brazil Without Poverty (*Brasil sem Miséria*), a national poverty alleviation plan launched by President Dilma Rousseff in 2011.

Considerable progress has been achieved but at different speeds and to varying extents in different areas. A much larger proportion of rural poor now have electricity, but the same is not true of sanitation,

Table 9.3 Social protection for rural population and rural development policies

Public Policies Realm	1985–1988	1995–1998	1999–2002	2003-2010	2011 ...
Education	Reformed	Partially reformed	Partially Reformed (**)	Partially Reformed (**)	Continued
Health	Reformed	Implemented	Partially Reformed (***)	Partially Reformed (**)	Continued
Rural Retirement/Pension	Incorporated	Implemented	Expanded (***)	Expanded (***)	Continued
Social Assistance/Care	Reformed	Implemented	Expanded (*)	Expanded (**)	Expanded (*)
Rural Development[1]				Created	Maintained
Pronaf		Created	Expanded (*)	Expanded(***)	Expanded (*)
Cash Transfer[2]		Created	Expanded (*)	Reformed and Expanded (***)	Expanded (*)
Agrarian Reform		Relaunched	Reformed and Expanded (**)	Reduced (*)	Reduced (**)
Programas de PAA etc.				Created	Continued
Pronat				Created	Descontinued
Crop Insurance (*SeguroSafra*)[3]				Created	Expanded
Brazil without Misery (*BrasilsemMiséria*)					Created

Source: Prepared by the authors based on Draibe (2003).

The number of asterisks (*, **, ***) indicates the intensity and depth of the reform and its coverage in terms of numbers of beneficiaries.

Note: (1) Include Programa Mais Alimentos, Programa de Aquisição de Alimentos (PAA); (2) Bolsa Escola, Vale Gás, Bolsa Alimentação, Bolsa Família, Cartão Alimentação; (3) Programa Garantia-Safra e Seguro da Agricultura Familiar (SEAF).

which remains deficient or entirely absent for many rural households. According to official figures, more than 500,000 rural households are not included in healthcare programs and a similar number of rural families are not covered by any public policies, so that they are completely excluded from the social protection system and rural development policies (Brasil sem Miséria, 2012).

Noteworthy progress has also been achieved in labor legislation enforcement, although much still remains to be done. Informality in the rural labor market is still significant, and there is no social protection for workers employed by family farmers. The latter issue is hard to solve under the existing legal framework and with the social protection instruments currently available.

Another gap relates to redistribution of income in rural areas. During the 2001–09 period, the growth in income accounted for approximately 80 percent of total rural poverty variation. Other research shows that incomes have risen among the rural poor thanks much more to retirement payments and cash transfer programs than to growth in earnings from agricultural production or employment (Neder, 2008). Given that these cash transfer programs are close to the limit in terms of the number of potential beneficiaries, further improvements in the welfare of the rural population will depend on their income-generating capacity and on access to social policies and their quality. This is true in general, but particularly so for health, education, housing and sanitation.

Bolsa Família is a mechanism for intervening *a posteriori* and is designed to reduce the negative effects of poverty rather than to eradicate poverty itself. The main vulnerability of the rural poor in Brazil is precisely the weakness of policies that prevent poverty risk, that is, policies that seek to prevent families in situations of vulnerability from becoming poor or extremely poor. It is a paradox that while most rural poor still spend their lives largely unprotected, those who survive to retirement age will receive a pension, the value of which exceeds the income earned by most when they were healthy enough to do paid work. Similarly for the youngest families – those with school-age children – who will receive the allowance, while couples without children or with adolescent children are unprotected. Even with the recent growth of formal labor relations in rural areas, a significant proportion that amounts to roughly 73 percent of the workforce and over half the wage-earning population, continue to work in the informal sector without any kind of safety net. Thus, a large contingent remains outside the public pension system, without rights to retirement pensions, health services, unemployment insurance and so on.

Another problem associated with social policies in Brazil, especially in rural areas, is intense fragmentation or lack of articulation. Interests and investments are still highly dispersed. Poverty takes multiple forms, from insufficient property and income to lack of qualifications, lack of access to public policy, lack of opportunities, and lack of citizenship in general. These lacks and insufficiencies are mostly addressed by specific sectorial and social policies without an overarching logic or framework grounded in a well-organized strategic plan.

Actions to promote development and combat rural poverty in Brazil have always been fragmented, comprising initiatives by multiple institutions and policies that endeavor to address the various facets of poverty without coordination or integration. However, the conditional cash transfer program in place is a promising embryo of the necessary coordination and integration, because it addresses two significant dimensions of poverty: extreme lack of income and lack of access to education. The Territories of Citizenship Program also points in the direction of building coordination mechanisms for the implementation of policies and programs originally designed with an essentially sectorial logic.

The post-Lula era: Brazil without poverty and the challenges facing Dilma

It can be said that the FHC administration laid the foundations for the programs now in place to combat rural poverty, which were massified by the Lula administration and extended to cover protection and productive inclusion. The Dilma administration is refining the legacy with two aims: to fill the gaps in the safety net and to make productive inclusion of the poor more effective through coordinated education and training policies. In this context it is possible to identify two main axes of Brazil's anti-poverty efforts. One is the explicit continuity of social policy reforms under the Lula administration. The other is a focus on the population living in extreme poverty, which amounts to more than 16 million people, 47 percent of whom are in rural areas (Brasil Sem Miséria, 2012). *Brasil Sem Miséria* was implemented with the latter in mind.

Brasil Sem Miséria breaks new ground compared with other anti-poverty programs, which award benefits in response to applications from families. The strategy underlying *Brasil Sem Miséria* is to reach out to citizens living in extreme poverty, most of whom are 'invisible' – not only because they do not even have identity papers – to understand their needs and potential, and to include them in protection and training programs designed to help them bootstrap themselves out of poverty. *Brasil Sem Miséria* comprises a set of global and regional subprograms. The global elements do not depend on regional characteristics, like those of the *Bolsa Família* as well as health and education programs, because these are basic rights for all citizens. The regional elements take into account the differences between town and country, given that conditions in rural and urban areas are different, and are based on three pillars: (1) guaranteed income, (2) productive inclusion and (3) public services. Specifically for rural areas, the highlights are technical assistance, funding and seed capital, the Water for All Program, market access, government purchasing of produce via the Food Purchasing Program (PAA), *Bolsa Verde* and so on. For urban areas the highlights are opportunity mapping and vocational training (Brasil Sem Miséria, 2012).

It is too soon to evaluate the strategy and results of the policies adopted by the Dilma administration. The government is clearly finding it hard to reform and enhance what exists without creating internal friction, but there would appear to be no doubt that adjustments are being made to improve the effectiveness and efficiency of social intervention. It is also undeniable that the scope of many programs is being extended while other programs, such as land reform, are on hold. Thus the major challenges of anti-poverty in Brazil are still to be addressed. They include improving public policy articulation and integration, sustaining the dynamics of specific programs, extending technical assistance to the poorest farmers, and increasing the amount of financing available for investment in agricultural properties, among others.

Notes

1. Brazil has 5,565 municipalities, 4,957 with a total population of less than 50,000 people.
2. The Gini coefficient improved from 0.584 in 1981 to 0.543 in 2009 (Ipeadata, 2012), but remains very high. In rural areas, inequality measured by the Gini coefficient fell from 0.542 in 1992 to 0.49 in 2009 (Table 9.1).
3. In Brazil, poverty is typically defined solely on the basis of personal income. Anyone who earns between 25 percent and 50 percent of the minimum wage is considered poor, while those living on less than 25 percent of the minimum wage are considered extremely poor.
4. The quality of the formal education delivered by public schools in Brazil is still low. Not only has it not significantly improved in recent decades, but it has failed to address in an appropriate manner the effects of poverty on teaching and learning (see Schwartzman and Bacha, 2012).

5. Irrespective of its virtues and defects, which are many, the 1988 Constitution was instrumental in the transition to democracy: in regulating simultaneously 'for and against' in almost all relevant issues, it reflected a divided society after decades of military rule, prevented polarization from exploding into open conflicts and obliged social groups to negotiate within the limits of democracy.

6. Social security expenditure was indeed responsible for the rise of social spending and has contributed to unsustainable public deficits that fuelled hyperinflation in Brazil at the beginning of the 1990s. It is still a major source of concern for fiscal policy in Brazil.

7. The basic land reform instruments are compulsory purchase of unproductive land for redistribution by INCRA to poor families (the traditional land reform programme), loans for associations of small farmers to buy land (market-assisted land reform), normal purchase of land for distribution by INCRA or other state institutions (Decree 433, 1992), and settlement on government-owned land.

8. *Bolsa Família* was launched in 2003 as a merger of four federal cash transfer programmes created during the FHC administration: *Bolsa Escola, Bolsa Alimentação, Auxílio Gás* and *Cartão Alimentação*.

9. Though one of the breakthroughs is actually the scale of its scope, it would be a misleading simplification to consider the BFP as a mere enlarged continuation of *Bolsa Escola*. In fact, in this kind of programme, the immediate goal of which is to provide basic shelter to the poorest, scale makes all the difference. The argument that scale does matter is applicable to almost any rural development policies 'inherited' by Lula from his predecessors. In fact, the change in scale by itself represents a breakthrough from past experiences.

10. Simulations show that the cash transferred to a typical family of two adults and two children corresponds in terms of purchasing power per person to only about 35 percent of the basket of food staples' (*cesta básica*) established by law in 1938 and still monitored today by DIEESE (2011). See for example Ferreira de Souza (2012).

11. Bridge loans help farmers cover running costs between harvests (inputs, electricity, and so forth).

12. Assets such as land, buildings, plant, equipment, and so forth.

13. Spatial econometric models with instrumental variables applied to census data were used for impact assessment.

14. Pnater was launched in 2010 together with Pronater, the corresponding programme. This new institutional framework enabled technical assistance and agricultural extension services to be provided by for-profit or non-profit organizations in the public or private sector via competitive bidding. The main aim of the model is to assure the continuity of these services. Since the policy and programme were launched, the government has accredited 437 organizations with over 18,000 technicians (Presidência da República, 2012).

15. Based on II Plano Nacional de Reforma Agrária (PNRA II, 2004).

16. The official numbers are subject to strong controversy. Still, all sources estimate that in 16 years of administrations of FHC (1995–2002) and Lula da Silva (2003–10) around 1.2 million of the families were settled, half in each administration.

References

Barros, R.P. and Carvalho, M. (2004) 'Desafios para a Política Social Brasileira', in F. Giambiagi, J.G. Reis and A. Urani (eds), *Reformas no Brasil: Balanço e Agenda* (Rio de Janeiro: Nova Fronteira).

Brasil sem Miséria. (2012) *Plano Brasil sem Miséria*. www.brasilsemmiseria.gov.br date accessed 14 August 2012.

Buainain, A.M. Braga, B. Garcia, J.R. and Buainain, V.P. (2009) 'Diálogo de Políticas para Inclusão Social e Produtiva em Alagoas: Pontos para Reflexão e Debate', paper prepared for the *Inter American Development Bank (IDB)*.

CEPEA/USP/CNA. (2012) *Agribusiness GDP – 1994 to 2011*. www.cepea.esalq.usp.br/pib date accessed 5 January 2012.

DIEESE. (2011) *Política de Valorização do Salário Mínimo*, nota técnica 93. portal.mte.gov.br date accessed 14 August 2012.

Draibe, S. (2003) 'A Política Social no Período FHC e o Sistema de Proteção Social', *Tempo Social* 15(2): 63–101.

Ferreira de Souza, P.H.G. (2012) 'Poverty, Inequality and Social Policies in Brazil, 1995–2009', Working Paper 87, *International Policy Centre for Inclusive Growth*. http://www.ipc-undp.org/pub/IPCWorkingPaper87.pdf date accessed 14 December 2012.

Ferreira, V. Sielawa, H. and Helfand, S. (2013) 'A Matter of Time: An Impact Evaluation of the Programa Nacional de Crédito Fundiário', *Working Paper*, University of California Riverside.

Giambiagi, F. Reis, J.G. and Urani, A. (eds) (2004) *Reformas no Brasil: Balanço e Agenda* (Rio de Janeiro: Nova Fronteira).

Guanziroli, C.E. (2007) 'Pronaf Dez Anos Depois: Resultados e Perspectivas para o Desenvolvimento Rural', *Revista de Economia e Sociologia Rural* 45(2): 301–328.

Guanziroli, C.E. Buainain, A.M. and Di Sabbato, A. (2012) 'Dez Anos de Evolução da Agricultura Familiar no Brasil: (1996 e 2006), *Revista de Economia e Sociologia Rural* 50(2): 351–370.

Hoffmann, R. and Ney, M.G. (2010) 'Evolução Recente da Estrutura Fundiária e Propriedade Rural no Brasil', in J.G. Gasques, J.E. Vieira Filho and Z. Navarro (eds), *A Agricultura Brasileira: Desempenho, Desafios e Perspectivas* (Brasília: IPEA).

IBASE. (2008) *Repercussões do Programa Bolsa Família na Segurança Alimentar e Nutricional das Famílias Beneficiadas*. www.ibase.br (home page) date accessed 14 February 2011.

IBGE. (2006) *Censo Agropecuário – 2006*. www.ibge.gov.br (home page) date accessed 14 July 2012.

IBGE. (2012) *Sistema IBGE de Recuperação Automática – Sidra*. www.ibge.gov.br (home page) date accessed 14 July 2012.

INCRA. (2012) *Famílias Assentadas: 1994–2011*. www.incra.gov.br (home page) date accessed 14 August 2012.

Ipeadata. (2012) *Ipeadata Social*. www.ipeadata.gov.br (home page), date accessed 14 July 2012.

MDA. (2012) *Programas*. www.mda.gov.br (home page), date accessed 14 August 2012.

MDS. (2012) *Bolsa Família*. Ministério do Desenvolvimento Social e Combate à Fome. www.mds.gov.br (home page) date accessed 12 August 2012.

Neder, H. (2008) 'Estrutura do Mercado de Trabalho Agrícola no Brasil: Uma Análise Descritiva da Evolução de Suas Categorias entre 1995 e 2006', in

A.M. Buainain and C. Dedecca (eds), *Emprego e Trabalho na Agricultura Brasileira*, Série Desenvolvimento Rural Sustentável 9 (Brasília: IICA).

Neder, H. and Buainain, A.M. (2012) 'Pronaf Impacts on Social Indicators of Agricultures in Brazil in the Period 2000–2010', *VI World Conference SEA* (Salvador, Brazil.)

PAN-Brasil. (2004) *Programa de Ação Nacional de Combate à Desertificação e Mitigação dos Efeitos da Seca PAN-Brasil*. www.ibama.gov.br/rn/wp-content/files/2009/05/PAN_BRASIL.pdf.

PNRA II. (2004) *II Plano Nacional de Reforma Agrária: Paz, Produção e Qualidade de Vida no Meio Rural*. sistemas.mda.gov.br/arquivos/PNRA_2004.pdf date accessed 14 August 2012.

Portal da Cidadania. (2011). Territórios da Cidadania. http://comunidades.mda.gov.br/principal/ date accessed 08 January 2014.

Presidência da República. (2012) Mensagem ao Congresso Nacional 2012 – Capítulo II: Desenvolvimento Inclusivo e Erradicação da Pobreza Extrema. http://www.secom.gov.br/sobre-a-secom/acoes-e-programas/publicacoes/mensagem-ao-congresso-nacional/mensagem-ao-congresso-nacional-2012 date accessed 14 December 2012.

Schwartzman, S. and Bacha, E. (eds) (2012) *Brasil: A Nova Agenda Social* (Rio de Janeiro: Editora LTC).

10

Environmental Policies in the Lula Era: Accomplishments and Contradictions

Fábio de Castro

The environment dilemma

In the last few decades, environment has become a contentious theme in Brazil's national politics. The country's environmental challenges are directly linked to its vibrant economic growth, which relies on primary industry with significant and growing energy demands. The increasing share of commodities in export value, from 23 percent in 2000 to 46.7 percent in 2012, has driven the so-called 're-primarization' of the economy (Figure 10.1). The national development program (Growth Acceleration Program), based on the expansion of agricultural land, energy production and infrastructure, has sparked harsh criticisms from civil society organizations and environmentalists regarding negative impacts such as biodiversity loss, erosion of ecosystem services and social disruptions (Fearnside, 2006; Zhouri and Laschefski, 2010). At the same time, the country hosts approximately 65 percent of a mega-biodiversity biome and important carbon sink, which makes land cover change a key environmental concern at the global scale. Pressured by its uncomfortable position as one of the top greenhouse gas (GHG) emitters, mostly from deforestation and land use (La Rovere *et al.*, 2013), the government faces major conflict between carbon mitigation policies and the national development agenda, based on expansion of extractive industries.

In this complex context, contestation over natural resources is closely connected to demands by rural social movements whose environmental justice discourse unites social, environmental and territorial issues (Acselrad, 2008). Despite a highly heterogeneous cultural background and social organizations of different social actors, their claims coincide in terms of fair distribution of land and resources, partnership in

229

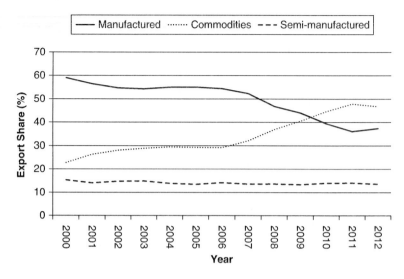

Figure 10.1   Share of exported products, 2000–12
Source: MDIC.

conservation policies, and improved territorial governance in a country with a highly skewed landholding distribution (Buainain *et al.*, this volume). Closely related to this political agenda are cultural-related claims of traditional identities and historical justice by ethnic communities such as indigenous, maroons, rubber tappers, coastal and riverine communities, to name a few. Such rural groups have been particularly successful in their efforts to show how poverty alleviation, increased equality and job generation are compatible with biological and cultural conservation (Acselrad, 2008).

In addition to rural populations, state governments have increasingly engaged in multi-jurisdictional alliances to attract funds for forest conservation and voluntary certification schemes (Toni, 2011). Environmental issues also reach foreign politics, as Brazil has become a key player in the international efforts for mitigation of biodiversity loss and carbon emission (Viola, 2010). The fact that a large proportion of the Amazon lies within its national borders gives Brazil leverage in global environmental governance as a major source of ecological services and as a source of innovative technologies and institutional arrangements to mitigate global climate change.

From a large range of traditional and peasant groups, to the increasing relevance of commodities in the national economy and the international demand for ecological services, natural resources have been highly politicized among different sectors of the Brazilian society. In this complex socio-environmental context, environmental governance in Brazil has gone through major institutional changes in the last two decades, from a centralized, national structure to a 'participatory' approach, in which ethnic groups have been engaged in the design and implementation of land tenure and land use in protected areas.

Considering the multi-scale, multi-sector connections of nature, it is no surprise that environmental politics in Brazil have been characterized by clashes between policies addressing environmental protection and social justice of rural populations, on one hand, and policies addressing infrastructure development and expansion of large-scale production systems on the other. A clear example of how environmental issues have become relevant in national politics is the presidential election of 2010, when the former Minister of Environment, Marina Silva, forced a second round by attracting one-fifth of the voters (Power, this volume). Although this event was more an expression of dissatisfaction at the options available than of a clear preference for the environmental agenda, the sudden increase of Silva's constituency revealed the potential for an alternative approach to the mainstream politics and for a development model in which 'environment' occupies a central position. More importantly, it raises questions about how the environment dilemma may influence national politics in Brazil. In this chapter I address this question by assessing the environmental policies implemented during the Lula government and during the outset of Dilma's government.

Due to complex connections across sectors and scales, a thorough accounting of environmental politics would deserve a full volume. Alternatively, I offer in this chapter a general discussion on how formal institutional transformations to tackle environmental issues have been connected to broader national politics in the last decade, and highlight some accomplishments and contradictions in the aim for sustainable development. The chapter starts with a brief history of institutional changes in pre-Lula governments, followed by a discussion of changes during his two terms. Following this, I provide an analysis of environment-related policies, grouped into three broad categories: (1) land governance with focus on territorial policies for protected areas and traditional populations; (2) energy governance with focus on renewable sources; and (3) climate governance with focus on the role of Brazil in the negotiation of global initiatives for mitigation policies. A final section highlights the prospects of environmental politics in the post-Lula era. The chapter closes with some final remarks linking environmental politics with development, democracy and citizenship.

Institutional legacies from previous governments

Environmental politics under Lula cannot be understood as an isolated process, disconnected from previous administrations. Since the democratization process, a few accomplishments have set the stage for recent political actions to take place. Needless to say, the Constitution of 1988 is a major benchmark in national environmental politics, defining rights to a healthy environment for all and responsibilities of the state and society to defend it and preserve it for future generations. In addition, a few biomes have been defined as national heritage to be protected, including the Amazon, the Atlantic Forest, the Pantanal wetlands and the coastal zone. The environmental legislation has also mandated participatory mechanisms in the design, implementation and monitoring of environment-related projects. One emblematic example is the Environmental Impact Assessment (EIA) for the approval of large-scale infrastructure projects, submitted to public hearings. The EIA has been a key instrument used not only by civil society organizations to fight against high impact projects, but also by the Public Ministry, an actor that has become fundamental in environmental politics (McAllister, 2008). The Public Ministry is in charge of 'diffuse and collective interests' and – due to historical factors and political demands – many prosecutors have specialized in environmental law and have become close allies of civil society organizations in the struggle against actions of the private sector and state agencies.

Another important element of the new Constitution is the multi-jurisdictional responsibility to preserve 'an ecologically balanced environment'. According to the Constitution, the three levels of government – municipal, state, and federal – are placed in the sphere of common and convergent competencies and none of them has exclusive power to legislate or implement environmental policy. However, despite this decentralized arrangement, the federal state holds some level of control in setting national plans to be adjusted by state and municipal governments according to their local contexts (Hochstetler and Keck, 2007).

The development of solid environmental legislation led to the creation of a federal environmental agency (IBAMA) in 1989, as part of a strategy to further develop and implement environmental policies. Brazil's government has shown bold signs of commitment to sustainable development by hosting the 1992 UN Conference on Environment and Development in Rio de Janeiro (UNCED Eco-92), and by signing international agreements elaborated in that meeting. The Eco-92 also opened new opportunities for both formal and informal national environmental politics. The Ministry of Environment was created as part of the national commitment to climate governance while national civil society organizations became more actively engaged with transnational networks of socio-environmental movements (Hochstetler and Keck, 2007).

Despite these institutional changes, it was not until Fernando Henrique Cardoso (FHC) took office that the federal government had a more active role in environmental policies. The Environmental Crimes Law of 1998 – addressing hunting, deforestation, pollution and damage to protected areas – gave the Public Ministry better institutional tools to issue complaints against individuals or legal entities who violate environmental regulations. In 1999, the Inter-ministerial Commission for Global Climate Change, composed of 16 ministries, was created in order to articulate governmental policies related to global environmental governance. Another important milestone during the FHC administration was the collaborative program among the Brazilian government, the World Bank and the European Commission, called Pilot Program to Conserve the Brazilian Rain Forest (PPG-7). The PPG-7 was designed as a participatory plan to mitigate carbon emission from deforestation, preserve biodiversity and promote sustainable development (Mello, 2006). Throughout the 1990s, approximately 200 projects were carried out in partnership with NGOs, including several community-based initiatives (Lemos and Roberts, 2008). Finally, two crucial innovations emerged during FHC's second term. First, in collaboration with the US Defense Department, the System for the Vigilance of the Amazon (SIVAM) was implemented, among other security goals, to control illegal land use activities in the Amazon. This cutting-edge technological surveillance system – comprised of more than 500 monitoring devices – covers 5.2 million km^2 of the Amazon, and is controlled by three observatory centers scattered in the region. Second, after nearly a decade of negotiation in Congress, the National System for Protected Areas (SNUC) was approved in 2000. The SNUC encompasses several categories of conservation units, including protected areas inhabited by traditional populations (Medeiros, 2006).

The advances before and during FHC were mostly reactive, pressured by demands from socio-environmental movements and international donors. From the creation of the Ministry of Environment on the eve of Eco-92 to the creation of a committee to articulate policies related to climate change after Kyoto, or the Environmental Crimes Law as a response to a sharp increase in the deforestation rate in 1998, the federal government was mainly responsive to political pressure from both below and above. By the same token, the PPG-7 program – designed when the environment was high on the global governance agenda – has been mainly undertaken by international donors. The limited involvement of the federal government suited the neoliberal perspective taken by FHC but did not fit the demands of the socio-environmental movements that called for increased institutional support from the state to empower marginalized groups. The Lula government fulfilled this gap by changing the perspective of national environmental policies. As part of the strong commitment to a social justice agenda and the repositioning of the state in the decision-making process, Lula took on a proactive approach that led to important accomplishments but also to some puzzling contradictions. The following section describes some important institutional changes under Lula and highlights the tension between socio-environmental and economic goals in three main domains of national environmental policy.

Institutional changes under Lula

The outset of Lula's administration was marked by a strong message of social inclusion and sustainable development. The appointment of senator Marina Silva as the head of the Ministry of Environment (MMA) in 2003 was a clear message that conservation, sustainability and traditional populations were at the core of Lula's environmental policy agenda. During this period, the MMA was marked by two main structural changes. First, following other Ministries (see Abers *et al.*, this volume), Silva sought close collaboration with civil society organizations, not only through improved channels for dialogue but also by appointing activists to positions in governmental offices. Secondly, the concept of 'transversal integration' was introduced in the MMA. According to Silva, environmental issues cross over different ministries and, therefore, engagement of the MMA in the planning process was crucial to ensure coherent national policies.

This new institutional rearrangement brought the state back to an active role in the decision-making process, but also set the stage for local actors to directly influence numerous state initiatives. It did not take long for the inclusive, transversal, integrated role of the MMA to be confronted by resistance from powerful political groups. The first lost battle was the institutional consolidation of transgenic soy in Brazil. After the embarrassing political situation of a decade of cultivation of irregular genetically modified (GM) soybeans in the country, Lula gave in to the agribusiness caucus and approved the regulation of the use of GM crops against the strong opposition of the MMA (Mueller, 2009). The major impact on MMA, however, came a few years later from inside the government.

The licensing process of hydroelectric power plant projects planned in the national development plan (PAC) was held back by the environmental agency in charge of the Environmental Impact Assessment (EIA), due to irregularities and violations of environmental legislation. Resistance to pressure from the secretary of state, Dilma Rousseff, to approve the projects led to a gradual isolation of MMA from the decision-making process. The tension between MMA and the government culminated in the resignation of Marina Silva in 2008.

In sum, the institutional arrangement of environmental policy has changed radically during both Lula terms, from close association with socio-environmental movements and a solid sustainable approach, through integration with other ministries, to a developmentalist, pragmatic perspective characterized by a national discourse of sustainability under deepened socio-environmental conflicts. Under this conflicting institutional arrangement, it is no surprise that accomplishments during the Lula government are marked with contradictions. Below I offer some illustrative examples of how discourse and the practice of sustainability have clashed during the Lula years in three different domains.

Rural land governance

During the Lula terms, the rural territorial configuration has undergone a major transformation, driven by policies targeting three broad categories of land use: (1) expansion of protected areas that recognize ethnic communities, to promote historical justice and social inclusion, and to help fulfill carbon mitigation targets; (2) expansion of production area, including small farms, agribusiness and extractive activities, to meet increased national and international demand; and (3) infrastructural development to promote regional integration and energy generation, and to facilitate transport of primary goods. I will focus on the first territorial category to highlight some accomplishments related to socio-environmental goals and I will refer to the production area and infrastructure to discuss some contradictions.

Protected areas have long been a key element in conservation policy in Brazil. Until recently, the northern model – focused on biodiversity hot spots and flagship species – has driven the creation of no-take conservation areas that restrict traditional communities from living in their territories and using local natural resources (Diegues, 1994). This picture started to change during the FHC terms, when manifestations of environmental citizenship among rural communities flourished in the country (Hochstetler and Keck, 2007) and the implementation of the National System for Protected Areas (SNUC) provided legal mechanisms to support local demands for rights to nature and land. Territorial rights claims resonated in the discourse of social inclusion, participation and empowerment deployed by Lula's government agenda, driving a boom of sustainable conservation units in the Amazon. Such areas comprise of a range of territorial models regulated by a Management Plan that is usually formulated by state agencies in collaboration with local residents. In addition, the implementation of indigenous and maroon territories, contemplated by the Constitution, was initiated in the new millennium as part of the PPG-7 program PPTAL (Projeto Integrado de Proteção às Terras e Populações Indígenas da Amazônia Legal) and the INCRA/MEC partnership, respectively.

As a result, Lula's terms have been marked by a major increase in protected areas and ethnic territories, the latter of which have grown remarkably in the last decade (Figure 10.2). Together with full protection conservation units, the spatial configuration of rural Brazil has been transformed into a mosaic of thousands of protected areas, covering approximately one-fifth of the national territory and almost half of the Legal Amazon. Supported by the PPG7 program, indigenous territories increased by over 400,000 km^2 during the FHC term and close to 200,000km^2 during Lula's years in office. Likewise, the national government formally recognized more than 100 maroon territories between the FHC and Lula terms, and approximately 1,000 communities are in different phases of territorial recognition. Finally, 57 extractive reserves have been created in both upland and coastal areas since 2001, while more than 240 agro-extractive settlements have been created along the Amazonian floodplain since 2006 (Table 10.1).

Protected areas combined with the surveillance systems (SIVAM) and enforcement measures implemented in the last decade have driven a positive result of a steady decrease in the Amazon deforestation rate since 2004 (Figure 10.3). Although this trend has been influenced by external factors such as the global economic crisis, it is clear that conservation policies have had an important impact on this trend. However, optimism about growth of protected areas and decline in deforestation rate in the Amazon contrasts with a few contradictions regarding patterns of land use on private lands, and deforestation in other biomes.

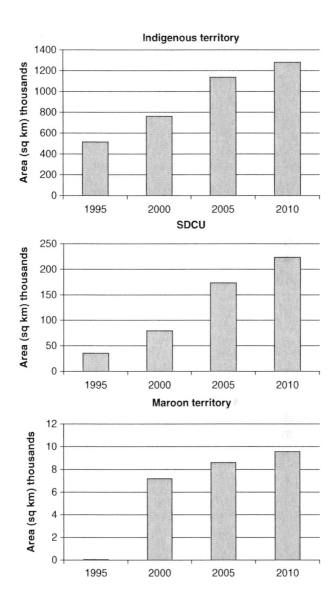

Figure 10.2 Expansion of ethnic territories in Brazil, 1995–2010 (SDCU = sustainable development conservation units)

Table 10.1 Number and area of ethnic communities created during FHC and Lula presidencies

	Indigenous[1]		Maroons[2]		SDCU[3,4]	
	N	Area (km²)	N	Area(km²)	N	Area(km²)
FHC (1995–2002)	145	412,269	42	7,753	20	29,377
Lula (2003–2010)	87	187,857	66	2,126	277*	93,454*

* includes 246 Agroextractive Reserve Projects (PAE) in the Amazon floodplain (INCRA).
Sources: 1 – ISA; 2 and 4 – INCRA; 3 – MMA.

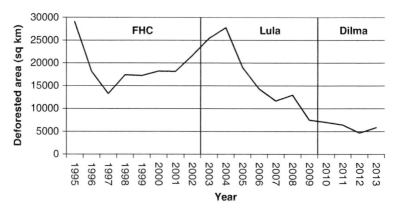

Figure 10.3 Deforestation rate in the Amazon, 1995–2013
Source: PRODES, INPE.

Rapid expansion of agribusiness has caused impacts on both protected areas and peasant territories. Land use in private territories is regulated by forest legislation, in which two sets of restrictions are of particular relevance for biodiversity conservation: Permanent Protection Area (APP) and Legal Reserves (LR). The former includes vulnerable terrains such as river fringes, hill summits and hilly areas; the latter includes a percentage of the property that must be protected, according to specific biomes: 80 percent in the Amazon and Atlantic Forest; 35 percent in the Savanna; and 20 percent in the remaining areas. The formal restrictions, however, have not stopped farmers from illegal deforestation in these areas. According to Sparovek *et al.* (2012), 25 percent of the private forest has not been effectively protected, which generated a deficit of 86 million hectares of forest in APP and LR. There was a consensus that the Forest Act needed to be adjusted to the new rural context, and to better tackle illegal deforestation in APP and LR. However, this process was captured by the rural caucus in the national congress and the decision was postponed until the following presidency (see Section 4).

Monitoring of forest legislation faced a chronic problem related to irregular land tenure. To tackle this problem, the Terra Legal Program was created in 2009 to foster the regularization of land tenure in the Amazon, where half of the territory is under unclear tenure status. However, civil society organizations have accused this program of facilitating land grabbing because it targets landholdings up to 1,500 hectares and provides formal channels to legalize a small number of large landholdings instead of providing land security to a large number of migrant small-scale farmers (Portal do Purus, 2012). According to Brito and Barreto (2011), although 70 percent of the illegal landholdings are less than 100 hectares, about half of the landholdings benefited by the program are properties of 400 hectares or more. In other words, while private landholdings reveal major flaws in compliance of forest legislations, protected areas remain the main source of forest protection and provision of ecological services in the Amazon.

Another contradiction in the conservation strategy is the political efforts to halt deforestation centered in the Amazon region, while other threatened biomes are overlooked. Lack of attention from both the national government and international community has allowed the rapid land cover change in the Savanna, which has gradually become a major source of carbon emission (Sawyer, 2008). Agricultural expansion and charcoal are the main drivers of increased deforestation in this biome, estimated to be as high as over 20,000 km^2/year in 2005 (Sawyer, 2008), although recent official figures estimate around 7000 km^2/year in 2009. About 80 percent of the territory has been degraded and only 2.6 percent is legally protected. Despite the high level of endemism and major carbon sink, the Savanna is not included on the list of national heritage in the Constitution.

In other words, accomplishments in forest protection in the Amazon contrast with growing socio-environmental conflicts mainly driven by the expansion of large-scale production and infrastructure in their surrounding territories (ISA, 2009). Lack of transparency, non-participatory methods and illegal practices have been some of the strategies used by private and public agencies to facilitate the implementation of large-scale infrastructure projects, which can render major socio-environmental impacts in the region (Fearnside, 2006). The focus on large-scale infrastructure and agribusiness in rural areas has directly affected the conservation agenda, enhancing environmental injustices in rural areas. While local social groups struggle for access to land and natural resources, rural development policies related to agribusiness, infrastructure expansion and extractive activities drive increased environmental degradation and socio-environmental conflicts (Sauer and Almeida, 2011). Along the new agro-pastoral frontiers mostly in the Savanna, the rural elite has gradually appropriated new agricultural lands and pushed rural populations into more isolated areas with limited access to market, infrastructure and information (Wolford, 2008). As a result, traditional populations in the Amazon struggle to protect their territory against large-scale projects, while large-scale farmers in the Savanna have freely violated the forest legislation to increase their production at the expense of environmental degradation. Ironically, under the label of 'guardians' of the global commons, traditional populations in the Amazon are not only excluded from the development agenda but also legitimize the expansion of highly impactful activities elsewhere (Castro, 2012).

Energy governance

The reliance of the Brazilian energy grid on a high proportion of renewables is well known worldwide. Two main sources compose the cornerstone of renewable energy, each targeting different purposes. Hydroelectric power is responsible for 74 percent of electricity generation, whereas biofuel is responsible for approximately one-third of transportation fuel for small vehicles. Together, they amount to 30 percent of the energy source, a figure much higher than the world average of 16 percent and 1.4 percent, respectively (Figure 10.4). Although these figures have been used by Lula to support the image of a green state in international climate governance, this unique feature had been established a few decades earlier as part of a strategy of energy sovereignty deployed by the military government. In fact, the proportion of renewables has been relatively stable in the last decade (Figure 10.5). Nevertheless, the accomplishments of Lula are related to initiatives to expand renewable energy production to meet the increasing demand. Below I briefly present these initiatives and discuss the implications of the recent finding of a large offshore oil reserve on the southern coast of Brazil for the future of renewable energy in the country.

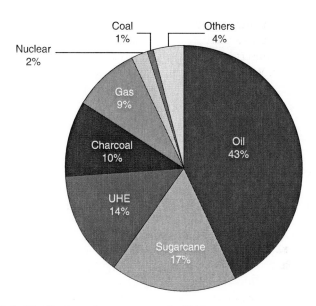

Figure 10.4 Distribution of energy source in 2012
Source: MME.

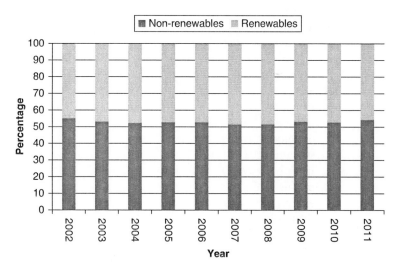

Figure 10.5 Proportion of renewables (hydroelectric power plant, sugarcane, charcoal, wind) and non-renewables (oil, gas, coal, nuclear) in the energy grid, 2002–11
Source: MME.

Hydroelectric power expansion

Brazil's abundant river basin systems and strong engineering capability have been the main pillars of the consolidation of hydroelectric power plant as the key energy source for electricity production. As part of the energy sovereignty policy implemented by the military government, a series of hydroelectric power plants have been constructed in the southern part of the country since the 1970s. Due to an overload of hydroelectric power plants in this region, more recent plans turn to the Amazon Basin as the new frontier for expansion of hydraulic energy. In particular, the electricity crisis between 2001 and 2002 pushed the national government to implement infrastructure projects to support increased energy consumption in the country. FHC's successful campaign to lower energy consumption among the population helped to avoid regular outages that could have affected economic growth. During his presidential campaign, Lula used this energy crisis ('crise do apagão') to accuse FHC of bad planning, and promised to expand energy generation under his presidency.

Lula's first term went relatively smoothly as the national government benefited from the inherited energy expansion program set up by FHC to address the energy crisis. A new energy expansion plan, released in 2007 and adjusted in 2010, anticipated a 4.5 percent annual increase in energy production, amounting to 40,000 MW by 2020, mostly from new hydroelectric power plants to be built in northern river basins (EPE, 2007). Needless to say, the expansion of hydroelectricity in Brazil became one of the major sources of socio-environmental threats in the Amazon. Considering the sensitivity of the Amazon region, dam construction has become an iconic example of the clash between development and conservation policies. On one hand, electricity generation is necessary to supply increasing household and industrial energy consumption; on the other hand, the reliance on large-scale hydroelectric power plants in the Amazon has triggered major debates regarding issues related to the actual sustainability of this energy source, unequal distribution of benefits and socio-environmental costs. The political discourse of renewable energy is confronted by empirical evidence of the social and ecological impacts of large-scale large dams in the Amazon, including high emission of greenhouse gas (Fearnside, 1995; 2005; 2006). Moreover, in the affected areas of Xingu, Tapajos, Madeira, Araguaia and Tocantins, the main rivers targeted for the hydroelectricity expansion overlap with territories of several traditional communities (ISA, 2009). As a result, new dam projects have driven reclassification of conservation units, which slashed more than 30,000 km^2 of protected areas (EcoDebate, 2012).

As discussed earlier, internal conflicts around the licensing process for the construction of hydroelectric power plants caused major institutional changes in Brasília, leading to the resignation of the environmental minister. Marina Silva justified her decision by accusing the government of a lack of political support for the Ministry of Environment, and overruling the democratic procedures of environmental licensing. Ever since, governmental agencies and the Public Ministry have been engaged in an arm wrestle between legal embargos and permissions. This issue is particularly relevant as it touches upon the tension between the democratic process and energy security. On one hand, the government promotes a large-scale plan to increase energy generation from renewable sources; on the other hand, the government has consistently overruled the national constitution, overlooked the claims of social movements, and promoted unequal distribution of the costs and benefits of these projects, as in the case of Belo Monte (see Section 4).

Biofuel expansion

Ethanol has long been a cornerstone of transportation fuel in Brazil (Wilkinson and Herrera, 2010), available in gas station pumps since the mid-1970s as special fuel (hydrous) or blended with gasoline (25 percent since 2007). However, the boom in ethanol production was possible only after the introduction of flex-fuel engines for small vehicles, which can run on both gasoline and ethanol. In addition, fuel demand has increased with the recent growth in car sales as a result of the emergence of the middle class combined with government incentives for the automobile industry. In the last decade, car sales grew 150 percent and the proportion of flex-fuel cars increased from 4 to 91 percent of total sales (Figure 10.6). As a result, biofuel production has proportionally increased far more than any other energy source in the last decade. Sugarcane-based energy (ethanol and bagasse) has grown 75 percent between 2003 and 2010, in contrast with a 38 percent increase in energy production in the same period. This striking difference reflects the aggressive policy that was implemented by Lula for the expansion of ethanol production from 12 to 27 billion liters between 2003 and 2010, bringing Brazil to the position of the world's second largest producer and first exporter of this renewable fuel (Figure 10.7).

Ethanol export has increased fivefold since 2003, peaking at 5.1 billion liters in 2008. The aspiration to tap into the new green energy market was hindered by two major trade constraints. First, competitive prices of Brazilian ethanol were curtailed by a protectionist US tariff set at $0.54/gallon

244

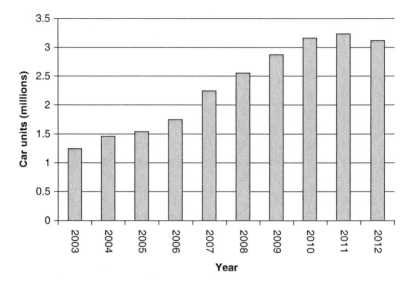

Figure 10.6   Car sales, 2003–12
Source: Anfavea.

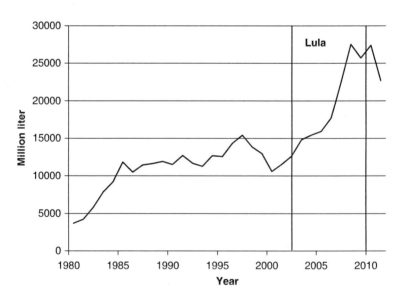

Figure 10.7   Ethanol production, 1980–2011
Source: UNICA.

of imported ethanol. Second, as of 2009 the European Union required certification of sustainable production from Brazilian ethanol producers. These restrictions brought the ethanol export figures down to less than two billion liters in 2010. As a response, the national government worked closely with main stakeholders (e.g., UNICA and CONTAG) to address the bottlenecks in the process of getting certification for the Brazilian ethanol. Voluntary agreements with the ethanol processing plants, mechanization of sugarcane harvest, and sugarcane zoning in non-forested areas are some of the outcomes of this process to address criticisms of labor conditions, harvesting methods and indirect deforestation related to ethanol production.

At the same time, the government was proactive in creating a certification scheme for the creation of a new market for biodiesel, which was implemented in 2005. The National Plan for Biodiesel Production and Use (PNPB), carried out by the Ministry of Agrarian Development, was primarily aimed at the inclusion of small farmers in the biodiesel production chain through a certification scheme: the Social Fuel Stamp (SFS). The SFS provides special benefits – such as tax exemptions, access to special rural credits, and privileges to participate in auctions organized by the National Agency of Petroleum, Natural Gas and Biofuels (ANP) – to both small-scale producers and biodiesel processing plants. Tax exemption was higher in poorer regions such as the north and northeast of Brazil. To facilitate the negotiations between small farmers and the biodiesel producers and distributors, the government carried out auctions in which amount, price and delivery date with winning producers were agreed upon. In a way, the biodiesel program was designed as an antithesis of the ethanol program, conceived with a very distinct production system, institutional arrangement, goals and socio-environmental implications. The program combined economic, social and political goals. In economic terms, it aimed at supplying the marginal biodiesel that needed to be blended with mineral diesel to reach self-sufficiency. In contrast to ethanol, the PNPB was planned only for domestic use and blending purposes, initially 2 percent of biodiesel (B2), with a gradual increase to 5 percent (B5) in 2013. The social dimension of the program addresses the criticisms of social exclusion in sugarcane/ethanol production. Issues related to poor labor conditions, food insecurity and environmental impacts were addressed by a provision for peasants to engage in a new market (Abramovay and Magalhães, 2008). Emphasis on large-scale, mono-crop, high-input agriculture and land concentration in the ethanol production system were replaced by small-scale, crop diversity and sustainable production of oilseeds.

The PNPB has been successful in reaching the biodiesel production targets but did not live up to its social goals. Biodiesel production reached two billion liters in five years, anticipating the B5 blending in 2010, three years ahead of the original plan. Figures on social inclusion, however, have been way below expectations. Four years after the implementation of the program, only 51,000 families were involved – one fourth of the target – and nearly 80 percent of the biodiesel was produced from soybeans cultivated in the southern region (Reporter Brasil, 2010). In 2008, the PNPB underwent a few adjustments to improve the social component of the initiative. Petrobras invested in three biodiesel plants in the semi-arid region of Brazil, raising the participation of small farmers to 109,000 families in 2010.

In sum, ethanol and biodiesel production are two faces of the same coin. Under the discourse of sustainable energy, they are both promoted by the national government as a unique opportunity for Brazil to use its large agricultural land, technological know-how and rural labor force to combine sustainability, job generation and energy security. In this national strategy, ethanol is targeted at the rural elite to expand the sugarcane farms and reach out to new international markets, while biodiesel is targeted at small-farmers to provide them with an opportunity to reach out to new domestic markets. However, both ethanol and biodiesel production have increased exponentially during the Lula years, and they have both relied on mono-crop feedstock: sugarcane and soybeans, which are key drivers of deforestation and social injustices in the rural areas. In other words, to what extent the biofuel program can be a sustainable and inclusive solution for energy production remains to be seen.

The expansion of biofuel in Brazil took place in the midst of major changes in the country's oil production profile. With a 7 percent annual growth rate in oil production since 1997, Brazil reached self-sufficiency in 2006. This accomplishment was followed by major news only a year later: the discovery of a deep offshore oil reserve below the pre-salt layer, a few kilometers off the southern coast. Estimated to be between 50 and 100 billion gallons, attention was shifted to this new opportunity, referred as 'the second independence of Brazil' by Lula and 'the passport to the future' by the Secretary of State at the time, Dilma Rousseff. Although the oil production profile has not been affected yet, a few socio-environmental concerns have been raised, such as increased carbon emission from the burning of gas during the oil extraction, risks of oil leakage (especially in high-depth drilling) and impacts on commercial fishing activities.

In contrast to the direct social impacts of hydroelectric power plants on rural territories, offshore oil reserves have no immediate social threats. However, Lula has adjusted his political discourse of a green state and has proposed a series of policy initiatives to justify the eventual change in the energy grid. A major benefit of the Pre-Salt program has been its coupling with social development through a proposal for a new royalties scheme. On the other hand, major changes in the energy grid may come from an impact on ethanol consumption in the case of the domestic price of gasoline being set too low, thereby limiting the use of ethanol to blending purposes only. In any case, possible changes in the energy grid may have a direct effect on Brazil's positioning in climate governance, a topic to which we now turn.

Climate governance

Brazil's positioning in global climate governance has always been balanced by the country's ambiguous profile, characterized by a high deforestation rate on one hand and a clean energy grid on the other. As mentioned previously, Brazil is the world's second-largest carbon emitter from land use change (La Rovere *et al.*, 2013). At the same time, the large portion of mega-biodiversity biomes (e.g., the Amazon, Atlantic Forest and Savanna), as well as the remarkable renewable energy program, have given Brazil leverage to play an active role in international mitigation-policy negotiations. The national government has used these two features strategically to strengthen Brazil's profile among industrialized nations.

Before Lula, Brazil played an important role in climate policy decisions. In 1992, the country hosted the UNCED Eco-92 and influenced the elaboration of the Biodiversity Convention, Agenda 21 and negotiation of the climate convention (Viola, 2010). In 1997, Brazilian diplomats teamed up with the USA delegation to propose the Clean Development Mechanism (CDM), perhaps the most concrete initiative of the Kyoto protocol, in which developed countries financially support projects for energy efficiency in developing countries. Brazil ranks third in reduction of carbon emission from CMD projects, half of which is related to renewable energy production from a sugarcane byproduct (bagasse), small hydro power plants and wind power (Friberg, 2009). However, it was not until the new millennium that Brazil took a higher stand on the climate agenda, both nationally and internationally.

At the national level, Lula built upon the Inter-ministerial Commission on Climate Change (created by FHC) to develop a more coherent domestic climate policy-making structure, by engaging ministries, private actors and civil society organizations in the process (Viola, 2004). At the international level, the climate governance diplomacy has been coupled with an ambition to become a leading voice that represents the Southern hemisphere in decisions regarding mitigation and measures to adaptat to climate change. By tackling deforestation more aggressively, the government shifted the Amazon question from a burden to an asset in the negotiations. The deforestation rate has dropped from over 25,000 km²/year in 2003 to less than 10,000 km²/year in 2010 (Figure 10.2). In addition, increased investment to expand ethanol production revealed the government's intention to shift climate governance from a threat to an economic and political opportunity. Steps to turn ethanol into a commodity, transfer of technology for ethanol production to other southern countries, and concrete measures to match international trading standards reflect the government's ambition to become a major supplier of ethanol and support mitigation policies set by industrialized countries.

In 2009, the Inter-ministerial Commission on Climate Change elaborated the National Plan for Climate Change (NPCC). The NPCC lays out a strategic shift from a conservative to a reformist position in climate governance, in line with industrialized economies. From the past position of adamant rejection to a set carbon emission target for emerging economies, the NPCC sets ambitious national targets to mitigate carbon emission by between 36 and 39 percent until 2020. Among several measures to reach this target are an 80 percent reduction of the deforestation rate and a doubling of planted forest until 2020; an 11 percent increase of domestic use of ethanol until 2018; and increased energy generation from an ethanol byproduct (bagasse) to 11 percent of the total electric energy by 2030 (CIMC, 2008). The proactive position of the government was supported by the important accomplishment of a steady decline in carbon emission. After a fast increase in carbon emission from 1.3 billion tons in 1990 to 2.2 billion tons in 2005, the country has experienced a continuous decrease ever since and has reached 1.8 billion tons of carbon more recently, mainly as a result of the lowered deforestation rate (Friberg, 2009). However, while land use change has dropped 20 percent between 1994 and 2009, carbon emission has increased 40 percent in industry, energy, agriculture and waste sectors in the same period, as part of the increased consumption pattern (La Rovere *et al.*, 2013).

With decreasing deforestation and carbon emission rates, a solid renewable energy grid, and a sound national mitigation plan, the Brazilian delegation arrived at the United Nations Framework Convention on

Climate Change (UNFCCC) in Copenhagen as a powerful player ready to push forward the proposal for reduced emission from deforestation and degradation (REDD+), a partnership between highly industrialized countries and mega-biodiversity countries. REDD+ is based on initiatives that create incentives to reduce deforestation and degradation (Tollefson, 2009). In 2008 the national government created the Amazon Fund, managed by the national development bank BNDES, to attract financial support from potential sponsors to support projects to prevent, monitor and combat deforestation in the Amazon. Until 2012, the Amazon Fund had attracted 128 million dollars, mainly from Norway. This initiative has been far from successful. The program has experienced problems in attracting effective projects in the first five years and only one-fifth of the promised funds has been transferred to the program. Notwithstanding these hurdles, the Amazon Fund has enabled the national government to re-centralize the negotiations for mitigation measures, and to engage international support in the governance of the Amazon forest without losing sovereignty over the region.

In sum, climate policy under Lula has shifted from a formerly reactive, conservative perspective to a proactive, reformist approach, to raise the country's political profile as leader of the southern countries. This remarkable progress in global climate governance contrasts with recent developments in the national environmental agenda under the new president, as discussed in the following section.

Environmental policies under Dilma

Dilma has inherited both advances and conflicts that emerged from the environmental and development policies carried out by the Lula administration. However, the heritage was mostly shaped by her, as she was the secretary of state and a key actor promoting development policies that triggered conflicts with the MMA and social movements under Lula. Although these policies are reason for debate among social scientists, there is a consensus that conservation policies have gradually become an even lower priority on the national agenda under the new government. Considering Dilma's poor record on environmental policies, it is no surprise that conflicts and pending issues left off by Lula have only worsened in the last two years. In this section I will briefly address three emblematic cases, which clearly show the high polarization between conservation and development policies. The three cases illustrate the three pillars addressed in this chapter. First is the decision-making process regarding the new Forest Act (related to rural land governance), which has long been contested by peasants, agribusiness and environmentalists. Secondly, the decision-making process regarding the construction of the Belo Monte dam complex (related to energy governance) is an old conflict between ethnic communities, the national government and NGOs. Third, the role of Brazil at the United Nations Conference on Sustainable Development (UNCSD) also known as Rio+20 related to climate governance was characterized by a return to a conservative approach, distancing itself from the European target goals and approximating the green economy model.

The revision of the Forest Act has become one of the main political battles between the rural and the environmentalist caucus in the National Congress. Although different proposals have been circulated, discussed and negotiated in the Congress since the 1990s, it was not until 2009 that concrete steps to vote for the new Forest Act were taken. Lula was able to drag out this process until the end of his term, and Dilma faced this highly politicized process in her first months as president. After several rounds of negotiation, the text from the opposition was approved by a massive majority on the eve of Rio+20. Among the changes are the flexibility of environmental protection on private land, related to the reforestation of illegally cleared areas, legal mechanisms to lower the Legal Reserves (LR) under certain conditions, and the decrease of Permanent Preserved Area (PPA). Despite a few vetoes from the president, the final text of the Forest Act became a formal instrument that encourages deforestation and is expected to lead to a 58 percent drop in reforestation, according to a recent estimate.

The construction of the mega hydropower scheme Belo Monte is a characteristic example of the tension between conservation and an economic development model. Formerly planned in the 1970s, civil society organizations were successful in silencing a few attempts to get the Belo Monte project off the ground. Under Lula, Belo Monte was not only revived, but also became a flagship project in his program to foster economic growth and to prevent energy shortages. Supported by a discourse of energy security, Lula stubbornly resisted repeated protests of civil society organizations; the environmental agency bypassed the mandatory environmental impact assessment, reclassified protected areas to accommodate the land to be flooded, and injected funding through the national development bank to make Belo Monte viable. Dilma followed Lula's steps to confront indigenous and peasant groups as well as national (Public Ministry) and international (Inter-American Commission on Human Rights of the Organization of the American

States) organizations, escalating to one of the most serious socio-environmental conflicts in the country (Hall and Brandford, 2012). The result was not only the reduction of protected areas, increased socio-environmental impact and unequal distribution of benefits to high-consuming mineral companies, but also the crushing of citizenship and overuse of state power, thereby violating human rights and the national constitution.

Rio+20 was the first global arena on climate policy after Dilma took office. The event attracted more than 45,000 participants and mobilized about 10,000 NGO members, and 188 national delegations, to discuss a document addressing institutional arrangement to support a green economy and to develop instruments and guidelines to foster global cooperation. As host of the event, the Brazilian delegation led the negotiations and the writing of the final consensual document. During this process, the Brazilian diplomats showed clear signs of reshaping the country's position on climate governance to a more conservative approach with strong support for a mainstream development model (Hochstetler and Viola 2013). The result was a document with a wish list and voluntary agreements with neither concrete decisions about actions nor commitments of governments regarding institutional arrangements, targets and monitoring mechanisms. This final document was highly criticized by social movements, researchers and some politicians as a regression in comparison with Eco-92. Perhaps the major achievement of the meeting was the prevention of concrete decisions regarding the establishment of a green economy, which could have led to even more inequalities and environmental degradation. Dilma's position was ambiguous regarding the final product. On one hand, the Brazilian delegation worked to remove major themes from the document, such as the scaling up of the United Nations Environment Programme (UNEP), reproductive rights and sustainable development goals; on the other hand, Dilma blamed other governments for lack of political will to allow more concrete decisions. In any case, the empty document seems to match the conservative position taken by Dilma's administration.

These three examples reveal how environmental issues have lost relevance on the national agenda, widening the gap between economic growth and sustainability. The new Forest Act creates opportunities for the consolidation of deforested land and an increase in deforestation and biodiversity loss. The hydroelectric dam complex Belo Monte deepens inequality, not only in terms of who bears the environmental costs of this high-impact infrastructure project, but also in terms of who receives the benefits of the energy produced. Finally, Brazil's position during Rio+20 not only reveals a missed opportunity to lead climate governance towards a progressive economic model, but also shows how the clash between the national government and the rural social movements is closely related to the increasingly carbon-intensive national economy. In all three cases, there is a clear prioritization of the neo-development approach, relying on short-term revenue from large-scale production of primary goods, and characterized by less sensitivity to long-term socio-environmental impacts.

Conclusions

The conservation agenda under Lula has moved forward in many ways. Environmental politics evolved to a governance perspective, in which different actors and policy sectors were engaged in different decision-making arenas. Furthermore, the national government moved from a reactive approach during FHC to a proactive strategy in both domestic and international affairs. The national government has used these achievements to overshadow conflicts and to improve its image as a green state within the international community. From the increase in protected areas and a drop in the deforestation rate in the Amazon, to expansion of renewable energy and a proactive plan to mitigate carbon emission, Lula succeeded in becoming a role model among emerging economies and mega-biodiversity countries. However, the development path taken by the government has often clashed with conservation and social inclusion measures. When contextualized in broader processes of reconfiguration of rural territories, environmental injustices and consolidation of a carbon-intensive development model, contradictions between conservation and development policies surface. The increase in protected areas has legitimized the expansion of large-scale farming and extractive activities, with direct impact on conservation targets. Renewable energy – praised by the government as a modern, low-carbon economy – contrasts with incentive measures to increase car sales and support for energy-intensive extractive industries. A national plan for climate change, including remarkable targets to mitigate carbon emission, does not match with the rules of the new Forest Act.

The environmental dilemma under Lula, and now under Dilma, goes beyond biodiversity conservation and carbon mitigation measures. It touches upon the development model, based on a gradual re-primarization of the economy, and reliance on energy – and water-intensive production activities. It touches upon citizenship issues and the role of the state in promoting the recentralization of political decisions regarding the environmental impacts of large-scale projects and limited participation of local communities and civil society organizations. Finally, it touches upon inequality issues as local communities, trapped in protected areas, are now in charge of reaching the zero deforestation targets, while private actors are allowed to continue their land use practices and the urban middle class increases its consumption of fossil fuel. In sum, environmental policy has become a battlefield where citizenship, democracy and sustainable development have been constantly challenged. As it seems, this picture will hardly change under Dilma.

References

Abramovay, R. and Magalhães, R. (2008) *The Access of Family Farmers to Biodiesel Markets: Partnerships between Large Companies and Social Movements* (London: IIED).

Acselrad, H. (2008) 'Grassroots Reframing in Environmental Struggles in Brazil', in D.V. Carruthers (eds), *Environmental Justice in Latin America: Problems, Promises and Practice* (Cambridge: MIT Press).

Brito, B. and Barreto, P. (2011) 'Regularização Fundiária na Amazônia e o Programa Terra Legal', in S. Sauer and W. Almeida (eds), *Terras e Territórios na Amazônia: Demandas, Desafios e Perspectivas* (Brasília: Editora UNB).

Castro, F. (2012) 'Multi-scale Environmental Citizenship: Traditional Populations and Protected Areas in Brazil', in A. Latta and H. Wittman (eds), *Environmental and Citizenship in Latin America: Natures, Subjects and Struggles* (New York: Berghahn Books).

CIMC. (Comitê Interministerial sobre Mudança do Clima) (2008) 'Plano Nacional sobre Mudança de Clima', http://www.mma.gov.br/estruturas/smcq_climaticas/_arquivos/plano_nacional_mudanca_clima.pdf date accessed 10 May 2013.

Diegues, A.C.S. (1994) *O Mito da Natureza Intocada* (Sao Paulo: NUPAUB).

EcoDebate. (2012) 'O Brasil perdeu mais de 45 mil quilômetros quadrados de áreas protegidas nos últimos 30 anos', *Eco Debate*. http://www.ecodebate.com.br/2012/12/21/o-brasil-perdeu-mais-de-45-mil-quilometros-quadrados-de-areas-protegidas-nos-ultimos-30-anos/ date accessed 10 May 2013.

EPE. (2007) *Plano Decenal de Expansão de Energia – PDE 2007–2016* (Brasil: MME, SPDE).

Fearnside, P.M. (1995) 'Hydroelectric Dams in the Brazilian Amazon as Sources of "Greenhouse" Gases', *Environmental Conservation* 22(1): 7–19.

Fearnside, P.M. (2005) 'Brazil's Samuel Dam: Lessons from Hydroelectric Development Policy and the Environment in Amazon', *Environmental Management* 35(1): 1–19.

Fearnside, P.M. (2006) 'Dams in the Amazon: Belo Monte and Brazil's Hydroelectric Development of the Xingu River Basin', *Environmental Management* 38(1): 16–27.

Friberg, L. (2009) 'Varieties of Carbon Governance: The Clean Development Mechanism in Brazil – A Success Story Challenged', *The Journal of Environment and Development* 18(4): 395–424.

Hall, A. and Brandford, S. (2012) 'Development, Dams, and Dilma: The Saga of Belo Monte', *Critical Sociology* 38(6): 851–62.

Hochstetler, K. and Keck, M.E. (2007) *Greening Brazil: Environmental Activism in State and Society* (Durham: Duke University Press).

Hochstetler, K. and Viola, E. (2013) 'Brazil and the Politics of Climate Change: Beyond the Global Commons', *Environmental Politics* 21(5): 753–71.

ISA. (2009) *Atlas of Pressures and Threats to Indigenous Lands in the Brazilian Amazon* (São Paulo: ISA).

La Rovere, E.L. Dubeux, C.B. Pereira Jr., A.O. and Wills, W. (2013) 'Brazil Beyond 2020: From Deforestation to the Energy Challenge', *Climate Policy* 13(1): 70–86.

Lemos, M.C. and Roberts, J.T. (2008) 'Environmental Policy-Making Networks and the Future of the Amazon', *Philosophical Transactions: Biological Sciences* 363(1498): 1897–1902.

McAllister, L. (2008) *Making Law Matter: Environmental Protection and Legal Institutions in Brazil* (Stanford: Stanford Law Books).

Medeiros, R. (2006) 'Evolução das Tipologias e Categorias de Áreas Protegidas no Brasil', *Ambiente e Sociedade* 9(1): 41–64.

Mello, N.A. (2006) *Políticas Territoriais na Amazônia (São Paulo: Annablume)*

Mueller, C.C. (2009) 'Agricultural, Agrarian, and Environmental Policy Formation under Lula: The Role of Policy Networks', in W. Baer and J.L. Love (eds), *Brazil under Lula: Economy, Politics, and Society Under the Worker-President* (New York: Palgrave MacMillan).

Portal do Purus. (2012) 'Relatório da CPT acusa o "Terra Legal" de favorecer os latifundiários', http://www.portaldopurus.com.br/index.php/cidades/boca-do-acre/7704-relatorio-da-cpt-acusa-o-terra-legal-de-favorecer-os-latifundiarios date accessed 10 May 2013.

Reporter Brasil. (2010) 'Family Farming and the National Biodiesel Programme: A Portrait of the Present; Perspective for the Future', http://reporterbrasil.org.br/documentos/FactsheetAGR_English.pdf date accessed 10 May 2013.

Sauer, S. and Almeida, W. (eds) (2011) *Terras e Territórios na Amazônia: Demandas, Desafios e Perspectivas* (Brasília: Editora UNB).

Sawyer, D. (2008) 'Climate Change, Biofuels and Eco-Social Impacts in the Brazilian Amazon and Cerrado', *Philosophical Transactions: Biological Sciences* 363(1498): 1747–1752.

Sparovek, G. Berndes, G. Barretto, A.G.O.P. and Klug, I.L.F. (2012) 'The Revision of the Brazilian Forest Act: Increased Deforestation or a Historic Step Towards Balancing Agricultural Development and Nature Conservation?', *Environmental Science and Policy* 16: 65–72.

Tollefson, J. (2009) 'Paying to Save the Rainforests', *Nature News* 460: 936–937.

Toni, F. (2011) 'Decentralization and REDD+ in Brazil', *Forests* 2(1): 66–85.

Viola, E. (2004) 'Brazil in the Context of Global Governance Politics and Climate Change, 1989–2003', *Ambiente e Sociedade* 7(1): 27–46.

Viola, E. (2010) 'A Política Climática Global e o Brasil: 2005–2010', *Revista Tempo do Mundo* 2: 82–117.

Wilkinson, J. and Herrera, S. (2010) 'Biofuels in Brazil: Debates and Impacts', *Journal of Peasant Studies* 37(4): 749–768.

Wolford, W. (2008) 'Environmental Justice and Agricultural Development in the Brazilian Cerrado', in D.V. Carruthers (eds), *Environmental Justice in Latin America: Problems, Promises, and Practice* (Cambridge: MIT Press).

Zhouri, A. and Laschefski, K. (eds) (2010) *Desenvolvimento e Conflitos Ambientais* (Belo Horizonte: Editora UFMG).

Index

Printed and bound by CPI Group (UK) Ltd, Croydon, CR0 4YY